MY HOPE
BUTCH

THE FURRY MEDICAL WONDER

DAVE CASSIDY

PORTLAND • OREGON
INKWATERPRESS.COM

www.inkwaterpress.com

ISBN-13 978-1-59299-437-3
ISBN-10 1-59299-437-7

Publisher: Inkwater Press

Printed in the U.S.A.
All paper is acid free and meets all ANSI standards for archival quality paper.

1

For Franzi

Table of Contents

Hope

*H*ope, as defined in Merriam-Webster's Dictionary, means, "to cherish a desire with anticipation."

Anyone who has ever had a dog as a family pet will be able to relate to the joy, heartache, and unconditional love that our furry, four-legged friend has brought to our lives. Little did we know that when we got the little pup from the breeder and saw on his papers that his official name was "My Hope Butch," how prophetic that tiny four-letter word would turn out to be. Over the last fourteen years, Butch has taught us more than we could have ever dreamed of learning about the feeling and true meaning of the word "hope."

Chapter One

Life Before Butch

*G*rowing up in Ontario in the early 70's, during the height of the Partridge Family craze, it wasn't easy to be blessed with the name "David Cassidy." My parents, ten years prior, with visions of naming their first-born after a famous king or the slayer of Goliath, had no idea of the harassment it would bring to my adolescent life. Walking the hallways of school, being serenaded by classmates with David's hit song of the week, often made me want to drive a multi-colored school bus at light speed in their general direction during recess break. Oh, what I wouldn't have given to have a nickname (or any other name for that matter) during those testing times of, "I Think I Love You," but little did I know at the time that a nickname was just around the corner.

When you grow up in Canada, you play hockey. That's not a generalization, but a fact. Another fact is that when you are the poorest skater on the team, you end up playing goalie. David Cassidy, Goalie.

1

It was really not the worst spot on the ice to be. If you played well, you were the hero of the game. But if you played poorly, the team didn't have much desire to speak to you in the dressing room afterwards. As fate, as well as a small fortune out of my parents' pockets for different hockey camps and goalie schools, would have it, I ended up playing well more often than not. This knack that I had for the wonderful position of stopping frozen rubber with my forehead soon had me moving up through the ranks of junior hockey. It was at a tournament in Brantford – the home of the Great One, *Wayne Gretzky* – where we ended up winning in a real nail-biter of a finale, that a local newspaper reporter penned this opening line to his column: "When you perform such tremendous feats of net-minding robbery, wouldn't your teammates call you 'Butch Cassidy' instead of 'David Cassidy'?"

The name stuck, and for the next fifteen years or so I became known as "Butch" to all who knew me. And secretly, deep down inside, I truly loved the nickname. Mostly because, during that awkward growing stage of adolescence, it just sounded really cool.

Around the age of twenty-two, my educational career had come to an end, with high school and then three years of college, studying business administration and majoring in marketing. It's not that I really enjoyed this area of study, but as with most middle-class kids, it was always drilled into my head that a decent education was necessary, otherwise I'd end up being a ditch digger. Although, ditch diggers probably earn more than many people in business anyway, but that's beside the point. I swam with the flow and, one May, ended up at my graduation ceremony with a piece of paper in my hand.

"Great, now what?" was the one question I kept asking myself. I could see how it was going to play out in my mind: getting an entry level position with some local marketing firm, going from door to door, begging people to fill out a survey about frozen breaded chicken nuggets, and inquiring what would entice them to buy these products of zero nutritional value. It's a strange feeling when you're in your early twenties and your future looks relatively bleak, so the path I chose was the only obvious one in my eyes – let's go backpacking in Europe for a year and put off the inevitable for as long as possible!

Needless to say, all my friends thought I was off my rocker. "Butch, what are you doing?"

"Butch, you just finished college! Who's going to take you seriously when you get back?"

"Butch, you're just running away from real life!"

Yes, I probably was in hindsight, but every day as I slaved away at a very menial task in a meat-packing company to save up some money for my trip overseas, the excitement inside of me grew larger and larger.

No one in my family – with the exception of my ancestors – had ever been outside of North America but that was probably about 150 years ago and they don't count. (Great-uncles fighting in world wars don't count either.) My parents, who at first I thought would be against my decision to go traveling, surprisingly supported the idea.

"Get out there and see the world. We never had the chance to do it, and besides, you're going to have plenty of time to earn a living during your lifetime," they told me encouragingly.

A lot of people I knew had gone backpacking overseas and they all seemed to have the same kind of stories: partying in this hostel, in this town, during this festival. But what I wanted was to get away from backpackers and do something on my own. If I wanted to hang out with other Canadians, drink beer, and talk about hockey, then I really didn't need to go overseas to do that, now, did I? Just a few blocks away was a pub where I could do that and save a hell of a lot of money.

One day, when I found myself drawn to the local library to do a little research on all these tiny countries packed into what is known as "Europe," I came across a book called *Cycling Through Europe*. After flipping through the first few pages, I knew right away that this was how I wanted to travel. I could turn down any road I wanted, wouldn't be dependant on public transportation, would be able to put up a tent and camp when and where I felt like it (with permission of course), and I could avoid the whole backpacker circus, where the same kind of people seemed to meet up in hostels, in every town along the beaten paths.

Not having done any serious biking in my life, I knew that it would be quite the challenge. And even though it sounded like a great idea in my head, would I actually enjoy it? There was only one way to find out, so out I went and bought one of the very first mountain bikes ever built, rigged it out for touring, and did a few short trips around southwestern Ontario. Aside from a really sore butt the first couple of days, I thoroughly enjoyed this self-propelled mode of transportation. I was covering what I considered great distances, under my own power, and not screwing up the environment at that. If I could avoid becoming roadkill, all the better. The *Cycling Through Europe* book said that "Europeans are very considerate of cyclists, because there are so many of them there," so I thought it shouldn't be a problem.

Soon enough, there it was. On a dreary October day, after a summer of watching 300 pigs an hour pass by on a conveyor belt, I found myself at the airport in Toronto, waiting for my flight to London, England, to start my big adventure. I was feeling extremely apprehensive, and at the same time incredibly excited about what was about to unfold. I knew there would be challenges, times of feeling homesick, times of fun, times of fear, and times of pure admiration.

Europe was old, right? We don't really know "old" in North America. If something is fifty years of age here, we tear it down. If, on the off chance a building makes it to one hundred years old, we have a big ceremony, call it a historical site, and then a few years later we tear it down. Our country has been a relatively young country since the time that we took it from the native Indians and claimed it as our own. More often than not, when you hear North Americans talking about culture, they are usually referring to yogurt.

Landing in London was a strange feeling because I knew that whatever happened from here on out was entirely up to me. There was an entire year laid out before me that looked like a blank canvas. *What was my Picasso going to look like twelve months down the road?* Once I had the bike entirely put together, my journey began. Since it was early October and autumn had already descended upon Great Britain, the only obvious choice was to head down south. This was about the extent of my plans. Having read many books and studied tons of maps, confusion had crept into my head. *How am I ever going to see all these great places, and how do I map out a route to do it all?* I had so many different configurations of routes in my little notebook that just a week before the trip, I threw it in the garbage. "Whatever will be, will be," I said to myself, and just set out like a rudderless ship, determined to go wherever the wind took me. In hindsight it was a good idea to take this approach from early on because plans were just made to be changed anyway. Besides, why put extra pressure on myself, right? Riding on a rock-hard saddle, sleeping in a tiny little tent, and eating from a one-burner camping stove was pressure enough.

The days passed by so fast that I couldn't believe that after only a month-and-a-half my chariot and I were lying on a beach in the southern part of Spain.

England had lasted only a few days before the ferry had taken me over from the White Cliffs of Dover to the port of Calais, and France was basically filled with eight-hour days of pedaling, with the exception of a few days in Paris. Winter was coming and south was where I wanted to be! This is how Canadians think: *If at all possible, get as far away from winter as you can.* Florida's and Arizona's populations swell by the tens of thousands every winter, just from the Canadian Snowbird migration. Winter is long in the Great White North, and with very minor exceptions, most of us dream of warm beaches during the windshield-scraping season.

The south of Spain was warm. The water temperature, though dropping ever so slightly, was still nice for a dip, and I was at peace with my life in the tent. I'd met and ridden with many different cyclists from all over the world, and the saddle sores on my rear end were now a thing of the past. My legs were even taking on the dimensions of a speed skater. It all looked great until I came to the realization that winter was on its way, and even southern Europe can get chilly in January and February. This dilemma had only two solutions. The first and colder option was to head back up along the Mediterranean, over the south of France, down through Italy, and then hit the Greek Islands. The second and stupider option of the two, which, naturally, I chose, was to carry on down to Gibraltar, catch the ferry over to Morocco, and then head east across Northern Africa. I remember a saying from college that went something like "God protects

7

the drunks and the children." He also protects the lunatics, among whom I counted myself after a few months in the Muslim worlds of Morocco, Algeria, and Tunisia. Fresh out of college, naïve as ever, and here I was alone on a bike, battling my way through parts of the Sahara Desert, and a culture that often made my own jaw hit the handlebars. Interesting travels indeed, but I wasn't sorry to hop on the ferry from Tunis to Sicily. File these two months under the category of *"Learning Experience."*

Sicily and southern Italy rolled by smoothly, and the calls of the Greek Islands were like Sirens in my head. After an overnight ferry from Brindisi to Patras, I was in the Land of the Gods. If you think that Europe is old, then that would make Greece really old, or at least it seemed to me. Just pedaling along the back roads was like a step back in time. Houses painted white with olive trees in the front, what appeared to be ancient ruins (or at least stone pillars) lying in their yards and the sheets on the clotheslines flapping in the wind. It was beautiful and exactly how I pictured Greece would be.

One night, as I was dozing off in my tent at a totally vacant campground just outside of Athens, I reminisced over the last four months of riding. I had covered a great distance with my pedal-powered chariot, and the time for some rest and relaxation was quickly approaching. *Get into Athens, phone the folks, check for mail being held for me at the post office, and finally, get out of the big city and scope out a nice island to chill out on for the next couple of weeks.* "Chill out" was a suitable term because it was only February after all, and the temperatures at night still took pokes at the freezing point.

The holiday from my holiday would be welcomed because life on the road, believe it or not, really does wear you down. People who haven't often traveled have a hard time getting their heads around the fact that it actually is hard on you. When I would tell someone that I had to hang out here or there for a few days due to pure exhaustion, I'd often hear, "How could you be? You're on bloody holidays!" True enough, but unless you've been there, you can't really understand it.

Often, as I came to discover, things don't go as planned. After packing up my tent, loading up the bike and drinking a really awful-tasting cup of instant coffee made on my little camping stove, I was on my way to tackle the Mega-Monster-Tropolis of Athens.

For the most part, drivers in Europe were courteous with cyclists, just as the book had said. They would pull out and give you a lot of space, wait to pass, or honk as a warning so you knew they were there behind you. Athens was in sight and the only road into it from the direction I was coming was a two-lane highway.

It all happened pretty fast on a fairly steep curve, but I'll always carry with me the image of a semi-trailer truck overtaking me on an uphill curve to the right, and then straightening out, all the while not knowing that I was right beside the connector on the two trailers. They swung towards me when he straightened out, and I just ran out of tarmac. I had one of two choices to make: 1. Let the truck hit me, and then I'd probably get tossed under the wheels and die or something like that, or 2. Go off the road and down the ten-foot rocky embankment. The rocky embankment came out on top, and I blanked out. I wasn't sure how long I lay there, but when I came to, my head felt like it had been slammed in a car door. I heard traffic zooming by, but when my vision cleared and I looked up, I couldn't see any cars – which meant that they couldn't see me either – hence the lack of help. I probably endured a concussion because of the size of the lump on my forehead, but there was a surprisingly small amount of blood. When I tried to get up, my ribs told me that I should probably think twice about that choice. But having had broken ribs before, I knew that they were bruised rather than broken. Still being able to breathe was a sure give-away there. Aside from all kinds of scrapes and aches, I knew I'd gotten off pretty easy. There was nothing broken inside of me that I could tell, but the chariot wasn't looking so hot.

The rear rim was probably the only metal part that wasn't bent. The frame, forks, and front rim were all mangled beyond repair; you didn't need to be an Einstein to figure that one out. Athens was only about a mile away and it would be great to say that it was my sense of determination that got me there, but it was probably just that I was operating on autopilot, in a state of complete shock. The bike, with all the pannier bags and one good wheel, made it into town in a blur that I can barely remember.

It was all over. Sitting in a cheap hotel room that same night with the dead chariot and my first aid kit beside my bed, the tears flowed.

As since the beginning of time, one day turns into the next and life goes on. I was heartbroken at my loss of transportation, but at the same time thankful that I was still able to function without serious injury. I could have easily gone under a tire and become a road pizza. I guess Lady Luck was on my side that day.

"*What to do next?*" was my main thought. As I sat there pondering, I realized that I really loved Europe and wanted to see even more of it. That very day, I set out in search of a new bike, but that search turned out to be futile. Sure, I had the option of buying a racing bike or even a junky little road bike, but neither of these options was very appealing. After five or so months on a new machine called a mountain bike, I couldn't see myself touring on anything else. The concept of a robust bike, which could handle the punishment and still be modified for touring, hadn't caught on yet over the big pond.

Going back home wasn't an option of mine, because when I start something I have to finish it. That's probably something I learned from playing hockey and all the discipline that goes along with it. If there's one thing I'm not, it's a quitter. I've also got an incredibly thick skull, which goes with being a Taurus, to prove it. So, as much as I disliked the idea of joining the backpacking crowd of North Americans and Australians, I decided I would give it a try anyhow.

There was a Syrian guy who was staying at the same hotel as me who had a little traveling business going, which consisted of buying used Eurail passes off of people who were headed home. Eurail passes are train passes, which will get you all over Europe with ease. They're bought and paid for before you head to Europe, and you can travel second class wherever there is room on the trains. Needless to say, he would change the travel eligibility dates with his forgery kit and resell them. Naturally I bought one from him and therefore had three months of train travel ahead of me.

As much as I tried to stay off the beaten track, it wasn't that easy. With a bike I had the freedom to pretty much set up my camp wherever I wanted, but this whole train-travel business took away a lot of that freedom and I found myself spending a lot of time in different hostels. After a while I got quite into it and saw it as a positive change. One thing I discovered was my love for Europe – the architecture, the people, the little villages, the old with the new, just everything about it. I loved it over there, but after about ten months of cramming my brain full of new things, keeping Kodak Film in business, and visiting about twenty-five different countries, my funds were running on empty and I was back on a plane to the land of strip malls and fast food joints.

There was no question in my mind about going back overseas again. It was a given, and all that was missing was the money to do it. So, for a year, it was back to the meat packing company working as much as I possibly could and living like Ebenezer Scrooge. That was one of the longest years of my life, which wasn't helped at all by working a job I absolutely hated. Luckily, the months rolled by quicker than I'd expected, and soon I was ready to head back to Europe on a brand new chariot.

"This time would be different," I said to myself. *"Why stop at Europe? Why not just bike around the whole world?"* So, once again I set off, but this time it was right from my parent's front door. The first destination was down to New York City, and from there over to Holland by plane. New York should never be experienced by bicycle. It was really white-knuckle riding on those roads, which brought back some not-so-fond memories from eighteen months' previous in Greece. I got in and out of JFK airport as quickly as possible and woke up the next morning in Amsterdam, ready for Phase Two. It felt so good to be back over there – just like I had never been away.

My plans were not entirely set out in black and white because plans change every day, and since it was the middle of summer, I wasn't in a rush to get south to the warmer climates like in the previous tour. I made my way in the direction of the Alps, sticking mostly to the narrow country roads. No more highways or busy roads for this camper. I was riding about sixty miles per day, just taking my time, and hopping over a lot of borders. On one particular day, I started off in the Netherlands, rode through the northern part of Belgium, back into the Netherlands, and then over the border touching into France just before veering off east into Germany, and finally finishing up in Luxembourg. Five countries in nine hours: Not even a Japanese tour bus could touch that one.

When I was a little further south and Switzerland was in my sight, I decided to visit the town of Interlaken, because I had met a girl a few months previously in Canada and she was working as a tour guide there. What I didn't know was that she was working as a tour guide for a company called Jungfrau Tours, which left Interlaken early in the morning and took tourists via train way up into the Alps, to the highest restaurant in Europe, called the Jungfraujoch. Up there, at 11,333 feet above sea-level, the guests were treated to a breathtaking view of the Alps, an unbelievable dining experience, guided tours out onto the glacier, and for those who wanted, even sled dog rides. Later in the afternoon, all the tourists would hop back onto the train and be brought back down to Interlaken.

When I did meet up with her, she invited me to stay at her place while I was in town and over the course of dinner one evening, she let it slip that they needed people to work up at the Jungfraujoch. She wasn't entirely certain of what the work would entail, but she asked me if I was interested, and without even thinking about it, I said yes.

The next morning I hopped on the train with her and headed up into the Alps for an interview with the director of the restaurant. Unable to speak a word of German, I was a little apprehensive, but when he started out in English, I felt much more at ease.

I never would have dreamt, when I left home, that I'd end up working in Switzerland, but after a ten-minute interview with the big guy, I became a dishwasher. There was no one higher up as far as altitude goes, and I was getting paid (quite well I might add, by Canadian standards) so I was able to make the claim that I was the highest paid dishwasher in all of Europe.

It was pretty mindless work as one can imagine, but I did get to learn a bit of the language as well as meet several very interesting people who were native to all different parts of the world. The staff accommodation provided for us was not up at the very top, but just a little ways down at a place called The Eiger Glacier, or *"Eigergletscher"* in German. This consisted of nothing more than a small restaurant, a common room with a television, and bedrooms for about 125 people. As all of our meals were taken care of, and there was really no place to go out and spend money, I found myself very quickly socking away a good stash of coin.

Plans are made to be changed, and this could not be truer than in the world of backpacking. Therefore, my grand vision of bicycling around the world quickly gave way to the concept of extended trips, and returning to work in Switzerland for the quick and easy cash. In 1988, I did a tour through central Africa, India, Nepal, Thailand, and the Philippines, before heading back to Switzerland to replenish the bank account.

Perhaps the big boss saw some potential in me, or maybe he was just a little short-staffed, but upon my return to the Eiger Glacier, I learned that I was going to be a waiter – a major jump up on the prestige scale, but this also meant that I had to begin taking learning the language a lot more seriously than I had during my previous time on the mountain. The lingo came slowly, although I was just learning how to speak it and not really read or write it. The base is German, but in Switzerland they have their own dialect of German, which even Germans can't fully understand. A good comparison between German and Swiss German would be like comparing high-class British English with Pidgin English. Naturally, I learned the bastardized version because that's what I heard all day long. In hindsight it was a dumb move, but I'm pretty proficient in dumb moves.

The season went well in 1989, so I decided to go home for the winter since I hadn't seen my family in over two-and-a-half years. Heading back "home" was different this time around because I knew that I wouldn't be staying. I'd found my new life calling as a travel bum and nothing was going to change that, as far I could see.

After a few months in Canada it was back over the big pond to Amsterdam to meet up with a Swedish friend with whom I had worked up at the Jungfraujoch restaurant. We had planned the previous summer on heading back to Southeast Asia, as this was a part of the world that fascinated me and I wanted to see some more of it. You could spend a lifetime traveling there and barely scratch the surface of all there is to see. As it turned out, when I arrived in Amsterdam, I learned that he'd be delayed for a couple of weeks coming down from Sweden, due to work commitments, so I decided to hop on a train and head down to Switzerland to visit a few friends.

Across the valley from Eiger Glacier where I previously lived is a sleepy little village called Muerren. There are no cars there because it is perched terribly high up on a cliff and is only accessible by either cable car or funicular railway. During the off-season there are about 300 locals living there, but during the ski season the population can swell up to around 5000; it is the epitome of a tourist-town. High above the village of Muerren is the famous Schilthorn Mountain with a revolving restaurant at the 10,000-foot high peak called Piz Gloria (made famous back in 1969 with the filming of the James Bond movie *On Her Majesty's Secret Service*.) Personally, I think it was one of the worst Bond movies ever made and you'd be hard-pressed to find many people who knew that George Lazenby was actually a Bond guy, but Telly Savalas made a great villain.

Anyway, it was here in the village of Muerren where the seeds would be planted that would shape the rest of my life, although at the time I was completely ignorant of the fact. My friend Brents, who I was there visiting, was very similar to me. He was a cook from Texas who did the whole seasonal work thing with six-month travel stints in between. I had gone up to Muerren for only a single night of visiting, which translated into a whole bunch of beers and catching up on the news of the foreigners working in the valley. Brents had just finished his winter season and was also heading to Southeast Asia for a summer of backpacking around, though he was going over there with three locals from Muerren. He asked me if I wanted to meet up in Bangkok and do some trekking up in the northern part of Thailand and, naturally, I agreed.

The next morning, before I left to start my way back to Amsterdam, Brents and I were strolling through one of the only two streets of the village, both feeling very tired from a night of catching up, when we met up with one of the girls he was going to be traveling to Thailand with. Her name was Franziska, and apparently I didn't make a very good first impression with her. She claimed that I didn't even say hello to her during that whole minute-long street conversation she and Brents had. Maybe it was the fact that my brain wasn't functioning on full power or that I just didn't want to look stupid with my limited German in front of this lovely Swiss lady, but I'll never live that first encounter down with Franziska, or Franzi as I like to call her. She turned out to be the woman I would marry.

Chapter Two

Wife, Marriage, and a Dog

*N*ot giving that chance meeting with Franzi on the street a second thought, I made my way back up to Amsterdam to tag up with my Swedish buddy Bengt. Bengt was a few years younger than I and, as a result, equally irresponsible. If it looked like fun, regardless of the act itself, he was in. When we finally met up, his first and only question to me was, "Where are we going anyway?"

"Trekking in northern Thailand," I answered.

"Well then, let's get on a flight and get there," was his oh-so-typical response.

So it went. We ended up taking what one would consider possibly the cheapest, longest flight imaginable, with stops in Athens, Cairo, Dubai, Delhi, and Bangladesh before finally touching down in Bangkok. When you're not on any time schedule, flights like these aren't a great concern. The more money you save, the more you have to spend when you eventually get there, though it tends to take a bit of a toll on the body, especially when you're jam-packed into the cattle-class section of the plane.

I told Bengt about my plans to meet up with Brents for trekking, which he was completely fine with, and a few days later, after checking out some of the sights in Bangkok, we did just that. The overnight bus up to Chang Mai was definitely not a jolly ride as our seats were directly over the back wheel well of the bus and we probably spent more time in the air than in the seats themselves due to the countless potholes. But arrive we did, even if it was with bruised butts and backbones.

There are tons of trekking companies in the northern part of this beautiful country, but being the cheap backpackers that we were, we decided to just find a guide and a cook on our own to avoid the big package deals that were plastered all over the windows of the travel shops. After asking around a bit, we found both a guide and a cook, and were finally on our way. Little did we know that our cook was an opium addict who had to take a two-hour break every four hours to replenish his state of mind, which is politely put, but it was a relaxing pace which didn't bother us much at all.

The north is very rugged and extremely green, and the exotic birds were unlike anything I'd seen, or for that matter, eaten before. Our guide, who carried a musket that looked like it came right out of the Civil War (complete with gunpowder and the little pellets), was quite proficient when it came to hunting. With one shot he nailed two very good-sized parrots – which went into the nightly stew – and the next day we dined on grilled squirrel, or at least some animal that resembled a squirrel. Kraft Dinner never looked so appetizing before, but we survived. After about ten days of hiking, camping, and eating a lot of meals that we stopped asking questions about, we had completed our trek.

As Bengt and I had no set plans for our next destination, we quickly latched onto Brents's invitation of heading down south to the warm, white, sandy beaches of Koh Samui. Three friends of his from Muerren were down there and he had promised Franzi that he would head on down for her birthday which was on the 25th of May. He went on ahead of us by a couple of days because we wanted to check out the floating market in Bangkok, which is a chaotic swarm of farmers selling their produce on long, narrow skiffs on a very narrow waterway. It's one of those things that attract all the organized tours, but it was still pretty interesting to see.

A couple of days later, Bengt and I showed up on the island of Koh Samui at Maenam beach, just as the directions from Brents had told us to. After checking into our two-dollar-a-night simple bungalows, we headed to the beach to see who we could find. Brents, Franzi, Martha, and a Frenchman named Remy were all lying on the beach beside each other, just likes strips of bacon sizzling in a frying pan. This time I actually said hello to Franzi, unlike the brief street encounter in Muerren. However, I could tell from her eyes that she was thinking, "Oh great, this is the idiot who didn't even have the manners to say hello to me on the street." Regardless, we all went out that night to a little restaurant just down the beach to celebrate her birthday. It was a nice dinner and a relatively quiet night. When you're backpacking, parties seem to happen spontaneously. When you expect them, they don't happen, and vice-versa. This was how Franzi's birthday went.

The next morning, after wishing her a happy birthday once again, the six of us had a relaxing day at the beach, followed again by dinner together and then, very unexpectedly, everyone seemed to have a great desire for the local Mekong whiskey. There it was, the unexpected party, and a good all-nighter it was. When the dust finally settled at sunrise, it was Franzi and I in each other's arms on the beach.

Travel romances, or one-night stands as they could be referred to, happen all the time. People have their own plans on where they want to go and what they want to do, so it's very seldom when two travelers who hook up in a fling actually end up traveling together. People just have the need for intimacy with others every once in a while. This time around was different, for me at least. Franzi and I spent the next few days non-stop with each other, doing different things together. I became hooked; this was the woman for me. I knew it in my heart, but my head was having a harder time getting around the idea. First, there was the language barrier, although she spoke very good English. Second, we were from two different cultures, with me being the city boy from North America, and she being the Heidi girl from the Swiss Alps. Third, it was a fling for her, because she already had a boyfriend back in Switzerland, and was very honest with me about that when we started off. Still, I *knew* that she was the one.

Franzi had planned on staying in Thailand for about five weeks, which meant that I would have had at least a couple of weeks with her, but she had to cut it short by about ten days. A single centipede bite on her leg was all it took. Within hours, this little round red spot on her shin developed into a bump about the size of a golf ball. After a few hours of messing around with the local doctors at the island's very understaffed health clinic, the decision was made by her best friend Martha that she had to get back to Europe for proper medical attention. So Franzi was taken back to Bangkok by ferry and put on the first flight out. It was a really sad farewell at the port, and we promised to write each other and keep in touch. However, deep inside, I wondered if I'd ever again see this wonderful person who, in such a short time, had managed to steal my heart away.

It took a few days of wallowing in self-pity and worrying about her health before I had my head back on relatively straight. There were no phones where we were, and this was long before the invention of the Internet and e-mail, so I was just praying that she would be okay. I continued to write her letters every day, hoping that someday I would see her again.

My plans were quite simple: Bengt, Brents and I would be flying to Hong Kong to travel around China.

From there, it was on to Australia. Plans change, but at least it sounded good and having something to focus on other than my broken heart was a welcome change.

Hong Kong was a place that I'd never been to before and I really wanted to see it before it reverted to Chinese rule in 1997. Vibrant, bustling, and hectic is how it bombarded my senses. It was hard to imagine that this nest of pure capitalism was straddling the largest Communist country in the world. With our visas in hand, we set off to explore this vast, and until very recently, closed-off country.

The time in China flew by quickly and believe me, it wasn't because we were having fun. It was the most difficult country I'd ever experienced in my backpacking days. Every day was a labor to get to different places, whether by bus, boat, rail, or plane. Not a word of English was spoken outside of the highly touristy areas, so that meant heavy usage of the phrase books and writing all requests for hotel rooms, bus and train tickets, and directions out in Chinese characters and sticking them in someone's face, hoping they'd understand what we meant.

Trying times those three months were, but the one constant throughout the whole thing was my desire to meet up with Franzi again. I'd written tons of letters to her and she even sent me a few responses, but just before I was about to leave China I got the shot to the head, the kick to the teeth, the puck in the groin, or better put, the "Dear John letter." To sum up an absolutely devastating note, she basically said that although we had a spectacular and unforgettable time together in Thailand, she felt it was time for me to put her in the memory column of my mind because she was still with her boyfriend (who, by the way, was a world-class mountain climber and guide.)

Being a travel bum doesn't exactly stack up against being a world-class mountain climber, though I wasn't going to be deterred by this minor technicality. It just wouldn't be as easy as I thought at first. With my "Dear John letter" in hand, I made it back to Hong Kong and straightaway booked a flight to Zurich. In hindsight, there wasn't a whole lot of thought that went into that decision. Nonetheless, it was what I wanted and there wasn't any doubt in my mind that Franzi was the woman for me. After booking the flight, my next stop was at the post office, where I made *the phone call*. Phoning from Mainland China was truly hit and miss, so I had decided to postpone the call until I returned to Hong Kong.

Time zones can sometimes work to your advantage, and I chose mine very strategically. I knew that if I called in the afternoon it would be early in the morning back in Switzerland, and that was how I wanted it to play out; get them before their brains start functioning at full capacity. The conversation was very abrupt, and I think she was truly caught off-guard when I asked her if she could pick me up in Zurich the following day. However, she actually agreed to come and get me (which I put into the optimistic plus column), but I was to find out later that she had had one tizzy of a day.

After she hung up and began her panic-filled day thinking about the travel fling that was going to show up in less than 24 hours, she hopped in her car and headed into town to pick up some groceries. Parking in Switzerland is scarce, so many of the larger shopping centres are built with parking garages underneath them. When she went down the ramp to enter the garage, the car in front of her stopped at the rising barrier, took the ticket from the dispenser, and proceeded into the garage. Franzi, who at that moment had her mind elsewhere, proceeded to follow the car in front, but was quickly shaken from her thoughts by the sound of the parking barrier crashing down on the roof of her car. The wood splintered pretty easily and luckily there was very little damage done to the car. Being in the daze that she was, she calmly parked the car and walked back to the automated ticket machine where the barrier was.

Switzerland is based on efficiency, so no one should be surprised to hear there was already a maintenance guy there fixing the thing. Franzi calmly told him that it was already broken when she came down the ramp and the machine didn't give her the parking ticket she would need to exit the garage. He fixed her up with the parking pass as he went about swearing in Swiss German about stupid, idiotic drivers and how this same thing happens at least once a week.

The next morning, bright and early, my plane touched down in the land of chocolate, cheese, and numbered bank accounts, with Franzi and her friend Martha there to pick me up. It was a very nice reunion, but I could see that she had a million things in her head about the complications that were going to arise with my arrival.

When I managed to get Martha alone, I asked her if I actually had any kind of a chance with Franzi, or if I was just spinning my wheels and wishing on an unattainable star. Her response lifted my spirits because she told me that although Franzi was still with Michael the "mountain man," they did very few things together and she was often left alone for long periods of time while he went off on his expeditions. It didn't sound like the perfect relationship – far from it actually – so with this glimmer of hope in my heart I decided to bide my time, get a job, and see just how this whole scenario would play out.

Up in the village of Muerren was where I decided to settle down this time. After finding an apartment, my search was now focused on a job. The job didn't come very easily this time around, but eventually, after Franzi spoke to a friend on my behalf, I found myself employed as a ski lift operator. A seasonal job, but a job nevertheless. The only problem was that I hadn't been on skis before. Luckily, due to my hockey and cycling days, my legs were strong and I had always had a great sense of balance, so within a few days I had learned enough about skiing to be able to make it down the hill without embarrassing myself too much. But the other people I skied with kept a good distance from me, and on a few occasions I was told that my style on the boards resembled someone squatting on the toilet.

As the year went on, Franzi and I spent some time together as friends, which was hard for me because I wanted so much more. But hope and patience were still on my side, though they were both starting to wear a little thin, and I had even come to the decision that if something didn't change in the next few months, then it was time to grab the backpack and head back to the open road. Not that I wanted to, but I was getting pretty discouraged at what was looking like a dead end, and there's also the manly pride to consider. Everyone I knew up in Muerren who had an idea of what was going on in my life, was telling me to give it up, in a nutshell. And give it up I almost did.

The summer season had just wound up and I'd finished a stint up on the Schilthorn Restaurant, running the self-serve cafeteria, when I started looking at my trusty map of the world. Australia and New Zealand were still on my mind, and with the crash of the Soviet empire happening, the Trans-Siberian railway route was very enticing as a method of getting back to Asia. From Beijing I could just grab a flight, make it down to Sydney ASAP, and then I would have seen the northern part of Russia, Siberia, and Mongolia along the way, adding another few notches in the travel belt.

All of these thoughts quickly flew out the window one clear October evening when my phone rang and Franzi told me that she and her mountain climber boyfriend had just called it quits. She was really down about the whole thing but if you had seen *my* face, you would have thought I'd won the lottery, I'm sure.

Finally, almost a year and a half after that brief encounter in Thailand, my chance had finally come along and I wasn't going to blow it. However, whatever pace Franzi wanted to take things was just fine by me, and that's exactly how we did it. Slow at first, a little quicker as we went along, living together a year later, and then the big marriage question popping out of my mouth one night in a very loud discotheque. How romantic, one might sarcastically say, but she didn't flat out turn me down, which I took to be a positive sign. What she did say was that the rest of her life was a heck of a long time to spend with the same person and she wanted to make sure I was the one. In her eyes, there was only one way for her to confirm to herself that she had the right guy, and that was by traveling together.

I had to agree with her because when you are on the travel road together, twenty-four hours a day and seven days a week, you learn the other person from the inside, out. Most couples date for a few years, move in together, and then spend their days off doing things with each other, all the while having plenty of time apart from one another. Whether it be going to work, going golfing, going out with the girls, business trips or any number of things, couples in a daily routine don't actually spend a lot of time together, technically.

When tramping around in strange, foreign countries, you're often faced with challenging situations

29

or crises that you just don't encounter in everyday life. This was what was important to Franzi and also to me. Whatever little tics he or she has that drive the other person crazy quickly surface when you're together literally non-stop.

With this train of thought, we set off on what would be a six-month trial run. It was kind of like taking a car out for a test drive before purchasing it, but this was going to be a hell of a long test drive. Our plan was to fly back to Ontario to visit my family for a couple of weeks and then head down to Ecuador and Bolivia. Franzi loved Ecuador because she had been there before, but truthfully, I wasn't that keen on South America. Having never been there personally, I still had stereotypical prejudgments on the entire continent. The thing that bothered me the most was probably the fact that the whole of South America was predominantly Catholic. Having been raised Catholic and spending thirteen years of my youth in private Catholic schools had nothing to do with my angst about traveling in these lands. It was merely experience that had me slightly wary. Crime was the key factor. Southern Europe, which entails Italy, Spain, and Portugal, were all devout Catholic countries, as were the Philippines in Asia, and these were the countries in which I encountered the most problems, hassles, and had to have my guard up the most. *"How could South America be any different?"* I asked myself, but this was my marriage trial run we were talking about here, so I was in.

Perhaps it was the negative vibes that I'd sent out, or it was just fate, but lo and behold, three days after we'd arrived in Quito – the capital of Ecuador – the crisis situation arose. The proverbial poop hitting the fan might be a more suitable term. We had just rented a jeep to go touring around the Andes and had only been on the road an hour, making our way up into the hills, when we started seeing rocks about the size of footballs on the road. The rocks looked like they had been placed there by humans, but not thinking anything was out of the ordinary, we just drove around them and kept on going. As we went further and further up, the rocks started to get a little larger, and the few people (who were all native Indians), that we did see along the road, all seemed to be waving at us, but in a strange kind of "screwing in a light bulb" motion with the palm of the hand turned upwards. Being the ignorant Gringos that we were, we just carried on and waved back at them.

The boulders on the road grew larger and larger as we climbed higher and higher, until we had to stop for the mother of all boulders, which was about 3 feet in diameter, and not having enough room to go around either side without dropping off a very steep and very high cliff, we were brought to a standstill. The road was so narrow that there wasn't even a chance of turning around and I wasn't relishing the task of driving about five miles in reverse, but all those thoughts quickly left my mind when we were suddenly surrounded by about 30 to 40 native Indians. *"This was definitely not what I'd signed up for,"* I thought to myself. They were holding shovels and pickaxes and were all pressing their faces against the windows of the jeep which, fortunately, were rolled up, and we had the doors locked. They started pushing and rocking the jeep and we honestly thought that we would be pushed over the edge of the cliff and end up tumbling down the mountainside like you see in the movies.

Considering the lack of any other option, Franzi put her window down an inch and started yelling at them in Spanish. The whole time, I hadn't taken my foot off of the clutch, which was good because it disguised how much I was shaking. *"We are going to die here, in the middle of the Andes, and no one will even know,"* were my thoughts. Finally, after persistent banging on the jeep and being rocked back and forth frightfully close to the edge, one of the older Indians put his head close to the crack in the window and started a conversation with Franzi. Her Spanish was pretty good because she had worked as a translator at the European Soccer Association for three years, but at this point she was suddenly quite fluent. The "Big Chief," as I'll refer to the ringleader, asked Franzi what we were doing way up here and why we didn't turn around when the people on the road were waving at us. "We didn't know what that signal meant," she said, and being the quick thinker that she is, told him that we had gotten lost and were on our way back to Quito to return to Switzerland. Not having any idea of where *Switzerland* was, she explained that it was over the "big pond," and the angry mood of the mob seemed to lessen when Big Chief spoke to them. I can only guess that he explained that we weren't Gringos from America, but just lost white people from a land a lot farther away than Gringoville. Franzi had never stopped talking to Big Chief and after a good half hour of non-stop banter between her, Big Chief, and the mob, they agreed to let us go free.

As we made our way back down in reverse, both shaking like leaves in a windstorm and completely dumbfounded that we were still alive, Franzi explained what Big Chief had said. Our timing for heading up into the Andes was impeccable. It was the first day of a native uprising. It was also the first day of the Copa Americana (a soccer tournament between all of the countries of North and South America), which was the absolute best time for the native people to disrupt travel throughout Ecuador, the country that was hosting the event. They are quite an impoverished group of people who receive very little support from the government, although the native Indian people make up around three quarters of the population.

After getting turned around and feeling at least a bit safer, we decided to head back to Quito, gather our thoughts, and plan out our next step. Along the drive back we passed a bus going in the direction that we had just come from and thought to ourselves that *that* was how we should have traveled, instead of making ourselves look like rich Americans. Wrong. We would come to learn a few days later that the bus was also ambushed and most of the people were killed.

Back in Quito, we nestled ourselves into the safety of a $30 hotel room, which was a definite splurge by our travel standards, but after dodging a bullet like we had on this particular day, things like money seemed very small on the grand scale of life. The big question here was, "what do we do now?" Franzi knew of my misgivings about traveling in South America, and she was no longer on the Ecuador-Bolivia bandwagon either, so we decided to cut and run. The interesting thing was that the same incident could have happened in many different countries, but it had happened in a Catholic one, even if that had nothing to do with it.

In my earlier travel days I probably would have pushed on and just put it down as an awful experience, but this was different now. There were two of us, and we both had to admit that even if we were to carry on, it wouldn't be enjoyable because we would be constantly on alert, and always looking over our shoulders, spotting dangers where no dangers existed. The plan therefore, was to get out of Ecuador, but not without a little five-week trip to the Galapagos Islands. You just can't be that close and not go see them. The time we spent there was so special. With very few people and lots of unspoiled wildlife, those islands are truly not just an Ecuadorian treasure, but a world treasure.

It was also while we were on the islands that Franzi came up with the idea of heading back to Canada to visit the Rocky Mountains. She'd been there before but I hadn't, so off to British Columbia it was. This idea didn't excite me all that much because one often tends to take one's own country for granted, but we had planned on traveling together for six months and that was what we were going to do.

British Columbia was a great experience in our little rented Volkswagen camper. The mountains were magnificent and we enjoyed camping wherever we felt like it. It was in the small town of Invermere, where we visited a friend of hers named Chris whom she had met about ten years earlier, that I said to her, "You know, honey, I could live here."

"I know," she said, "I could too." We spent about ten days at Chris's farm – a big 3000-acre cattle ranch – and truly had the time of our lives.

After a quick stop back in Ontario at the parents' place, we were back on the plane bound for Switzerland, both convinced that we could love, honor, cherish, and simply put up with each other until death do us part, so we quickly set about getting the ball rolling for our hitching ceremony. We wanted to put a rush on the entire thing because if we were married, then my whole status within Switzerland would change. I would be given a different visa allowing me to stay for the whole year instead of the nine-month working visa which I had always had as a seasonal worker. With a nine-month visa you are required to leave the country for a three-month period before returning, but I never paid any attention to that regulation; those were always just my three months of laying low and studying German.

The wedding took place on a cold and dreary November afternoon in a small village school classroom with just the Justice of the Peace. Franzi, Martha as Franzi's maid of honor, Brents as my best man, and I made up the whole wedding. This is how Swiss weddings work: just a five-minute technical thing and then you're married in the eyes of the law. The majority of couples have the big church ceremony a few days later, which we also wanted to do, but we put it off until the following summer when my family could be there, along with the nice weather.

In June of 1994, we were married not only legally, but also before the eyes of God in a Catholic ceremony, I must add. No one was hurt or robbed. It was a beautiful sunny day and the ceremony took place at Franzi's uncle's old farm courtyard with a wonderful view of the Alps. The reception afterwards was even more spectacular because it was in a thirteenth-century castle with a moat, drawbridge, and everything. My family and friends who had made the long journey for our special day were completely blown away, as was I.

The swinging single days were now a thing of the past and I honestly enjoyed the feeling of having a companion to share every up and every down with. It made me feel whole and I was happier than at any previous point in my life. The thought of having children was something that I had put into the back drawer of my mind, because Franzi had had some serious medical issues with her stomach (and by medical issues I mean three major surgeries within the past six years) so we weren't even sure if she would be able to carry a baby to term. But we were happy together, so that was all that really mattered.

It was late in 1994 that we were sitting at home one evening in front of the TV when we saw a National Geographic program about the diverse wildlife of British Columbia that stirred up a lot of memories about our camping experiences there, just over a year before. We are quite spontaneous people by nature, and over a bottle of wine we had basically made the decision that we were going to live there one day. We didn't exactly know when or where, but we decided to give ourselves a goal and we set a rough date for the big move to happen in 1997. "What the heck, that's three years down the road. We'll just save every penny from now until then and do it," we said.

It was with this goal in mind that we went about our daily lives. We lived very simply and watched every cent that we gave out. In a day and age of microwaves, VCRs, stereos, and all kinds of other toys, we were quite content with our little radio and 14-inch TV. We used our car as little as possible, opting for our bicycles, and every purchase that we contemplated ended up being a major discussion of whether we *really* needed it or not. A log home on a nice piece of land was just what we had in mind, like in all the travel magazines at the doctor's office. It was going to happen, and our plan was to give ourselves the best possible start when we got over there. The best way to do that was to have a good reserve in the bank. I knew that in Canada the wages were poor in comparison to Switzerland, so by sacrificing now we'd be paving a much rosier street when that big move finally came along.

The following spring was a tough one because Franzi's stomach started giving her problems again. Sharp pains that would double her over and keep her up at night seemed to be the norm, so after a trip back to the specialist it was decided that they'd have to open her up again, go in and clean out the scar tissue from previous operations, and see what could be done with the holes in the lining of her stomach wall. It all sounded routine, but with every operation there can be complications and you never know what they'll find until they actually get in there. This was no exception.

Franzi had several holes in her stomach lining and as a result it took quite a while for the surgeons to fix her up. To make matters even worse, they had found more than they had expected, so the question of ever having children was now laid to rest with a definite negative. Even though neither of us had really given any thoughts to having children, it still came down like a sledgehammer on our heads when we were faced with the reality that it could never happen – ever.

Franzi spent over a week in the hospital in the town of Interlaken, which was where we were living, and when she finally came out she looked like she'd been through the wringer. The doctors said she shouldn't even consider returning to her job as a shoe salesperson for a couple of months.

At that time I was working evenings in a pub as a barman and not starting my shift until around four in the afternoon, which was perfect because I could spend all day with her, fix her something for dinner, and then head off to work. She wasn't staying up very late, as she needed a lot of rest, so her evenings were occupied with a little TV and looking after our new kitten, aptly named Maenam, for the beach in Thailand where we had really met. It was a cute little thing without a care in the world, and a good distraction for Franzi who was trying to rebound, but not having such a good go at it.

I had the opportunity of two weeks of holidays that I decided to grab when Franzi started feeling a little bit better, so we decided we would go up to the village of Muerren where her parents had a holiday apartment. We planned to spend some time up there and do some easy walking to build up her strength again.

It was during one of those leisurely walks that we came across an extremely pregnant acquaintance of ours, waddling along the main road of the village with two children in a stroller, and a very rambunctious black Labrador Retriever, named Shadow, at her side. We stopped and talked for a little while about this and that, as people often do when they just meet on the street. Eventually she asked us where we were heading and if we wouldn't mind taking her dog for a walk. She was having an extremely hard pregnancy and didn't have the energy to look after the two toddlers and give the one-year-old dog the exercise he needed to get him down to the level of mildly wild instead of incredibly wild.

We agreed to take him for a few hours because we were just going to walk for about 45 minutes, make a stop for a drink at a little mountain restaurant, and then head back. I'd never had a dog in my life, or even walked one for that matter, but she assured us that he was well-trained, would come when he was called, and wouldn't give other dogs a hard time. It sounded good enough to me so we set off with our new rental dog. Sure enough, Shadow behaved like a saint. He'd go running off in the bushes and forest, digging for whatever dogs dig for in various holes in the ground, splashing around in the creeks and ponds, chasing birds and squirrels. However, as soon as we called his name, he'd be right back at our side. If we told him to sit, he'd sit. If we told him to lay down, he'd lay down. We were quite amazed at how well he listened, but then I remembered learning that Labs were really intelligent dogs, as they were often used to lead the blind as well as being involved in search and rescue missions and such.

Franzi loved having the dog with us on our walk and when we finally brought him back to his owner, she was ecstatic to hear that we'd love to take him again the next day. And so we did. Every day we'd go and pick up Shadow, take him with us wherever we went, and bring him home towards the evening. He was quite the wild and crazy young adult dog, but it never ceased to amaze us how well he listened when given a command.

After a two-week period of pretty much the same routine, Franzi finally came out and asked what I had half-expected her to ask at least a week earlier. "Why don't we get a dog?" she threw at me one night at the dinner table. Wow! My mind was really racing here because having a dog was a lot of commitment and responsibility. Sure, we just had a great two weeks of leisurely afternoon walking with Shadow, but that was kind of the same as going to a Dude Ranch and riding horses for a few hours everyday. We enjoyed the fun parts, but what about the feedings, the walks when we didn't feel like walking, the trips to the vet, cleaning up the never-ending piles of poop in the yard, the complications it would throw into our social lives, and certainly not least, the cost. Dogs in Switzerland are very expensive, as is their food, and besides that, what did I really know about owning a dog? Taking someone else's dog for a walk was one thing, but training and raising one was a whole new ballgame.

The other problem with having a furry little friend in our household was what to do with him or her if we decided to visit my parents in Canada. The first thing I thought about if we were going to go away on holidays and couldn't take the dog with us, was that we could just put him in a kennel and not worry about it, but that was shot down quite quickly by Franzi, both barrels on fully automatic. "If we get a dog, it won't be staying in any kennel!" This was basically the only answer that I expected, being the caring soul that she is. If she committed herself to an animal, it was going to be the full one hundred percent and nothing less.

A big concern of ours was when we *actually* moved to Canada. Would the dog have to go into quarantine? If this was the case, then there was no way we'd be getting one. This worried us quite a bit as we sat there that night having our "pros and cons, should we or shouldn't we?" discussion. When we finally put our heads on the pillow that night it had been decided that if there was no quarantine required and that if we could find someone very reliable and willing to look after the little one, then and only then, would we start searching for the little puppy of our dreams.

Our first thought was of family. There had to be someone, whether it was either of her two brothers, or her parents, that would look after the dog if we went away on holidays or in the event of an emergency, and it didn't take a lot of convincing with her parents before they agreed to be our backup plan. Franzi's father always had had dogs in his younger years, but when he started up his butcher shop he just couldn't have one anymore, because he was unable to devote the time to it that was required without it being neglected. Now that he was retired, he said he'd be more than happy to help us out in a pinch.

The second concern was quickly put to rest with one phone call to the Canadian embassy in Bern: no quarantine. All that was required to bring a dog into Canada was a valid rabies shot and a certificate of good health from our veterinarian. It all sounded simple. Luckily, we weren't planning on moving to Australia, because there the dogs have to spend their first six months in quarantine, or at least that's how it was in the mid 90's. Everything seemed to be falling into place for a new family addition and we were both pretty excited about the whole prospect. There was just one hurdle left to overcome, and it was one we hadn't even thought of at first, but it was a hurdle that could throw a monkey wrench into the whole grand scheme of things.

What we'd overlooked in all of our planning and excitement was whether or not we'd even be *allowed* to have a dog. This was just one of those oversights that was so obvious, it didn't even register in our minds. The house that we called home in Interlaken didn't belong to us. We were renters, just like about seventy percent of the whole population of Switzerland. Due to the fact that land is outrageously expensive, as well as building costs, people just don't even bother trying to own their own homes. If someone has their own house, it was probably passed down to them from their parents, who had it passed down to them from their parents. Sure, there are people with oodles of money who can afford to buy the land and build, but these people were in the small minority of the population.

Being a renter means following the rules of your landlord. What he or she says goes. That's just the way it is. Now our big mission was to suck up to ours to see if he'd let us have a dog in our house or not. It didn't seem like such an unreasonable request, but we were still quite nervous when we went to talk to him about it. This was mainly because our house wasn't just any old house, but a newly restored wooden farm-house that was built in 1599, as well as a protected heritage site. The restoration was a major job and I could see him not wanting a puppy in there, chewing on wood that had been growing around the same time that Columbus discovered the New World. I sure as heck wouldn't.

He didn't exactly say yes, but he didn't turn us down either, which was a good sign. The decision actually didn't even sit with him at all, but rather with his wife who, it seemed, wore the pants in the family. He was just one of these resigned, henpecked husbands who would find any excuse to get out of the house and away from his wife. He even had a little field right beside our house with about eight sheep and he was constantly there, not really looking after the sheep, but just avoiding his old lady. I felt sorry for the guy because that's just not how marriage is supposed to be.

After a couple days of sitting around and won-dering if he'd forgotten about our puppy wish, we finally got the knock on the door that we'd been awaiting. Following a lot of hemming and hawing about the damage a little puppy was capable of doing, he finally relented and gave us the go ahead to get a little camper. If there was any damage to the house, we'd be on the hook for it, and we had to make sure that he didn't upset the neighbors with excessive barking. The last rule was that the puppy couldn't give his precious, time-out-from-the-wife sheep any problems. Franzi and I were both on the same page with all of his requests and it took us about four seconds to agree with every condition he threw at us. We were nearly at the point of starting the canonization process into sainthood for our little puppy-to-be.

When he finally left, all we could do was sit back, take a deep breath, open a bottle of fine Italian wine, and contemplate what kind of a little saint we were going to get. It was a great feeling, passing the last hurdle.

Did we want a big dog or a small dog? With long hair or short hair? Should it be a mutt or purebred? What about exotic or run-of-the-mill? There were so many things to figure out, although we'd already been doing some research through dog magazines and library resources to try and figure out what kind of a dog we would end up getting. I wanted a dog with an Einstein level of intelligence because I sure as heck didn't know much about them, and Franzi was in the same boat as I was in that department. Poodles are supposedly the smartest of the canine race, but if they were so smart, then why would they let their owners shave them to look like cheerleader pompoms?

Border Collies and German Shepherds are right up there on the intelligence scale as well, but after a little reading on the Border Collies, we had to admit to ourselves that we were after a dog that was just a few notches down on the hyper scale. The German Shepherd, although very majestic looking, strikes fear into the hearts of many (myself included and not to mention Franzi, who was attacked by one as a child), so that type was quickly scratched from the list as well.

As we sat there at the table going through our list of potential spoiled, pampered house pets, we both agreed that Shadow was one great dog and that we couldn't really go wrong with getting a Labrador Retriever, even if everyone else AND their brother seemed to own one. Our thoughts of getting something a little different and original didn't seem to hold up a lot of weight when stacked beside the most popular breed in the western world. There had to be a reason why they were the most popular breed, and since we were just getting our feet wet in the dog ownership pool, we decided to go with simplicity.

There it was, the decision made. Now all we had to do was find a breeder and get the wheels of puppy-hood in motion.

It was around this time, the spring of '95, when the news on TV seemed to be filled with horror stories dealing with puppy mills, both in Switzerland and much of Western Europe. We knew that we had to find a reputable breeder with a good track record. The easiest solution we could think of was to just ask the owners of Shadow where they got him from. He was the perfect dog, and knowing his owners, they would have fully examined the breeder before buying Shadow, which they had. They told us that Maya (the breeder), takes the whole process extremely seriously, has about 18 dogs, and treats them all like they are her children.

This was exactly what we wanted to hear, so with her phone number in hand Franzi gave her a call. I let Franzi take care of all the dealings here, because first of all, she was Swiss and there wouldn't be any misunderstandings with the language. And second of all, she always knows the right questions to ask. My train of thought tends to wander at times, getting off track, and I often leave out a few important questions or details. My German was pretty good at this point, but I was quite relieved I wasn't the one on the phone, as the conversation went on for a good hour and a half. It was a never-ending talkfest and when it finally ended, Franzi looked about as drained as if she had written a nuclear physics exam.

Maya wanted to know basically everything there was to know about the two of us: where we lived, what our jobs were, what our working schedules were like, did we go away on holidays or business trips, had we had a dog in the past, why we wanted one now, etc. etc. etc. The list was virtually endless. She asked all these questions because, as she put it, "her puppies deserved the absolute best and they weren't going to be going to just anyone." I remember looking at Franzi with a raised eyebrow, not saying a word, but she knew exactly what I was thinking. Her reply was, "I know, adopting a baby probably would be much easier." She really nailed it on the head.

We weren't given a straight answer from the breeder during that first conversation, but we both had to admit afterwards that she sure took the breeding process and selection of potential candidates extremely seriously. This was a good thing, because it was a reflection of how she ran her business. Perhaps "*passion*" would be a better word. We wanted a top-of-the-line, Rolls Royce, Labrador Retriever, and judging by the way she spoke, Maya's sounded like the best. Almost every one of the dogs in her kennel was a Swiss or European champion of something or another, all with very distinguished bloodlines. It wasn't like I knew anything about any of this, but I played along just the same, acting my knowledgeable best.

A few days later the breeder phoned again with another barrage of questions for Franzi, which she must have had all the right answers to because we were invited over to view the puppies. It looked like we'd passed the "telephone" test and were now onto the "what do we look like" test. Actually, I totally understand the reason for wanting to meet with us. You can only tell so much from a person over the phone. A visual image gives you much more perspective. She was looking for potential people who could give her puppies all the love and activity that they needed. If we had shown up both 80 pounds overweight wearing biker jackets with tattoos on our necks, she would have surmised that we were not very active and probably had intentions of turning her cute little puppy into a vicious guard dog.

We set out on a sunny Tuesday morning filled with anticipation and an uneasy nervousness of whether or not we'd be found worthy of raising a furry little munchkin. It was a beautiful two-hour drive through the Swiss Alps to a small village named Sarmenstorf in the province of Aargau, which is quite close to Zurich. We arrived a little early, which is always a good thing, because the Swiss pride themselves on their punctuality. Showing up late for an appointment is often met with stern frowns and is seen as a sign of unreliability. If you can't be where you're supposed to be, when you're supposed to be there, then you probably can't feed or let your dog out for a pee when you're supposed to either.

When we pulled up to the house/hobby farm, Maya wasn't around, so we just set out on our own and followed the sounds of yelps and barks. The setup she had there was really something else. The kennels were large and spacious with natural trees in them for the little ones' piddling pleasure, as well as small, man-made, freshwater ponds. There were lots of toys and plenty of shade, and I'm sure that even *I* would have had a good time in there. It was, more or less, a little paradise for the dogs.

It was in the last kennel that we heard the yelping of puppies and as we were just about to head over in that direction, Maya came around the corner and introduced herself. She was a very pleasant lady and if she was eyeing us up, she was doing it very covertly. There were a few more questions for us about our feelings towards natural and homeopathic medicines, because this was what she often used on her dogs. When we told her that we were all in favor of natural medicines, her mind seemed to be more at ease and her manner opened up considerably.

She took us over to the last kennel where a few of the pups were peeking out of their spacious doggy mansion and the mother was laying half asleep under the shade of a tree. The moment that she opened the gate it was as if she'd set off an alarm clock. There was literally a stampede of little feet and different colored bodies all trying to reach her as quickly as possible. The mother just lifted her head, saw that it was the proper human with her puppies and then went back to sleep. It was a litter of eight, with three yellows, three blacks, and two browns. That was quite an assortment of colors when you consider that the two parents were both black. After a couple minutes of scratching and petting the little ones, they all settled down and went about playing with each other and their toys. If the sight of a bunch of puppies doesn't melt your heart just a little bit, then you've got a pretty hard heart. Ours were certainly melted.

Maya knew that we wanted a male and she also knew that it didn't matter which color it was, just as long as it had a good temperament. But up until this point, we still didn't know if she had planned on giving us one. Had we passed all prerequisites for puppy ownership? The question was quickly answered when she pointed to the yellow one chewing on its mother's ear and said to us that that one will be ours. It had the best character suited to our needs. Both Franzi and I were pretty speechless and I had some guilt go through me for my previous thoughts because all Maya had been doing was gathering up info on us to give us the best possible match. The real magical moment came when Maya told Franzi to step into the kennel with her. The little yellow guy that was to be ours did a full sprint to Franzi and gave her a full lick on the face as she bent down, while all his brothers and sisters just continued on playing their puppy games amongst themselves. Our little pup just wouldn't leave Franzi's side and Maya gave us both a look that said, "You see? I know what I'm doing." She sure did.

It was really hard to leave, but we had a two-hour drive back and didn't want to get caught in the rush-hour traffic. I would have loved to have taken the little one with us right then and there, but he was only four-and-a-half weeks old and the law in Switzerland says that breeders cannot give away a puppy until it has completed its ninth week of existence, otherwise the breeders could risk losing their breeding licenses. Yes, literally everything is regulated over there, which in this case was a good thing.

I don't think that we stopped talking once the whole way home. Franzi was in a kind of a shock that OUR dog just ran right over to her while none of the other ones could be bothered. "It was meant to be," she said. After the initial shock of being granted the right of ownership of the little guy, and the secondary shock of his 1,800-dollar price tag, the conversation quickly swung around to what to name him.

We probably picked out about 120 different names during that two-hour drive, giving each one a full minute of consideration before discovering a better one. As it turned out, we arrived back home without a clue of what to name him. Lying in bed that night we said to each other that the perfect name would come. "We'll just sleep on it and it'll come. What's the rush anyway?"

The rush came the next morning. I had a few things I needed to address early on and Franzi was just about out the door and off to work when the phone rang. It was Maya, and she needed a name to put on the registration papers for our little guy, as well as something to call him so he could get used to his new name and learn it. Franzi was in quite a panic at this point because we hadn't decided on anything the day before and had agreed that this was going to be a mutual decision. She tried explaining everything to Maya, but was told we had to decide on something that day because she was on her way to the post office to file the papers with the Swiss Kennel Club. There it was – Franzi's decision all alone, with every consequence that name would carry. As I later learned when I arrived home from work, she gave it all of about three seconds thought and then blurted out the name "Butch."

"Butch?" I yelled, "That's my name! What the heck were you thinking? You can't name the dog after me; we don't look anything like each other. It's going to be constant confusion because I'll always think you're calling me to come or telling me to sit or yelling at me to stop chewing on shoes!" It was just too weird. That was *my* nickname and had been for quite some time now. I loved that nickname and now I felt like I'd lost some of my identity – like it was being ripped away from me and just given away frivolously like a quarter being thrown into a street musician's guitar case.

So, there it was, a new "Butch" on the block. When I asked Franzi what made her say that name, she really didn't have a good answer. "It was all I could think of and the pressure was on! Maya didn't really like it either until I told her that it was the name of a famous bandit cowboy in America, who was quite the legend by the way, and was played by Paul Newman in the movie. That seemed to warm her up to the name, sort of." "Butch" wasn't even one of the 120 possible names that we'd kicked around on the drive home the day before. Wow.

It took a few days to get used to the idea that I'd either be losing my nickname or sharing it with a furry, four-legged camper, who would have no idea about the bandit legend, hockey goaltending robbery, or even who Paul Newman was. Butch was his name, and that's how it would stay.

The really funny thing about the name Butch is that 99% of the Swiss population can't actually pronounce it, as there's nothing in Swiss German even relatively close to it. When they say it, it always comes out sounding like the word *pooch*. Franzi was probably the only person who could pronounce it properly, but we had to work on it.

The weeks went by slowly as we waited for the fifth of September (which was the end of Butch's ninth week of existence) to arrive. We were so looking forward to bringing the little guy home, and Franzi and I set out rearranging our household to bring it to a safe level of puppy destruction. Anything that sat three feet or lower from the ground suddenly found a new home higher up on shelves or window sills. The stairs leading to the second floor where our bedroom was now had a dog-proof gate at the bottom to prevent Butch from having free roam of the house, and to give us a little better chance of keeping an eye on him. Right under the stairs I built him a bed out of wood with a thick blanket for him to lie on, and a chain attached so that he would stay in it at night and wouldn't head into the living room to relieve himself. Many of our friends had told us that a dog or a puppy would not soil the area in which they sleep, so if he was stuck in this bed, he would either bark or yelp, or do something to let us know that he really had to go outside and take care of business.

The last weekend finally rolled around and you would have thought that we were about to have a baby; that's how excited and nervous we were. We were both rookies in the field of dog ownership with really no idea of what to expect, despite all the reading we'd done, so in a way, I guess it was pretty much the same as first-time parenting. It was going to be quite a new experience as well as a very sharp learning curve, but we kept telling ourselves that we were ready for whatever this little puppy was going to throw at us. Yeah, right!

We had actually planned to pick up Butch on a Sunday, which would have made him eight weeks and six days old, but when we spoke to Maya about this idea, she politely informed us that it was not the full nine weeks and that she could lose her breeding license if she allowed us to take the puppy even one day early. So be it. As it turns out, she had some business to take care of in Bern the next day and wanted to know if we would meet her there, which was quite the blessing because it meant only one hour of driving each way instead of two, and we really wanted to get the little guy home and into our family. Therefore, we agreed to meet at a restaurant parking lot just outside of Bern, right on the highway.

Naturally, we arrived half an hour early, because as I stated before, being late was tantamount to being a convicted felon on the social stigma scale, and sure enough she too was fifteen minutes early, apologizing for keeping us waiting. The Swiss are so polite.

When she went around to the back of her station wagon and opened up the dog crate door, I thought that there'd been some sort of mistake. This wasn't the same dog that we'd seen just four weeks before. This thing was *twice* the size – a full ten kilos or twenty-two pounds of yellow fur. He was afraid, as I'm sure it was his first car ride, and just wanted to tuck his head under Maya's arm, praying this whole nightmarish experience would come to an end. She told us that he'd been yelping and whining the whole way. He'd just been separated from his parents and all of his siblings, so it was understandable. The world, as our little Butch knew it, had just been drastically altered.

Maya wanted a photo of the two of us with our new puppy, so I took the little guy from her arms as he trembled in fear. I felt so sorry for Butch because there was no way in the world he knew what was going on, and after our farewell to Maya, all he did was whine. When we got him in the car with us, Franzi sat in the back with him, trying to give comfort the best she could. Sadly, just a few miles down the highway the yelping stopped and gave way to vomit, all over the back seat. That was the start of our doggy parenthood.

Chapter 3
Who Rules the House Now?

That simple, one-hour ride home turned into quite the adventure when you took into account the multiple vomit or dry heave stops, as they eventually became. The poor little guy would drink a little water from his bowl at the side of the road and have a pee, but a few miles later history would repeat itself. They never showed these kinds of scenarios in Disney movies.

When we eventually turned into our driveway and put on his leash to bring him into the house, his next big panic attack started. I guess there was no way to prepare him for the full-grown sheep that he was about to encounter on the other side of the wire fence separating our parking spot from a tiny field. But he had to meet them sooner or later, so I guess that was as good of a time as any. Franzi walked him over to the fence, which was really more of a drag, but after a minute or two of shaking and hiding behind her legs, he eventually came around and stuck his nose through the fencing. For all we knew, he was probably checking them out to see if he was related or something. Perhaps they told him what was going on and that it wasn't such a bad place to live because soon his little three-inch tail was going back and forth like he was the happiest camper in the world. All the vomiting was forgotten.

The first thing we showed our little Butch after finally getting him into the house was his bed under the steps, complete with soft blankets and pillows, and a hot water bottle so it felt like he was still close to his mom. He wasn't in that bed for ten seconds and he was out like a light: big day, heavy stress.

Having lived with his litter in an outdoor kennel for all nine weeks of his little life, Butch's first educational goal would be to learn how to make it known to us that he had to go outside to take care of his business. Ha! Much easier said than done! For him it was a simple matter; if he had to go, he had to go. Our job was to anticipate just when that might be. To be on the safe side, we would take him out about every half hour when he was awake. If he was sleeping in his bed and just woke up, out he went. For the most part, this system seemed to work pretty well, but what we also soon learned was that during playtime, all bets were off. When he went into his wild puppy mode, ripping around the living room, he would actually squirt while he was running. If he suddenly stopped on a dime and we were only a few feet away running to pick him up and take him outside, it would often be too late. That first day, when I scooped him up after one of his whirling dervish moments, he was in my arms like a baby and as I tried to get to the door, the little floodgates opened right up. Suddenly, I was wearing the water that he had been drinking just a short time before.

The first night was not really what we had in mind, either. After one last play round, we took Butch out, he did his business and we thought that would be the end of it for the evening. However, we had no sooner laid our heads on the pillows after tying him up in his bed when the whining began. At first Franzi wanted to bring him up to the bedroom with us, but after discussing this in whispered tones, we decided he had to learn that his bed was where he was meant to sleep when we went to bed.

After about 15 minutes of whining with the occasional yelp thrown in, the noise seemed to subside, for all of three minutes. We thought that it was better to be safe than sorry, so I got up and took him outside for another little round of business. At least I *thought* it would be a little round of business, but when I got him outside the little pee machine known as "Butch" seemed to go for an eternity. I was really at a loss in regard to explaining where all this fluid was coming from, but I sort of caught onto the idea that if he whined, we'd better take him seriously. When I got him back into his bed, he zonked out right away, as did I.

The blissful sleep that we were both enjoying lasted a whole two hours before the whining started again and the whole process repeated itself. That's how the first night went for us and when morning finally came, little Butch was the only family member looking chipper and ready to meet the day. For the first time in my life, I was able to sympathize with what new parents have to go through. The good thing was that with a puppy, this stage of life didn't last nearly as long as it would with a newborn baby.

This whole process went on for about a week, with our nightly bed conversations consisting of only "it's *your* turn to take him out." After that, the periods in between his calls of nature seemed to get a bit longer, which was great because sleep can be a wonderful thing.

The other big lesson that we learned during that first week was that puppies don't just promenade like adult dogs do when you take them for walks. The whole world is a new experience, with new things to check out, different smells that just have to be smelled, and anything that a puppy comes across has to be tasted. This was the big one. Whether it be a leaf, a plastic bottle, a wrapper off of some food, or another dog's poop, it all had to pass by the nose first and then the mouth. This was a habit we wanted to break him of right away.

Despite the reputation the Swiss have of being polite and law-abiding, there is still an element out there that will poison dogs. I was really shocked when Maya told us this, because who in their right minds could poison a dog? Sure enough, there was the occasional article in the newspapers about this happening, which made us ultra alert anytime Butch grabbed something on the street and started chewing. A lot of the poisoning incidents appeared to be related to farmers, and I'm sure that their reasoning was that the dogs were stealing feed and had to be dealt with, but it still made me sick to my stomach. Another factor is probably the situation in which people live. Houses are right next door to each other with very tiny yards and people are extremely protective of the small spaces they have. If your dog gets into their garden they can do whatever they like to the dog. It's for this reason that you would never see a dog just roaming free. Every dog is on a very short leash, as was Butch.

The first command that he learned was "phooey," pronounced like Hewey, Dewey, and Louie but with an "F"; this meant NO. Every time something went in his mouth that didn't belong there he heard a loud "phooey," followed by "give it out!" He seemed to catch on to this command pretty quickly, but there were still times when we had to pry his little jaws apart and manually confiscate the object of his pleasure. He would often give us his best pissed-off puppy look, but we were of the opinion that we knew best and that it was for his own good. Puppies never stay pissed off for very long.

Without a doubt, the most intriguing thing to ever cross his pallet in those first few weeks was the head of our kitten, Maenam. We had just finished dinner and were settling onto the sofa to watch the news when this yellow blur went running by us with a pile of fur in his mouth. We must have both yelled

61

"Butch, phooey!" at the same time because he stopped dead in his tracks and just looked at us like we were from another planet. There he stood, with the head of the cat in his mouth, the body dangling, and all four of her paws desperately searching for any foothold they could find. I think the way that we freaked out startled him into dropping her on the spot. It was a sight to behold. Her whole head was covered in slobber and as soon as she got her bearings she was under the couch faster than you could believe.

This was an isolated incident and for the most part the two of them got along with each other just dandy. They would play together, and sleep together, and when one of them wasn't around, the other would frantically search all over for the other. The kitten, Maenam, was only a few months older than Butch, so the pair had a lot of wild playing moments together, and Butch really enjoyed digging in her litter box as well.

During that first month, we fell into a pretty good routine, with me walking Butch in the morning, Franzi and me walking him together when she had her lunch break, and when I left for work at around 3 P.M., I'd let him out again for a security pee. Then he was normally good until Franzi came home from work at around 5 P.M.

We quickly learned that Butch was not a morning dog. Normally, once he started sleeping through the night, we'd hear a little yelp around 6:30 or 7 A.M., which was just a nature call yelp, because after we'd taken him outside he'd go right back into his safe little bed. "Don't even think of talking to me until you've had your first cup of coffee" was the look he'd give us before dozing back off. As the day went on, though, his energy level seemed to gradually increase. The morning walk was sort of slow motion, with a lot of dragging and pulling. The noontime walk was as a walk should be, with the little guy running in spurts and trying to smell and eat everything, but the evening walk, when Franzi would take him out to the abandoned airfield or in the woods, was something to behold. It was like his whole day was building up to this running crescendo. She'd normally let him off his leash when there were no other dog owners around to get angry with us for not having him under control, but what the heck; he was just a puppy after all. "Let him have some fun and enjoy this stage of life" was our attitude.

And so it went for those first two months. He wasn't a big fan of going into lakes or rivers, but we weren't concerned about that because everyone told us that eventually he'd come around and would love swimming, as did all Labs. What he seemed to enjoy the most was shocking us. We hadn't had any company over to our house since we got the little guy, preferring to spend all of our time with him, and when we finally did have people over, Butch decided to express his jealousy and disapproval in the most indignant way possible.

Friends of ours had come for dinner and everything got off to a good start that evening. We greeted them at the door, as did Butch, and for the first fifteen minutes or so, he was the absolute center of attention, which was all he had ever known in our home. When we settled in around the table for dinner, he was quite put out. "Why aren't my humans playing with me? Somehow I've got to get their attention."

With this thought in his little mind, we were suddenly greeted at the table with a yellow whirling dervish brandishing our toilet brush between his teeth, circling the table at the speed of sound. It was really quite comical, but we decided that his bedtime had arrived. After wrestling his version of a stick away from him, I walked him out of the room, took him outside for a quick pee, and then led him to his bed and tied him up for the night. Or so I thought.

The first two minutes were quiet, but then the yelping started. It wasn't just normal puppy yelping, but a painful-sounding "I'm such an abused animal" form of yelping. At first we tried to ignore it, thinking that it would taper off with time, but that just wasn't happening. When it got to the point that it was starting to drive us all a little crazy, Franzi went and unhooked his little chain and gave him his freedom to come back in the room with us. Big mistake! No sooner had Franzi sat back down but there was Butch, right beside the table, showing us his disapproval at not being the main focal point, by having a dump right on the carpet. It definitely wouldn't be classed as a "boring evening."

It was around this new puppyhood time of our lives that old patterns started to emerge. Franzi, who had gone through yet another stomach surgery only five months earlier, started having a lot of pain again. This wasn't an ongoing pain, but it would just come out of the blue, in the form of colic. It could happen once a week or once a month. There was neither rhyme nor reason to when the attacks occurred, but when they did, they came pretty ferociously. She'd be doubled over in bed, or wherever she was when they came, with her eyes rolled up into her head and groaning like a truck had hit her. When this happened while I was at home, I'd help her to the car and get her to the hospital as quick as possible, where they knew exactly what to inject her with to get the cramps to ease off. However, when I wasn't at home, she couldn't even reach the telephone and therefore ended up suffering through a long and painful period until the cramps subsided.

The one constant was that when the attacks happened, Butch never left her side. He'd always be right there, lying against her if he could, with a low whine in his voice and knowing that something wasn't right with his mom. He was the only thing in the world that could bring even the slightest semblance of a smile to her face while these ordeals were happening. When the pain would eventually subside, she'd just lie there with him in her arms. Even at this young age, Butch and Franzi were bonding very closely.

The strangest thing, which we didn't realize right away, was that a day or two after these colic episodes happened, when Franzi was feeling better, Butch would end up really down. He'd have no energy at all on his walks, and often he wouldn't even touch his food, or if he did eat, he'd throw it back up. It was only after about three or four times of this pattern repeating itself that we picked up on it. That's when we knew that we had a very sensitive dog on our hands, despite the unruliness that ran through his veins. Franzi was the person who spent the most time with him and treated him like he was her own child, so I guess it only made sense that he connected with her like he did, so quickly.

I'd known since the day we first met that Franzi had medical issues with her stomach, and it was all part of the "For better or for worse" vows that we took upon getting married, but I was feeling guilty that all of these attacks seemed to be happening at night when I was at work. Bartending was a well-paying job, but money isn't everything, and it was for this reason that I decided to quit my job and try my hand at something new.

Franzi seemed extremely relieved when we talked about my change of direction because she was never at ease with me working until two in the morning in a bar. The big question was "What am I going to do now?" The options for foreigners in Switzerland were pretty limited because all employers wanted to see Swiss diplomas. If you went to school in another country, there was an equivalency examination that had to be taken to be accepted on the same level as if you had a Swiss education. It made sense, and it's a policy that a lot of countries employ, but for me it was a great big brick wall. Yes, I had a diploma from a college in Canada where I majored in marketing, but that was ten years ago. If you factor in that I could speak Swiss German but couldn't read or write it, the brick wall just got a little thicker.

The only way that I was going to better myself and my chances would be by learning to read and write German, so this was the path that we decided to go with; back to school it was. I enrolled in a four-month intensive German language course in Bern, which meant an hour commute every morning and afternoon. I loved it. I was able to get home by mid-afternoon, take Butch for a walk in the woods, do my homework, make dinner and then spend the evening with Franzi. The peace of mind of knowing that if something happened to Franzi, I – or someone at her place of work – would be there for her, was priceless. It also felt like we were a real family, spending our evenings together.

Having weekends off was a real treat also. I hadn't had a weekend off in a long time, so we made the most of it. We'd go up to the village of Muerren where we'd both worked in the past and had many friends, and Butch would just love this. Up in Muerren he didn't have to behave like he did when we were at home because there were no cars on the streets. Everyone up there knew us, so they wouldn't get too choked when Butch ran through their gardens or gave their cows a little scare. It didn't take him long to figure out that cows don't like to play. Butch even learned how to ride cable cars and gondolas.

It was just before the ski season was about to start up in Muerren, but as it's been known to happen in

Europe, there was not a speck of snow on the ground, so we decided to take our five-month-old puppy for a real Swiss mountain hike. We had his food packed up, as well as his portable water dish and all kinds of little treats, and off we went. It was a gorgeous day with warm sunshine beating down on us, totally unseasonable for November, and we were out there to enjoy it. Up we went for a couple of hours, stopping here and there to check out the scenery or have a nibble on the granola bars we'd brought with us, and we'd covered quite a bit of distance since starting off. Butch seemed to be having the time of his life. For every step that we would take, he'd have about six under his belt, zigzagging all over the place. There were lots of new smells that just had to be checked out up at the higher mountain altitudes.

After stopping for a picnic lunch for about half an hour, we decided that it was time to start heading down towards the village since the days were getting shorter and as soon as the sun disappeared behind the mountains, it got cold very quickly. It all sounded like a good plan, but our little four-legged friend, who'd been ripping around for the last three hours, decided that he'd had enough. He just lay down and no amount of coaxing or prodding was going to get him going again. Even standing ten feet away, holding out a piece of sausage, wouldn't get him up. It was at this point, faced with a two-and-a half hour hike back down, that we realized we'd overdone it with our little friend. He was toast.

The prospect of having to carry him down the mountain was a daunting one, but that's exactly what I did. He was only twenty weeks old, but he was big for his age. The 45 pounds that the scale read felt like more like 65. It was slow going with him in my arms and every ten minutes or so I'd put him down to see if I could get him to walk, which he would for about two minutes, but then he'd just park his butt on the ground and the whole dead weight haulage would start over. Needless to say, when we got down close to the village and I set him down for a rest, he took off in front of us and ran the last three hundred yards like he had just woken up. My arms felt like they were falling off and all my thoughts were on a nice, cold, frosty beer, but inside I had to laugh at how I'd just been played by man's best friend.

We stayed up in Muerren that night at Franzi's parents' place and the next morning, although he looked like he'd been out partying all night, Butch was still up for a Sunday walk. We didn't want to tax his tired little legs with another hike, so we just went for a leisurely stroll around the village. The fact that it was a Sunday and that we both knew so many people up there meant that we didn't do a whole lot of walking. Walk ten steps, stop and talk to someone you know for five minutes, walk another ten steps, talk again, and so it went. Butch had no patience for this incessant gabfest, so he would go off cruising on his own and we'd just keep an eye on his whereabouts. He never seemed to get into trouble so we kind of let our guards down a little bit, and before we knew it he was running down the road with a big block of cheese in his mouth that he'd stolen from a family of four that were sitting on a bench having a picnic.

Embarrassment doesn't begin to describe our feelings as we walked up to the family with Butch in tow. The cheese was a distant memory for him, as his new mission in life now was to lick his lips and try to look innocent, but unbelievably the family wasn't upset about it one bit. They even said that it was their own fault for leaving the cheese out in the open. You just have to love Swiss politeness at times. I was tickled pink and just howling inside, despite the stern look on my face, but Franzi still had a few harsh words for our little friend.

Chapter 4
The First Big Hurdle

*C*hristmas came and went and we all had a great time. We spent it up in Muerren with Franzi's family, and it was the first real Christmas that I could actually enjoy with them. Before, I'd been working over the holidays, which was one of the busiest times of the year in the food and beverage industry. This Christmas brought back a lot of memories of a lifetime ago when I was a student and spent the holidays with my own family. The snow arrived just in time for the holiday rush and we even had a few days when we could do some skiing in between our dog walks.

Butch just loved the snow. When there was a big dumping of the white stuff, he made it his mission to find out what was underneath by walking with his head half submerged in it. If one of us threw a snowball into a snow bank, he could spend fifteen minutes searching for it. I often tried to figure out what was going through his brain during this process, because it was like trying to retrieve a glass of water that had been dumped into a swimming pool. I didn't get it, but somewhere in that little canine brain, he had his reasons.

With the holidays at an end, it was time to head back to school. The daily commute was a drag because it meant getting up at 6:00 to catch the train at 6:30, but it allowed me an hour to do some studying or homework, which was also the case on the ride home. Having not been in a classroom setting for over ten years, I found it a little difficult at first because you have to retrain yourself how to learn. However, once I got my concentration on track, the whole process seemed to go fairly smoothly. Going into the Christmas break, which was the halfway point of the course, I was even up in the top ten percent of the class. Not too bad for someone who dropped out of French after only half a semester because I thought it was a "waste of time" and would "never use it in real life."

Butch, who seemed to be growing on a daily basis, was soon approaching his six-month birthday, and that meant it was time for him to get his first rabies vaccination. The appointment was set for January 8th, and it was a time in his life that neither Franzi nor I will ever forget.

After I got home from school, Franzi and I put Butch in the back of the car, which he really loved because it had a big back window and everything that we passed seemed to excite him, and we headed off to our veterinarian appointment. Interlaken had a few vet clinics and our whole decision-making process of which one to choose when we got our cat, Maenam, was based on how busy they were. It only made sense that the busiest one had to be the best one, right? Otherwise they wouldn't be busy. They treated our cat well, so Butch would be just fine there. It could be that they were a great clinic and we just happened to be the fraction of one percent that had a problem with them, but a problem we had.

We took Butch into the waiting room where there were a few other dogs waiting for their various treatments as well, and he was just the happiest little camper. New bums and crotches to sniff and smell always put him in a good mood and got the ol' tail wagging. Butch just loved other dogs, and the others in the waiting room all received a lick on the face. Only Butch could make four new friends in a two-minute period.

Finally, it was our turn to head on in to the examination room where the white-coated doctor met us and introduced himself to Butch and us. The tail was still wagging, which was a good sign. The rabies shot was the only order of business for us that day and the vet had the syringe all prepared in advance. Two minutes later, after receiving his injection in his left rear hip without even flinching, we were settling up the tab and heading back home.

That evening started off like all others, with Butch being fed first and then the two of us enjoying some quiet time before we sat down to eat. His meal was no problem for him as it disappeared from the bowl in a matter of seconds. Franzi called his whole feeding process "Hoovering," after the vacuum cleaner. Normally, after we finished our meal and settled to the sofa to watch a little TV, Butch would determine it to be playtime on the carpet. One by one, he'd transport every squeaky toy and stuffed animal that he possessed from his bed out into the living room, placing them in front of us before heading back for the next. When all were accounted for he'd sit down in front of us and let out a low to medium level bark. "It's time. Let's go. Play with me. Now!"

On this particular night, that didn't happen. At first we didn't even realize that he hadn't come for his nightly ritual, but after a while Franzi tuned in and said, "What's up with our little holy terror?" I found it strange too, so we both went to see what was up with him. Seeing him lie there in his little bed, which he was very close to outgrowing, made both of our hearts sink like stones in a pond.

He was panting, with both eyes looking unfocused and distant, and showing no recognition at all that we were kneeling down beside him, which for Butch, who thrived on attention, was virtually unheard of. *What the heck had happened to our dog who was licking every other dog's face in the waiting room just six hours earlier?*

"No panic," we said to each other, but deep inside we were both worried because we'd never seen him like this before. This just wasn't our dog. Something had happened to him today, whether it was vet-related or food-related we couldn't tell, but the smart money was on the vet. After a few minutes of trying to coax him into feeling better with no results, Franzi was on the phone to the clinic. 9:00 in the evening is a bad time when you're trying to get hold of a professional, and this was no exception. The answering machine naturally told us their office was closed, but did give us a phone number to call in case of emergencies. This, in our eyes, was a major one.

Franzi, who did all the important telephoning because it was her mother tongue, dialed the number. It was the same doctor who answered the phone at home who had given Butch the vaccination. He seemed a little put out that we were actually interrupting his evening, but we really didn't care. After a few questions as to Butch's symptoms, he determined it to be a reaction to the rabies shot that he'd given him earlier that afternoon. Without studying five years of veterinary medicine, I'd also come to that same conclusion. *Duh!* Our biggest question was, "What do we do with him?" The vet seemed to think that the whole reaction would just work its way out of the system and in the morning he would be back to his normal self. He did, however, want us to keep an eye on him and observe him. Yeah, like we were going to go out bar-hopping and just forget about our Butch for the night. *Oh, please!*

The one thing that still had to be dealt with was getting him out for a pee because he hadn't had one since right after his dinner, four hours earlier. This was no easy task. Butch laid right back down in his bed the second we got him standing up, so we knew that wasn't going to work. He had to be carried out. When I set him down I thought for sure he'd just lie down again but to my surprise he didn't. He took about two steps and squatted the way a female dog would do her business. A few drops and that was good enough for me. When I carried him back into the house, it came as no surprise to me whatsoever that Franzi already had a hot water bottle in his blanket and a sleeping bag and air mattress right beside his bed.

I loved this dog, but no one was as close to him as Franzi was. She has always been an absolute animal lover, but the bond that she had formed with Butch in the four months that he'd been with us was definitely rare. It was almost as if they could understand what the other meant or wanted just by looking at each other – like a mother-son relationship.

Butch didn't seem to be either getting any worse or improving by the time I left Franzi beside him with her arm over his head and went up to bed. Sleep came very fitfully that night for me and I'm sure it didn't come at all for Franzi because when I went downstairs at 5:00 A.M., she was just sitting there beside him with watery eyes and our eight-cup-coffee machine only had about one cup left in it.

"Our little guy doesn't deserve this," she sobbed. "Just look at his belly, Dave. This isn't right." *No, it definitely wasn't right.* He still had the distant stare, although the panting had now been replaced with what I can only describe as a guttural whine. What was also different from the night before was that his whole left side, from the front leg back to his testicles, was grotesquely swollen. He was lying on his right side with his head out of the bed and on her lap and it just ripped my heart in two to see both, Butch and Franzi, suffering.

The decision to phone the emergency number again was an easy one, but we decided to wait until 6:00 A.M. to give the doctor a decent night's sleep, as he was probably going to be the one to take a look at our dog. When we phoned him, he just told us to bring Butch and meet him at the clinic at 7:00 A.M., which was still two hours before the posted opening times. When I carried him out to the car I thought it might be best to see if he could do his business, but that just wasn't going to happen. Something was seriously wrong because Butch had never gone for twelve hours without having to squirt like he was putting out a four-alarm blaze. He just laid down beside the car and continued that sorrowful whine. That was that for screwing around, so I bundled him into the back of the car, which, luckily, was a hatchback, and off we went.

When we arrived at the vet clinic the doctor was already there, just opening the door. It only took one look at our little camper and he, too, knew that this puppy's world was not a very nice world to be living in at the moment. After getting him up on the examination table, there was a lot of poking, pressing and probing, followed by a lot of side-to-side head shaking. You could see that he didn't really know what the problem was either, so his course of action was to do some blood work to see if that showed any irregularities, put him on some infection fighting antibiotics, hook him up to an IV to keep him hydrated, and then just observe his status over time in what we called the "Doggie Intensive Care Station." The Doggie Intensive Care Station was off limits to us non-medical people, so it was with very heavy hearts and tears in our eyes that we said goodbye to Butch, who tried to raise his head up and look at us, but just couldn't manage it as they rolled him away into the back room.

We left the clinic after making the doctor promise to phone us right away if he found something or if there was any change in his condition, and drove back home in total silence, with both of us lost in our own thoughts and silent prayers. I guess I wasn't going to be attending classes that day.

Franzi left for work at around 9:00, which was probably a good thing because she needed the distraction, and I was left with the task of sticking beside the telephone.

As we didn't have an answering machine, I wasn't going to leave the house for fear of missing the call, and what really struck me was how empty the whole house felt; all the action was missing. Butch had only been with us for a little over four months, but during that time there was always something going on at home. He loved being the center of attention whenever he was awake, and it seemed so strange to sit back on the couch without the yellow fur ball poking me with one of his play toys. Maenam was still hanging around but that just wasn't the same. Cats don't fetch tennis balls. I actually didn't even see her that whole morning, which I hadn't realized until I started looking for her. The fact that her cat entry window was closed meant that she had to be inside somewhere, but she was being very quiet. After an indifferent search I finally found her in a place where I'd never seen her before, under Butch's blanket in his bed. It was as if she was trying to keep it warm for him until he came home.

Franzi burst through the door when she came home for her lunch break, and the first thing she asked was whether or not I'd heard anything. I didn't even have to say anything and she already had her answer. Waiting has never been one of her strong suits so she decided that if we didn't have any response from the clinic by 4:00, she'd give them a ring to find out what was going on. Neither of us knew how long all these tests were going to take, but we wanted to stay on top of it, and we really needed to know if our little friend was getting any better and if his swollen side had started to go down in size.

The afternoon dragged on just as slowly as the morning had, with still no word on Butch's condition. Around 4:30, Franzi finally phoned. The news we received from the vet wasn't what either of us had hoped for. The initial blood work had come back inconclusive, he was running a fever, and the swelling on the left side of his body had actually increased. Butch had gotten worse in the last twelve hours, and thinking back on that little face we'd seen earlier in the day, I couldn't even imagine what he was looking or feeling like right now. There was no question he'd be spending the night at the clinic and that made it even worse on Franzi and me because of the thought of him being there all alone, and the confusion he must have felt being sick and in a strange place without even his humans to tend to him. However, we both knew it was for the best.

The next morning Franzi was on the phone as soon as the clinic opened, but his condition hadn't changed very much at all. The fever was down a bit, and the swelling had seemed to stabilize, which meant that it hadn't gone down but was still the same. Being absolutely desperate for some good news, we took this as a positive. "At least he's not getting worse," was the line we said simultaneously.

This whole ordeal began on Monday, with Butch being admitted early Tuesday. Wednesday came and went with still no change in his condition, and on Thursday we got the call from the vet that neither of us wanted to receive. Butch was still the same, but the doctor said that there was nothing more they could really do for him. They didn't know what was causing the swelling and everything that they tried just didn't help at all. The impression we got was that he was basically saying, "Your dog is on the way out and it might be best if he spent his last time with the two of you."

So be it. Late that Thursday afternoon we went and picked up Butch. He looked so pitiful, with sunken eyes, shaven patches from the IV and even a partially shaved side and belly. When he saw us, there was a quick glimmer of life in his eyes, but it disappeared as fast as it had come. We got him home and carried him into the house and then straight to his bed. Curled up in one corner of his bed was Maenam, who hadn't left it during the whole week except to drink and use her litter box. Even *she* had stopped eating while Butch was away. After we moved her out of the way and got him situated as comfortably as we thought he could be, she crawled back in, lay down on his front paws, and started purring.

I was really at a loss as to what could be done for him except to keep him comfortable. I just couldn't wrap my mind around the fact that there was a good chance that he could die. That just wasn't fair. Franzi, on the other hand, is the consummate problem solver in our relationship. Often she'll come up with ideas or solutions that might seem outlandish at the moment, but end up succeeding. She has a stubbornness about her that will not accept failure, and her new mission was to bring our dog back to good health no matter what was involved.

The world of Western medicine had let us down, and not even knowing what the "Internet" was at the time, she went to the next best source of information known to humankind – her mother. Not all remedies are available with a simple prescription at a drug-store. Some are just known to a few and are passed on through the generations. I believe the correct term for these is "Grandmothers' Remedies." Her grand-mother was no longer with us, but Franzi's mom had a fair bit of knowledge, and the method of getting rid of excess fluid that she suggested sounded really strange, but we were willing to give anything a try.

What her grandmother used to do to get rid of the fluid buildup in her husband's legs and ankles during his later years was to get a cabbage, rip off a bunch of leaves, and crush them up with a rolling pin. These would be applied to the areas retaining water and held in place by wrapping them in bandages. Apparently the cabbage pulls the water out of the pores.

I was in the car and on the way to the grocery store and pharmacy so fast that it would make your head spin. As strange as this whole home remedy thing sounded, I totally embraced it, because to doubt it was a road that I didn't want to go down.

Armed with cabbages and bandages, we set about the procedure just as Franzi's mom had prescribed. We weren't quite sure how many leaves to use but we went with the theory that "more is better." It wasn't an easy chore getting Butch to stand up so that we could hold cabbage leaves on his belly and wrap bandages around his body, but he must have known that we were trying to help him. At one point, when Franzi was wrapping his chest, he gave her a lick on the face as if to say "thanks." This was the first semblance of Butch that we'd seen in days; we weren't ready to say goodbye to our friend yet.

Franzi stayed with him the whole evening and before bed I managed to get him outside for a little pee before laying him back down again. When I picked him up I couldn't help but notice that the bandages were quite moist. *"Maybe it's working,"* I thought, but not wanting to raise false hopes, I decided to keep this to myself and see what the morning brought.

The next morning we were both up at 5:00 and right down the stairs to our little companion. He was awake, with eyes that were a lot more focused than on the previous days, and to our delight, the bandages were just soaked. When we unwrapped him, his belly and side were very wet but it was a little discouraging because neither of us thought that the swelling had gone down at all. *Could it be that the bandages were just wet because of him sweating?* We couldn't tell, but we weren't going to stop in case it was actually working and we just couldn't see it.

This went on for another few days with very minimal, if any results. His belly was still monstrous and although he was looking a little bit livelier in the face, Butch still had no desire to leave his bed or even try to get up.

After dinner on Sunday evening, we were sitting at our table in the kitchen where we'd eaten so we could keep an eye on the little guy, trying to figure out what to do next. Finding another veterinarian was our first thought, and then Franzi said we should phone the breeder, Maya, to see if she had any ideas. Why we didn't think of that one before still escapes me to this day, but sometimes you can't see the forest for the trees, you know? Maya had years of experience with dogs and puppies and had probably seen the majority of all canine illnesses, or at least had a degree of knowledge about them, so since we had nothing left to lose, Franzi had her on the phone in a matter of minutes.

The conversation continued for quite some time and although I couldn't understand every word that Franzi was saying, because of the sheer tempo and speed of her frantic talking, I had a good idea of what was going on. The simple fact that she wasn't breaking down and crying was a good sign.

When she finally got off the phone, I was right in her face with "What'd she say?" but my dear wife had to first sit down and take a few deep breaths before she could fill me in on our next plan of attack. It seemed that Maya was not a big fan of traditional Western medicine, and although she had all of her dogs vaccinated with the regular shots because of breeding regulations, she treated their illnesses for the most part with homeopathic medicine. This was something she hadn't elaborated on, despite the questioning about our feelings towards homeopathic treatment, when we first had gotten our little guy, for the simple reason that a lot of people don't believe in that route.

We'd seen first-hand that Western medicine, and even grandmother's recipe, hadn't really helped him, so this looked like our only avenue left open. Maya had given Franzi the name and number of a lady who treated her dogs when they were sick, but she also said that we'd have to be very open-minded about the whole procedure because it took a lot of blind faith and it wasn't exactly explainable. It all sounded extremely strange, but with our interest tweaked, we gave her a call. No one answered and no answering machine picked up the call. It was going to be a long night with our little cabbage-wrapped buddy, wondering about this mysterious lady who took care of Maya's dogs.

Since Butch had come home three days earlier, his condition hadn't changed very much. He'd let us change his wraps without complaint, and he was able to do his business outside with our help carrying him up and down the stairs, but he would just take one or two bites of his food, which was beside his bed, and leave the rest. The two positive signs were that the swelling didn't seem to be getting any larger and that he would drink a bit from his water dish. His whining didn't let up except when he was able to find a little peace through sleep, and you could really see that he didn't want to let go. He was a fighter with a strong will and there was still a flicker of life in those sunken brown eyes.

The next morning I skipped out on school again. I'd missed four of the last six days, but I'd been keeping on top of the exercises on my own. It was a good distraction to do the home study thing, because my emotional sanity wouldn't have been able to handle the feeling of helplessness from not being able to get our dog back to even a mediocre state of health.

As soon as we thought it was late enough in the morning to phone the mystery lady without fear of waking her up, Franzi made the call. Luckily, she was home. After the initial introductions, and explanations of how we got her name and number, Franzi set about telling her the whole story, with every little detail, about what had transpired with Butch during the past week. There were a lot of questions Franzi had to answer, and then there were long periods of silence as she was told what was to be done. I saw a lot of note taking, talk of money, and then the goodbyes.

"I don't care if you believe in this or not, Dave. I know it sounds freaky, but this is what we're going to do," Franzi told me straight up. Well, with those two opening lines, she definitely had my interest. It turned out that the lady, who I'll call Frau K., practiced *Fernbehandlung,* or, as it's known in English, "distance healing with the mind," as well as homeopathic medicine.

"Great," I muttered, not feeling all too positive about what was to transpire in the quest to heal our dog. "Now it was all in the hands of some psychic," I thought. Things that I can't explain have a real tendency to bother me, and now we were heading down a weird path that, for me, envisioned witchcraft and voodoo. All these thoughts I kept to myself because Franzi seemed to be into it, and we really had no other options.

What we had to do was cut off a good piece of hair from the tip of his tail, put it in an envelope along with a recent picture of him, fifty Swiss francs, and send it to her by express mail so that she got it the next morning. After a thousand franc vet bill, this was peanuts, so within the hour we had everything on its way in the mail.

Not having any idea of what to expect from Frau K., we did the only thing that we could: we waited and prayed.

The next morning I went to school and Franzi used up another one of her holiday days to be with

Butch. We knew that Frau K. would only be getting our letter this day and then it would probably be another couple of days before she got back to us after doing her whole hocus pocus thing, but I was so badly hoping that we'd hear from her sooner rather than later. And sooner it was.

Our phone rang around five o'clock that same evening, and before Franzi picked the phone up, we both looked at each other and crossed our fingers. Frau K. had gotten our letter that morning and had a chance to examine the hair. For her, it seemed like a simple matter. She came right out and said, "Your dog was injected with a needle that was not sterile, directly into his lymph node, which has become infected and is causing the fluid build-up. You should be getting a letter tomorrow with some small homeopathic tablets in it to take care of the infection. Give these to him as directed, keep on applying the cabbage presses, and I'll work on the swelling from here."

Now, if someone had told me two weeks earlier that I'd be putting all my faith in some woman I'd never met who could give me a whole diagnosis of an illness, the cause of that illness, and the medication to deal with that illness based upon a little tuft of hair and a photograph, I would have opened the yellow pages and started searching for a good psychiatrist for that person. This was just a little too strange for my black and white thinking. I wasn't sure whether I should be elated that we'd finally figured out what was wrong with Butch and were on a path to a cure, or to dismiss it all as absolute rubbish.

That night we went to bed not knowing what to expect, except for a letter in the mail the next day with homeopathic medicine in it. I wanted to believe in this lady so badly, but my logical thinking just kept holding me back. Franzi seemed pretty convinced that it would work because she's the one who talked to Maya and heard the testimonials about how Frau K. looked after Maya's dogs. Time would tell.

Butch seemed to have a little better appetite the next morning and his eyes seemed a bit livelier. The bandages were fairly wet when we removed them but neither of us could say for sure that the swelling had gone down. The letter that we'd been so expectantly waiting on arrived around noon, just as Franzi came home for lunch, and after reading all of Frau K.'s instructions, we started on the homeopathic regimen of little white pills.

After Franzi had gone back to work, I left Butch sleeping alone to go and do some badly neglected grocery shopping, which took over an hour. The minute I walked back in the door I was greeted by my dear friend who'd gotten out of bed on his own and was walking, in all his bandaged glory, over to the door to greet me. I knelt down to give him a hug and was met with a big lick on the face. He still looked terrible, but it was one of the most beautiful sights I'd seen in a long time. He didn't even head back to his bed after that; instead he went and lay down on his cushion in the living room – something he hadn't done since the beginning of his illness.

Franzi was on cloud nine when she came home and saw that Butch wasn't in his bed, and I told her all about the greeting that I had received earlier that day. She came right out and said that we just have to believe in this lady, even if it goes against all our senses and we can't explain it. Belief and hope are two very powerful emotions, as I was quickly learning.

He stayed with us in the living room that night, and when bedtime rolled around and we changed his cabbage wrap, we were shocked to see how soaked the bandages were and how the fluid buildup down his whole left side seemed to have shrunk a bit. Not a lot, but a noticeable bit. For the first time in over a week, we both had a good night's sleep.

After getting up early the next morning and changing his wrap, which was, once again, soaked, I headed off to school. The whole way there all I could think about was Frau K., the distance healer. *Could it be that the tablets were working their magic with helping to rid his body of the fluid, or was there something else going on here that I didn't have a grasp on? Was it really possible to heal with the mind from far away?* Butch still had a monstrous belly, but not as monstrous as 24 hours ago, that's for sure.

School came and went. I'd gotten myself a little behind in the lessons but it wouldn't take long to catch up. All that was on my mind during the train ride home was whether or not Butch had improved even more. I was hoping that he'd be at the door again when I walked in, but that wasn't the case today.

He'd rediscovered his bed again and was just lying there panting and looking extremely uncomfortable. After putting the water dish next to his bed again and throwing a blanket over him, I thought it best to let him rest. So I set about doing my homework despite the fact that my interest in learning German at the moment was about the same as my interest in learning to knit.

Franzi arrived home and said that he had been just like that at lunchtime today. It was all like a roller coaster ride. One day the emotions were up and then the next, they came crashing right back down. I wanted off the ride at this point, to be honest. I think we both did.

Maya phoned us just after dinner that night to check up on Butch, one of her many pups scattered all over Europe. After we told her the events of the last two days, all she could say was, "He's still with you and he's fighting as hard as he can. Frau K. knows what she's doing and she'll fix him up. Don't the two of you give up on him, because dogs can sense these kinds of things."

It reminded me of a coach's pep talk between periods when we were down by a couple of goals. "There's still time to go in the game and it's in your hands whether you win or lose, but you had better give it your absolute best shot until the final buzzer goes. Because if you don't, you'll have a hard time living with yourself knowing that you could've affected the outcome."

We had to admit that it made sense. There were going to be good days and bad days; this just wasn't one of the better ones.

As we were sitting on the couch that night watching a little mindless television, something very unusual happened. Something we hadn't heard in a very long time: Butch barked.

Actually, he barked three times. This completely caught us off guard, since it was a sound we hadn't heard in the last eight days. We darted from the living room toward the kitchen hallway where his bed was, and there was our Butch, actually standing up and looking more alive than we'd seen him in a long time.

Franzi was the first to get to him and she just gave him a great big hug and then backed off with a strange look on her face. "He's all wet!" she exclaimed, with a great deal of excitement in her voice. Sure enough, his bandages were actually dripping and his bed looked like someone had dumped a bucket of water in it. We quickly ripped off all of his bandages, with pieces of cabbage flying everywhere, and sure as day, his whole swollen side was almost back to normal. This was too good to be true. Butch even got out of his bed, took the few steps to his food dish and started "Hoovering" down, just like he used to do. After gulping down the whole bowl, he proceeded to the door and gave out another little bark that told us it was time to head out and take care of his business. And so he did.

That night, after bandaging him up again, our heads hit the pillows but sleep didn't come easily. Both of us were too excited to sleep and too busy giving thanks to the higher powers that were bringing this nightmare to an end.

The following morning we found another soaked bed, and saw that the swelling had virtually disappeared. Butch was also back to about 90% of his old, trouble-making self. He wanted his breakfast right away, had to sniff every corner of the yard when I took him out, and even gathered up all of his play toys and brought them in the kitchen for us to choose from as we were having our morning coffee.

Thank you Frau K.! From somewhere in the southwestern part of Switzerland, over an hour away, this homeopathic distance healer had done for us what the trained, Western medicine doctors couldn't; she had saved Butch's life.

It wasn't until almost a week later, when he was back to his normal self again, that I noticed a freshly scabbed over scar on a part of his belly that hadn't been shaved. It was about an inch long and looked like it had been done with a scalpel. This totally freaked me out and I was instantly on the phone to the vet clinic. The doctor told me that they had not made any incisions whatsoever on Butch, and that he hadn't seen any fresh cut or scabbed-over scar when we brought him in to the clinic.

The next phone call was to Maya, and she didn't seem surprised at all when I told her about the cut. All she said was, "Frau K. has some interesting ways of healing."

Chapter 5
Butch the Scholar

*H*aving pulled through this major illness, there was newfound joy in all of our lives. Franzi and I were still having some trouble digesting the way in which Butch had healed, and we didn't talk much to people about the whole scenario for fear they'd think we were nuts, but nevertheless, we had our good friend back and he was his old, rambunctious self again.

There were times during the whole illness when we could have given up hope on Butch, but that was something we just couldn't do. The commitment that we undertook when we got him meant that we had to give Butch the best life that we possibly could, and just like with children, there are good times and bad. You have to accept them both and try to make the best out of every situation, no matter how hard or impossible that may seem at the time.

My intensive German course finished at the end of February and I ended up sitting at the top of the class. Although this surprised me a bit, I'd worked awfully hard at it the last six weeks and spent a lot of time with my nose in the books.

During the final two weeks of school, Franzi and I went up to Muerren for the weekend, and it was up here that we ran into my old bosses, Anna and Andreas, whom I'd worked for as a bartender a few years previously. Anna and Andreas were a middle-aged Swiss couple with a very young and open outlook on life; they didn't really fit the mold of the typical Swiss "establishment" crowd. They tended to put more emphasis on what you could actually do as opposed to what school you attended, what kind of grades you had and what your diploma said. They'd given me a great letter of recommendation after I worked for them, and they completely understood my reasons for leaving; I simply wanted to be down in the valley with my fiancée at the time.

We sat down on the outdoor patio of the hotel they were running and had a bottle of wine together while shooting the breeze. I told them about the schooling I was just about to complete and their response was, "Well, that would be why you can speak German three times better than you used to!"

The day was sunny and the patio was extremely busy with skiers and snowboarders, so Anna and Andreas both had to get up from the table to go help out their staff for a short time, but they told us not to go anywhere. When they returned about a half-hour later, they both sat down to their glasses of wine once more, and then proceeded to tell me about an opening they had at the reception desk. It involved a lot of correspondence, basic accounting, and quite a bit of contact with the public. "Was I interested?" they asked.

I knew that they had probably talked to each other about this while helping out their servers, but knowing how hard it was to get a decent job as a non-Swiss person, I was really taken aback at this sudden offer of a very respectable job. I was speechless, actually.

My first thought was that it would be the same as before: long night hours and being unable to finish work in time to catch the last cable car down to the valley. After they explained that the working hours would allow me to be home at night with my lovely wife, things started looking a lot better. Still, this was uncharted territory for me. Luckily, Franzi was at my side and gave me the kick under the table that I needed. I graciously accepted their offer and before leaving the patio, thanked Anna and Andreas profusely for having enough faith in me to fill the position.

The new job started off well, with an extremely sharp learning curve. After a few weeks, all the anxiety I'd felt going into it was gone, and I found I enjoyed working a job that involved using my brain again. With either a seven to three shift or a three to eleven shift, I was always either waking up early or coming home very late, but the nice thing was that I could lay my head on my own pillow at night.

The winter came to an end and it was time to get the hiking boots out of the closet and hit the trails again.

Whenever Franzi and I had a day off together, we'd be out exploring the countless trails in our area, with our once again healthy Butch leading the way. Normally, after a day in the mountains, we'd stop at the lake, which Butch loved more than life itself, to give him a cooling-off swim. The water was always freezing because it was all glacial runoff, but Butch didn't seem to mind, thanks to his trusty fur coat. He could be in that water for a good hour, and when he'd come out he'd be shaking like crazy, but when it came time to leave he would always try to prolong the process. "Are you talking to me? I want to swim some more!" was what the expression on his face looked like.

One time, on an extremely hot afternoon, he was digging in the shallow water right beside the shore and actually struck gold. Well, technically, it wasn't gold, but a nice cold bottle of beer that someone must have left to keep cool and had forgotten about. Normally, anytime Butch retrieved something, he'd bring it right to Franzi because he knew there was a better chance of her playing with him than me, but this time he just seemed to know where that beer belonged. He came straight to me and didn't even drop it at my feet. *What a dog!*

There were many times, however, when we'd call him and he'd forget his name, and although we weren't very discipline-orientated, we did recognize that this could be a problem in the future. *What if there was a farmer coming at him with a shotgun because he was digging up the farmer's carrots?* That would be a very good time for Butch to know his name and come when we called him, now, wouldn't it?

So, it was with heavy hearts that we enrolled our wild little guy into obedience school. If I could handle four months of language school, he could surely make it through eight weeks of once-a-week doggy university. And if he passed the obedience course, we'd even get a twenty-franc discount on his annual dog license fees. Butch didn't seem to care a whole lot about that.

The course was every Wednesday night and held at the abandoned airstrip close to where we lived, which meant we could walk there, relieving Butch of some of the excess energy that he always seemed to have bundled up inside of him. When we arrived there the first night, there were about twenty other dogs, all with their humans in tow, and, for the most part, they seemed to be under control. It's not always desirable to be the exception, but that's exactly what we were. As soon as Butch caught sight of all these other playmates, we knew we were in trouble.

At this point in his life he was clocking in at around 75 pounds of rambunctious muscle, and when he wanted to go, it was all you could do to hold on to his leash and keep your shoulder in its socket. Unfortunately, Franzi happened to be the one holding the leash, or trying to at least, and when I turned back to ask her something, she was gone, dragged off in the direction of Butch's twenty new best friends. I really had to concentrate so that I didn't burst out laughing, because I knew that if she saw or heard me, I'd be the one sleeping under the stairs. So with a straight face, I ran after her to give her a hand.

Butch had met the pack and was doing his best to lick every face and sniff every rear end he could before the big bellow came.

"Get that dog under control!" I guess we'd just met the instructor of the course. I think we were both wondering at that moment why we ever decided to subject ourselves to such a degree of embarrassment. The twenty other dog owners were all looking at us with a slight look of amusement mixed with conde-scension. Our faces were probably a tad bit red at that point. With a great deal of force, I held onto Butch, but his mind was far away from obeying me at the moment. His tail was going so fast that it was almost a blur; no flies were going to land on this bum!

First things first – only one of us would be allowed to participate in the training course with Butch. As we were told, the animal needs to have a distinct Alpha person who is the ultimate master. This didn't exactly fit into our plan because we *both* wanted to be the master. We wanted Butch to listen and obey both of us, equally. It didn't really make a lot of sense to me at the time, but I gave the instructor the benefit of the doubt and we quickly concluded who would be Butch's Grand Alpha human master: it would be Franzi.

This decision came about due to the simple fact that I wouldn't be able to attend every single Wednesday night training session during the eight-week period. There were a couple of weeks that I had the afternoon shift, so with the passing of the leash to my terrified-looking wife, I took my place on the sidelines and wished her all the best.

The first drill was walking heel, with the dog on the left side of the owner. All the owners were asked to walk with their dogs at their side to a pole about one hundred yards away, go around the pole, and come back; simple enough. Franzi and Butch were among the last ones in line and when they started off, Butch felt it was his duty to catch up to the dog in front of him. The soles of Franzi's shoes must have lost at least a quarter of an inch, because for most of those one hundred yards she was in total braking mode. Dogs who'd already gone around the pole and were on their way back presented another problem. This quickly became known as the sideways lurch. Upon completion of this ultra-demanding obstacle course, I saw the instructor pull Franzi aside and have a few words with her. She just looked over at me and shrugged her shoulders in resignation. This was going to be an interesting eight weeks.

As we were walking home, I asked why the instructor had pulled only her aside, because despite Butch's total degree of disobedience, there were a few other dogs there that weren't exactly "perfect" either. Franzi said that the instructor told her she had to work with Butch every single day, because in all her years of training dogs, our dog was one of the most uncontrolled that she had ever come across. I had visions in my head of Butch standing up on the podium with a big blue ribbon pinned to his collar with the words "'Most Uncontrolled' – 1ˢᵗ Place."

For the next few weeks I wasn't able to attend doggy boot camp, but Franzi filled me in on the newest embarrassments as soon as I came home each Wednesday night. She'd been working with Butch on a daily basis, as did I when he walked with me, and although he was starting to get a little bit better in the obedience department, he still had a long way to go. When I'd give him a command, he'd look at me and tilt his head a bit to the side, as if pondering whether or not it was in his best interest to listen to me. I can't say for sure, but at the time I could have sworn that he knew he was so damn cute. That, and the fact that I always got sucked in by his innocent face, made life for Franzi much harder when she had to line up with the twenty other four-legged Einsteins.

The absolute highlight of the whole course came during week seven – one week before the big final exam. This was going to be the "how to behave around humans who don't have dogs in their surroundings" lesson. What this entailed was a trip into town on the public transit bus, and then going into a restaurant for a beverage, with the dogs in tow.

In many parts of Europe, dogs travel just like humans. They're allowed on buses, trains, cable cars, gondolas, boats and ships, and the only form of transportation where dog and master are separated are the airlines. As for the "dogs in restaurants" part, well, that was more of a central and northern European thing.

Luckily, on this evening, I was able to attend the lecture. Having already travelled many times with Butch on trains, buses and cable cars, Franzi and I had no fear for the first part of the tutorial. Butch would simply lie down and go to sleep on most forms of public transportation. Perhaps it was the movement that calmed him down, or the fact he didn't always know where he was going, so he figured it was nothing to get excited about. Travel by car was another story. He knew the roads well enough to know which ones led to the lake. And as soon as he sensed a familiar road, all hell would break loose in the rear part of the car. The barking would start and just wouldn't stop, and no amount of scolding helped. In the back of the car he had the safety of his doggy divider bars, which kept him from jumping into the back seat, and it was almost like a prisoner talking back to a guard. If you wanted to do something about the prisoner in the back, you basically had to stop the car, get out, and open up his cell. We were too lazy for that.

As we expected, Butch was one of the better-behaved dogs on the bus ride into town, much to all the other dog owners' astonishment. Up until this point, he'd developed quite the reputation, and not many of the other owners wanted to be around Franzi and Butch during the drills. Probably because he resembled that little hellion in elementary school that always got the others into trouble.

The next part of the evening was about taking all the dogs into a restaurant where they were expected to obediently lie under the tables while their owners had dinner, or drinks, or anything else. We'd tried this a few times up in Muerren, but it was not a great success. Butch would usually end up under the table, but one of us had to have his leash wrapped about three times around our own leg as well as having a firm foot on the part of the leash that was closest to his collar. We called it the "pin him down so he can't move" approach.

The restaurant was forewarned about the canine banquet they were about to host, and they had a table for about twenty waiting for us when they arrived. Since I wasn't the Alpha human, a few other non-Alpha observers and I had to sit at another table, away from the group, but I still had a good view of all the events.

When the group began arriving, they all came in one after another, putting the dog under the table first and then seating themselves. There were a few dogs that were reluctant, but for the most part it went well. Even Butch, to my absolute disbelief, lay down perfectly at Franzi's feet.

The waitress who was taking everyone's drink order was a young lady, probably in her early twenties, and quite attractive in her little black miniskirt. She was doing her absolute best to make it all the way around the big table without stepping on any tails or paws, because not all the dogs could fit underneath without some body parts sticking out.

Franzi, who seemed to be quite proud of both herself and our dog, gave me a little wave as well as a look that said, "You see, he's not always such a wild camper!" All I could do was nod my head in agreement. Just the fact that Butch was lying half under the table, not bothering the other canines *or* barking *or* yelping had left me pretty speechless. I really didn't think that he had it in him to be still and quiet for such a long ten-minute period of time, and sadly enough, that all came to a screeching halt shortly thereafter.

The drinks the waitress was delivering were all on a large serving tray being delicately balanced on her left hand. Around the table she went, from person to person. When she finally reached Franzi, with about a third of the tray still loaded up, Butch made his move. As the waitress was bending over to set Franzi's drink on the table, she suddenly seemed to rise up about four inches and all the drinks on her tray were no longer standing upright. "Whoa!" she yelled, startling everyone, who all jumped up to see what had happened. Butch had decided it was finally time to say hello to the young lady and did it in the most self-pleasing way he knew how – by sticking his nose between her legs, under the miniskirt, and then lifting up.

I just sat there watching the whole scene play out in front of me, in absolute disbelief. Franzi was grabbing Butch, the others were knocking over their drinks trying to get a better view, and the waitress was back-pedaling as fast as she could. No longer able to watch for fear that I might burst out laughing, I turned away from the whole fiasco and pretended to have nothing to do with the lunatic dog people. My darling wife happened to notice that I'd disowned her and our four-legged miniskirt stalker. That was one of the major mistakes in my life and something I had the pleasure of hearing about for a long, long time.

Everyone helped the waitress clean up the mess and she didn't seem at all bothered by the ordeal. After Franzi finished shooting daggers at me with her laser beam eyes, and apologizing to the young lady for our overly-friendly Butch, she had a really great response about the whole thing.

"As long as it's only dogs sticking their heads up under my skirt, and not the customers!" Now, if only the dog trainer could have been so easy-going about it….

Not a lot was said that night between the two of us. I really wanted to laugh hysterically, but my sense of self-preservation was stronger. Embarrassment was no defence against disowning your loved ones, even if only for a brief moment.

The final obedience exam was only a few days away and we were both really nervous about Butch's chances of actually pulling it off. What we needed was a strategy, so we racked our brains for a couple of nights, trying to figure out what in the world would entice our dog to make all the right moves when the pressure was on.

As with many of our great ideas, it came to us while enjoying a bottle of wine. The doggy instructor had said that it was alright to reward your dog for a job well done with a small treat and a lot of praise. Taking this whole reward thing and twisting it around a bit, we came up with something even better. We'd starve Butch the whole day, and then cut up about six sausages into bite-size pieces while he was watching, and then put them all in the left side pocket of Franzi's windbreaker, again, while he was watching. Butch loved sausages, so in our eyes, this plan seemed foolproof.

When the big day finally arrived, we followed our plan to the letter. On the walk to the airfield Butch never ventured more than a step or two away from the sausage lady. He was hungry, and after a few little samplers, he seemed to figure it out.

The first test was walking heel, which he did surprisingly well, finishing the exercise with a large sausage belch. The next test was sit. Butch always did this, even as a little puppy, so it came as no surprise when he parked his butt immediately down on the asphalt as soon as the command came out of Franzi's mouth. The third leg of the exam was to get him to lie down on command, which, despite all of our efforts, he had never done in his life. This time around was no exception. Not even the sausages helped here. Perhaps he was just behaving like humans would? If you walk into the boss's office, or a medical office, you're normally told to "have a seat" or "take a seat," and unless you're really ticked off, you usually do sit down. If you were to go into those same places and hear "lie down" or "take a bed," chances are that you wouldn't do it either.

Two out of three tasks had gone well at least, but there was still another tough challenge coming up – the agility course. This involved walking up and down ramps, jumping over small obstacles and crawling through a long tunnel. With the sausage supply at his side, Butch breezed through the ramps and cleared all of the small jumps. But, when it came to the tunnel, it was an instant freeze-up. With the instructor standing right beside her, Franzi could not very well have thrown a handful of sausage bites into the tunnel because that was, for some odd reason, not allowed. It probably ranked right up there with doping, so after a lot of coaxing and prodding, the instructor decided to end the fourth and final test.

Having only passed the two easiest of the four tests, we felt like parents who somehow knew their child was going to have to repeat kindergarten. He was a good dog who'd already been through a lot during his first year on the earth, and the fact that he was again healthy was really all that was important to us. If he had to take the course again, then so be it. We'd just work a little harder with him.

When all the participants had finished the testing, the instructor gathered us all around and triumphantly announced that each and every dog had passed the obedience class of 1996.

"Although for some it was very borderline," she added, looking over at Butch, who was trying to pull Franzi in the direction of a squirrel that had caught his eye.

If the truth were told, we were sure that she never wanted to see our dog in her class again.

Chapter 6
Time for the Big Move

With our new graduate demonstrating on a daily basis that he hadn't learned or retained a lot of knowledge during his time at school, we started to research everything that would be involved in immigrating to Canada.

The subject was always in our heads and often absorbed the majority of our dinner conversations, but that's all it was – talk and conversation. Now, though, the time had come to make a conscious decision to do it.

With summer slowly coming to an end and the hotel reception business winding down, it seemed like the perfect time to set the wheels in motion. There were so many factors to consider that the only way to start was with the almighty list. I'm a true believer in making lists, which is probably to compensate for my inability to remember anything.

We already had a general idea of where it was that we wanted to live, or at least start off, and that was in the small village of Invermere in British Columbia. We loved it when we visited there in 1993, and with the lakes and mountains that surrounded it, it was very similar to Interlaken, where we lived in Switzerland.

Franzi, and the whole residency process, was at the top of my forever-growing list, and it had never occurred to me that getting her legalized in Canada would be such a big deal. She was married to a Canadian and had been for almost three years, so it wasn't like she'd married me just for the passport – having a Swiss one of her own – but it still felt like I'd been punched in the gut after visiting the Canadian Consulate in Bern.

"Up to a year?" I barked at the desk jockey, forgetting that he was just another public servant doing his little cog part in the big red tape–infested government cogwheel. *How could this be?* It seemed like everyone got into Canada, and for the most part they did, but what I failed to realize was that it actually took some time. Unless, of course, you showed up on the shores in a boat and said you were a refugee. It made absolutely no difference whether you were from Zurich or Timbuktu – the wait times were the same for everyone.

The initial fee that we had to pay was $1475 and that was just to receive the immigration forms. This was only the start of the expensive process. Obtaining government copies of birth records and police background checks, as well as a full medical examination from the Canadian consulate doctor, were starting to hit the pocketbook hard. The man whom we'd spoken with at the consulate told us that a lot of applicants deal with private immigration services to ensure that all of their information is complete and forwarded on to the proper channels. That made sense to me; it was a lot like taxes. If you were clueless at doing your income tax return, you took it to someone who did it for a living.

Finding a private immigration service to help us out proved to be another matter. Most of them were actually situated in Canada, which meant that I was going on a little overseas road trip. Getting two weeks off work in November was very easy because the village of Muerren was asleep, and the ski season didn't get going until mid-December. So armed with all of Franzi's paperwork, I set off for a quick visit with my family, and to further the business of moving us across the pond.

This all went off without a hitch, and I was told that now it was just a waiting process while the wheels of government churned. Also, that Franzi should have all of her necessary documentation to legally enter Canada as a landed immigrant by the beginning of the following summer, meaning late June or early July. It was a relief to be able to put this whole process on the back burners and not have to think about it for a while.

Next on the "extremely important things we had to figure out before we move" list were the animals. We had checked this out previously, but government regulations can change all the time. Luckily, it was all still the same. Butch and Maenam would be able to enter Canada without any quarantine, providing they had all their shots up-to-date and a letter from the vet stating that they were in good health. If only it were that simple for Franzi.

Winter arrived rather early, with plenty of snow to bring smiles to the faces of both the locals and tourists alike. With both of us being busy at our jobs, doing a lot of skiing, and walking the snow monster Butch, there wasn't a lot of time left for planning the "over the pond" move. There were still some serious matters to be ironed out, like which of our worldly possessions we'd be selling off and which ones would be following us, and of these items, how would they be following us? We needed a shipping company, and we needed to have a garage sale as well.

Having set our departure date for mid-September, we knew that the time would fly by rather quickly, so we had to stay on top of all these detail-demanding particulars. After all, they weren't going to look after themselves. The other thing we hadn't considered was that we'd have to organize a couple of going away parties; one for all of Franzi's family and the other for all of our friends. When we thought of this aspect of the move, I think it really hit home for us that the time was quickly approaching when we'd have to say goodbye to a lot of people we loved and cared about. For Franzi, this was going to be a big step, and we talked about it quite a bit that winter. She reassured me that this was the direction she wanted our lives going in, and that although it was hard at the moment, the four of us were going to have a great life over in Canada.

Winter rolled along, just as we thought it would, and our search for a transport company to ship our belongings was actually a relatively easy one. There was a company in Basel that shipped all over the world and all that we had to do was box up everything that we were taking with us, bring it to Basel, and they would build a wooden crate to the required size, which in turn would be put into a container. We would be paying for the volume rather than the weight, which meant that there would be some very strategic packing involved with each and every box. The container would go by train to the port in Rotterdam, and then by ship to Montreal. And finally, from there by train to the final destination of Calgary. After that, it would be up to us to find our own transportation to bring it the final three hours over the Rockies to our new home. The whole process would take about three months we were told, so that meant having everything packed and ready to go by mid-June.

The big decision that now faced us was what we wanted to take with us over to Canada. If we packed up everything that we owned, life would be a lot easier when we got there, but the expense would be enormous. If we just took the basics of our household (including everything of sentimental value), the shipping costs would be greatly reduced, allowing us to buy new things in Canada. All of our appliances and anything that involved electricity quickly fell out of the equation because Europe was on 220 volts and North America was on 110, so they would be useless in Canada, anyway. We debated the pros and cons of this decision again, over a bottle of wine, and when the last drop had been drained, we were going with the bare minimum as well as the sentimental items. Another step had been taken.

The ski season up in Muerren typically comes to a halt as soon as Easter has passed. If Easter should happen to fall particularly early, the hotels and ski lifts will stay open another week. Most of the hotels shut down until the summer tourist season starts in mid-June, and I was fortunate enough to be working at one that stayed open year-round.

It was on the Easter Monday, after a busy morning of people checking out, that I received a phone call from Franzi's mother. Her whole family was up in Muerren for the holiday weekend and Franzi had gone out that day skiing with her brother Beat. After she had made it through the whole winter suffering from only one colic attack, I was beginning to think that maybe her health problems were slowly coming to an end, but it just wasn't meant to be. Her mother told me in very frantic terms that Franzi had just been taken to the hospital after blowing out her left knee on the slopes. She's a great skier, but these things can happen to anyone.

I left work right away and dashed to her parents' apartment, which was only about three minutes away, where her brother was just bringing her back from the hospital, on crutches. What was supposed to look like Franzi's knee had a lot more in common with a watermelon from what I could see, but she said she wasn't in any pain. A combination of painkillers and shock will do that to a person.

Surgery was in the cards, but they would have to wait for a few weeks until the swelling had gone down. Butch, who hadn't left Franzi's side since the time we propped her up on the sofa with an ice pack, looked especially gloomy. He knew that her world had been turned upside down and wanted to do something, but his low whines and licks on the face weren't getting her up off the sofa. He never left her side that afternoon and when I went with him for a walk that evening, he was just not the regular Butch I knew. No one can ever tell me that dogs don't sense the distress of humans, or know depression; Butch was down.

Fortunately, with the season at an end and slow times ahead for the hotel, I was able to use up some of my holiday time that I'd built up over the last year. Many people would have simply cut out a few of the daily dog walks, but having watched on a daily basis how Butch stuck on Franzi and gave her all of his love and companionship while she was laid up on the couch, I felt that there was no dog more deserving of his exercise. So at the crack of dawn, early afternoon, and each evening, we spent our time together out in the forests. It probably wasn't the same for Butch, not having his mom along, but he seemed to enjoy it nonetheless.

The surgery came and went and was pronounced a success by the doctors who performed it, so now we were onto the recovery period. Franzi had gotten very proficient on her crutches and even started joining us on our walks, as long as they were on flat surfaced roads and not out in the bush. Just ten days after the operation, Franzi even took Butch out on her own, which absolutely terrified me because I knew how he could pull on his leash. It was something she felt she had to do despite the fact that I was at home and wanted to go with her. "No, this afternoon is for Butch and me," she said at the end of our driveway. She then bent down and said to him, "Butch, I know this sucks having to walk like this, but I'm making a promise to you right now. Someday, you will never ever have to walk on a leash again." And then they set off.

Waiting at home on pins and needles, I half expected Butch to show up on his own with a human-less crutch attached to his leash, but just over an hour later the two of them came home, both with smiles on their faces, and Franzi proceeded to tell me that he hadn't pulled on his leash even once. He knew. That one walk had done more to renew Franzi and her whole spirit than a month of physiotherapy could ever have done, and it wasn't long afterwards that the crutches were a thing of the past.

The whole packing process went along smoothly and we were able to sell off most of our furniture, power tools, appliances, and other electrical items. We even had a buyer lined up for our car – a two-year-old

Fiat – which we had first thought about bringing with us. We decided against it due to the fact that the Fiat is a virtually unknown brand in Canada, so getting it serviced would be a monumental problem.

Between packing and selling off possessions, our cosy little home was starting to look pretty bare. An old kitchen table with two chairs, a sofa facing a small television set on the floor, our bed, some clothing, and a few other small items were all that we had left.

Butch seemed totally confused by the whole process. He'd walk around from room to room, smelling where things had once been, and then he'd give me a look as if to say, "What are you doing? You'd better not touch my bed, because I know where yours is."

It was now early June and all of our possessions that were being shipped to Canada had to be brought to the shipping company in Basel. Knowing how movers often handle boxes and packages, I spent literally hundreds of francs on roll after roll of bubble wrap and tape in order to pack up, as best I possibly could, all of our dishes and glassware, which had been wedding gifts.

With the help of a few friends, we loaded up all our boxes into a truck that Franzi's boss had loaned us, and we set off for Basel. Once there, we were reassured that our items would be handled with the utmost care and attention, but I wasn't taken in by their promises. These guys weren't going to be travelling with our stuff all the way to Calgary keeping an eye on its safe passage. After a couple of days they would never even see it again, or for that matter, care about it again.

So it was with a silent Hail Mary that we said goodbye to everything that held a major degree of sentimental value for us.

"It's only stuff, Dave," Franzi began. "Sure, it means a lot to us, but we just have to have some faith in the universe that it'll show up intact in three months' time, and even if it doesn't, there's nothing we can do about it. So there's no point in losing any sleep over it, now, is there?"

Being a very hands-on person, having blind faith was never an easy thing for me, although I knew she was right. The most important thing was that the four of us make it over there safely. At the end of the day, the rest was just stuff.

The lease we had on our rental house was finished at the end of June, which was still a few weeks away, but it didn't feel very comfortable to be living there anymore. Our closest friends were all up in Muerren and we had the use of Franzi's parents' apartment, so it only made sense that we should spend the last three months in one of the most beautiful places in all of Switzerland, surrounded by people we cared about.

The big dilemma we were now facing was the fact that Franzi still hadn't received her immigration papers. It had been roughly nine months since we'd put the ball in motion and the immigration broker back in Canada told us that our application was progressing along quite nicely and it should just be a matter days before we received the papers.

Those words weren't at all reassuring, because as most people discover at some point in their lives, the wheels of government can turn at a very slow pace, and sometimes they can come to a complete halt.

With only three months left before we wanted to leave, I kept having this strange scenario play out in my mind. *What if, for whatever strange or bureaucratic reason, Franzi was somehow denied landed immigrant status?* I knew that there was a 99.99% chance that this wouldn't happen, but still, "never say never." What a nightmare that would turn out to be. Everything we sent out would have to be shipped back, as well as finding another place to live, which was not an easy task at that time in Switzerland.

As Butch's second birthday arrived we decided to take him on a hike, similar to the one a year-and-a-half earlier when I ended up having to carry him all the way back down, and then finish it off with a barbeque. This time around I knew that there'd be no carrying involved because Butch was now a full-grown Labrador who was very large, by Lab standards. People would always ask us if he was a purebred because his body seemed so long compared to regular Labs, and his weight was around 90 pounds.

Our breeder, Maya, almost lost it on us when we told her his weight, thinking that we'd turned him into a small hippopotamus. In all her years of breeding Labs she'd never had a full grown male over 85 pounds. Although, after sending her a photo of

Butch standing beside us, she realized that he was just a very large bundle of muscle, without an ounce of fat on him. She even went so far as to say that he was one of the most beautiful Labs she'd ever seen.

Franzi and I both had the day off work, so we made a whole day of it: stopping for picnics, letting Butch play in the streams, and just allowing him to be himself on his birthday.

Throughout the course of the hike, Franzi and I talked about our hopes and dreams for our new life in Canada, and about how exciting new beginnings were, and then, as we sat by a little stream, watching Butch dig up rocks from the water and bring them to us, she blurted out, "Dave, we can't go over to Canada together. That'll never work."

"What? What do you mean we can't go over together?" I responded instantly.

"Think about it. How are we going to get to Invermere? Where are we going to stay? We've got a couple of animals here that we have to think about. They'll need a home when we get there. You'll have to go ahead of us."

She was right of course, as she usually was, and I could have kicked myself for overlooking something so completely obvious. That was exactly the way it was going to have to be.

We hiked on that afternoon without saying much more about it, but my mind was racing. If I were to go ahead, the first call of business would be to find a place for us to live so that when they got off the plane, they had a place to come home to. The other thing I had to think about was that I would need some wheels to go pick them up at the airport in.

These were straightforward things to deal with when I got there, but still, they all had to be in place. The thing that bothered me the most was that I'd be alone over in Canada. No Franzi, no Butch, no Maenam. This was going to be one of the biggest steps in Franzi's life – leaving her family, friends, and homeland – and it tore at my heartstrings knowing that I wouldn't be there for her.

The hike came to an end with Butch looking quite exhausted after spending his big birthday tramping through the Alps. So after finding a public barbeque place just outside of Muerren in a wooded area, with a wonderful view of the famous Eiger, Mönch, and Jungfrau mountain ranges, we started a fire, opened a bottle of wine and settled down for the Birthday dinner.

The bratwurst, steak, and potato salad, which had all been frozen solid when we started off earlier in the day, were now at body temperature from being in the backpack all day. The two-legged hikers enjoyed the bratwurst, and our yellow, four-legged friend got his birthday steak, which Franzi had promised him the day before. Not everyone would give a steak to a dog, but this was to become a birthday ritual, and he never complained that it was over- or under-cooked.

Over our camping dinner that night, we played around with dates in our heads, and decided that I'd book a flight for September 9th and Franzi would follow about three weeks later. That would give me just enough time to find a roof for over our heads, and a car to get us around.

The days on the calendar quickly turned into weeks and soon we were approaching the end of August. We'd had a big going-away party with all of our friends and family, which was both heart-wrenching and heart-warming, because of all the goodbyes and how obvious it was they cared about our well-being and us.

With only a week left before my departure, Franzi's papers still had not arrived, and answers from Ottawa, the capital of Canada, as well as from the private immigration service we hired, were not forth-coming either. The whole situation had my nerves frayed, but strangely enough, Franzi didn't seem too concerned.

We'd booked her flight for the 25th of September, on a direct flight from Zurich to Calgary. Butch would have to travel in the cargo hold, but Maenam could be in the cabin if her cage was stored under the seat. Naturally, they'd both be zonked out with sleeping drugs, but twelve hours seemed like a very long time for them to be under.

The solution that Franzi had come up with seemed logical and I wasn't able to poke any holes in it. If her papers didn't arrive by the time she was set to leave, she would just enter into Canada with her Swiss passport, as a tourist. Tourists were allowed to bring animals into the country, and she could stay for up to six months. When the papers arrived, we'd have them sent to Canada and then she could just make a quick trip over the border to the United States and re-enter Canada with the landed immigrant papers all rubber-stamped.

There probably were some kinks in this plan, but we weren't immigration gurus, so it all made perfect sense to us. The main thing was that we were able to sleep a little better at night, and we weren't giving the poor lady at the post office, where our mail was being forwarded, the evil eye everyday as if it was her fault that the papers hadn't shown up yet.

Tuesday, September 9th, 1997, finally arrived. This was it. This was the day that my stay in a country that I'd truly come to love, where I'd lived for the last ten years, give or take a few travels, was to come to an end.

Having first stepped foot in Switzerland with only a backpack to my name, I now found myself heading back to my country of birth, again with a backpack, as well as half a container full of stuff, a wife, a dog, and a cat to follow, and a growing level of nervousness which I hadn't experienced in a long time.

Canada, although it was my home and native land, was a country that I had spent very little time in during the last twelve years, having left home right after graduation from college, and I'd still been living at home at that point. I'd never rented my own place in Canada, had a phone hooked up, did my own taxes, or any number of the mundane tasks that people do on a regular basis without even thinking about. To put it bluntly, I really had no idea of how the daily nuts and bolts of everyday life functioned. Franzi was our bill payer and had dealt with all the officialdom of daily life in Switzerland, but now that we'd be living in my land, it was my turn to step up to the plate. Although there was quite a bit of anxiety about how the scenario would play out, it couldn't be any worse than being surrounded by an angry mob of South American Indians who wanted to erase you from the earth.

With my overfilled backpack and a suitcase that was bulging at the seams sitting beside the door, Franzi and I had breakfast together. This was going to be our last meal together for the next two and a half weeks and although we didn't speak very much, with each of us lost in our own thoughts, I felt so close to this lovely woman who'd chosen to spend her life with me.

Sir Butch, on the other hand, had his nose a bit out of joint. He was smart enough to know that when a backpack or a suitcase was pulled out, someone was going somewhere, and he didn't like having the family unit disrupted in any way. There he stood, with the saddest of looks on his face beside the door and let out a little yelp, as if to say, "please don't go."

"I have to go Butch, I'm sorry," I told the little guy.

After saying goodbye to Maenam, who was in one of her cat-like "don't you dare touch me" moods, and receiving a scratch on my arm that drew blood, the three of us set off for the cable car station, with

Butch walking beside me on his leash like a perfect gentleman.

With only about two minutes to spare before the cable car left, Franzi and I said our tearful goodbyes. Butch watched us, patiently waiting his turn, and then when I crouched down to give him a hug he covered me in big, wet licks.

We waved goodbye, with Butch standing up to look out the window of the cable car station with his tongue hanging out of his mouth, and as the cable car started to slowly descend, even knowing that I'd be seeing them all again in a few weeks, my tears just flowed.

The Swiss chapter of my life had just come to an end.

Chapter 7
New Beginnings

*J*ust getting to the airport was quite an exhausting procedure in itself. The journey involved two cable cars, one bus, and four trains. With two large pieces of luggage as well as a carry-on, changing between all of the different transportation modes was really starting to stretch my arms.

The afternoon was clear and sunny as I took off from Zurich, and I could see from the airplane window the mountain range where I'd started my journey just six hours ago. I knew that Franzi would be out walking Butch and that she'd be looking up at the skies because we actually took off on time, so I gave her a little wave. *"See you soon, honey."*

The stopover in London's Heathrow was quick, with only an hour to change terminals and catch the Calgary-bound flight, which I managed with only a few minutes to spare. Heathrow is normally an absolute nuthouse, but during this short and intensive stopover, the mood was very sombre. Princess Diana had passed away a few days before and it looked like the majority of the people were still in a state of shock.

Franzi had a second cousin who had emigrated from Switzerland to Calgary about 30 years previous, and during our travels of 1993, we'd stopped and visited him for a couple of days. His name was Jurg, and he's the one who picked me up at midnight in Calgary. I felt bad that he had to come so late, and even worse when I waited for my luggage that failed to arrive, but he welcomed me quite warmly back to Canada.

It was Jurg – a confirmed bachelor – with whom I spent my first few nights back in Canada. My luggage arrived two days later, as I expected, because I knew that there wasn't much hope of it making it on the Calgary flight when I, myself, barely did. The world of backpacking teaches you to carry at least three days of clothing in your carry-on bag.

During these few days in Calgary I was able to get some of the important things done, like contacting the warehouse where all of our worldly possessions were just sitting and waiting for us to pick them up. I was also able to get in contact with Chris, our friend with the cattle ranch in Invermere, who said that he could drive out on Saturday with his one-ton flatbed truck, pick up our stuff, and bring me back to his place, which I could use as a home base.

Having these two people help me out from Day One was an incredible bonus and very much appreciated. I hated to think how it would have been if I'd had no one in Calgary or Invermere to help me out in the beginning.

I phoned Franzi everyday, mostly because I missed her so much and I wanted to know how Butch was doing, but also to keep her up to date on what was going on over on this side of the pond. It was on the Friday when I phoned that she gave me the great news that her landed immigrant papers had finally arrived. It was almost a year to the date from the time that we first started the immigration proceedings.

That was an extremely large load lifted from our shoulders. Everything seemed to be falling into place. Her papers came, our container arrived and was waiting to be picked up the next day when Chris came to get me, and even Butch was back to his old self after a couple days of moping around, looking for me all over the apartment up in Muerren. It's certainly a great feeling when everything goes well, but it also makes me a bit nervous because you just know that sooner or later something has to go wrong or sideways.

Chris showed up at Jurg's house the next morning at 11:00 A.M. in a flatbed truck that reminded me of the one Redd Foxx drove in the TV series "Sanford and Son." It was not only old and beat up, but it also looked extremely tired. It was good to see Chris again and I kept my opinions to myself about his farm vehicle, but somewhere in the bottom of my gut, I didn't have a good feeling.

Jurg and I said our goodbyes and I promised him that I'd stop by and see him again when I came to pick up Franzi, and then Chris and I were on our way to the warehouse to retrieve my worldly possessions.

It took close to an hour of red tape and paperwork, along with a lot of Canadian Custom forms which had to be filled out, but finally the guy in the blue overalls pointed over to the corner of the warehouse and said, "There it is, take it."

It wasn't quite what I'd had in mind from these helpful folks.

"Do you think it might just be possible for you to use your forklift and perhaps set it on the back of the flatbed truck that's sitting right outside of the loading dock?" I asked.

"Well," he drawled, "we normally don't do that, but it's getting pretty close to lunchtime and I'm the only one here, so if I were to wait around for you two to unpack everything and then load it yourselves, I'd be here for the next two hours. Okay, I'll get the forklift."

"Great!" I thought. *"Toto, we're not in Kansas anymore."* Swiss efficiency had definitely spoiled me and I could see that the Canadian work mentality was going to take some getting used to.

Once the crate, which happened to be a whopping 2,200 pounds, was loaded on the truck, Chris and I set out for Invermere. I hadn't noticed during the drive to the warehouse, but as we pulled out onto the main road, Chris was using hand signals to indicate a turn.

"What's up with the blinkers?" I asked.

"Haven't worked for a few years now," he replied. "Don't worry, most people in Calgary don't even know that their cars are equipped with them."

After a few minutes of driving and observing, I realized that he was right. The traffic was bumper to bumper as we made our way through the city, and it was as we were stopped for a red light that an explosion, louder than anything I've ever heard, shocked us almost out of our seatbelts. People were getting out of their cars, looking around with puzzled faces, when Chris turned to me and said, "Dave, I think we just blew a tire."

When I got out of the truck, I didn't see it at first, but sure enough, it was one of the inside tires on the back. Not wanting to look stupid, I didn't ask him if we could make it back with just five tires, but as luck would have it, we were in the right hand lane at the stop light, right at the entrance to a gas station with a garage attached. If you're going to have a breakdown, there was no better place to have it than where we did, so Chris pulled in and after a few hours we were on the road again with a brand new tire that didn't quite fit in with the other five nearly bald ones.

The ride to Invermere was a slow one, with the old truck never exceeding fifty-five miles per hour due to the extremely heavy load that it was labouring with on its back. Chris would downshift a lot when going downhill, which I found to be a little strange and it wasn't until we were almost in Invermere that he confessed to me that the brakes were pretty much shot. At that point, after an eight-hour trip that normally should have taken only three hours, I didn't care anymore. We'd made it with our cargo intact, and that was all that was important. Later, when I looked back on the trip, I couldn't help but laugh at the whole adventure.

Back at his farm, we parked the truck in a big garage, leaving the crate on the back. There was no point in unloading it, because with a little luck in the apartment search, we'd be moving it again in a very short time. But for now, it was bedtime.

My first night in Invermere was spent sleeping on the floor of Chris's mobile home. He was in the process of building his dream home, and he also had another houseguest, so with the only bed and sofa spoken for, the carpet was to be my place of rest. The floor was still softer than some of the beds I'd slept on in China.

Luckily, there was an abundance of beat-up old cars at the farm, with a few of them even licensed for use on the road, so Chris handed me a set of keys the next day, because he knew that I wouldn't get far in my apartment and auto search without a mode of transportation.

Armed with the local newspaper, that only came out once a week, I set out on the five-minute drive into town, found the only coffee shop open on Sunday, and started going through the classified ads.

The pickings for accommodation were slim, with a few one- and two-bedroom apartments, but they all wanted references, which didn't seem like a monumental hurdle to overcome. I'd just have to talk to the people, and explain that we'd just moved here from overseas, and didn't have any references.

After circling five potentials, I went to the pay phone in the coffee shop and began dialing. The first four had already been rented and taken off the market, due to the fact that the newspaper was already five days old, but there was a glimmer of hope with the fifth one, which was also the most expensive. The lady agreed to meet with me later that afternoon, and didn't seem too concerned about the lack of references, or the fact that we had a cat and a dog. Perhaps the high rental price she was asking had deterred a lot of people, but I was still thinking in terms of Swiss prices, so it looked dirt cheap to me.

The next call I made was to my dear wife, who was eight hours ahead of me with the time change. She'd just finished her dinner and was getting ready to nestle in beside Butch, who was stretched out on his back in the middle of the couch, in the process of recharging his batteries from a big three-hour walk earlier in the afternoon. She sounded pretty relieved that I'd made it safe and sound, as well as our crate. I refrained from telling her about the adventure of the eight-hour drive with Chris, because that would have just made her wonder more about this path she'd chosen for her future. After letting her know about the apartment I was going to look at later on, her only words of advice were, "If it looks even half decent, take it. We need a roof over our heads and we can always look for something else afterwards." As usual, she was right; again.

The local paper didn't have many cars or trucks advertised, and the ones that they did have were either monster-sized pickup trucks that actually allowed you to watch the gas gauge move as you drove, or small sports cars, which would be absolutely useless during a typical Canadian winter. *"No problem,"* I thought to myself. *"Something will come along, and in the worst case scenario, I can always rent a car to go pick the family up at the airport."* Asking Chris to borrow the truck I was using at the present time was out of the question, for the simple reason that I didn't think it would make it there and back. Farm vehicles are great, but only for around the farm.

The prearranged time of three o'clock rolled around as I sat in the truck waiting for the landlord to arrive. The large house didn't look too bad from the outside, and from what I could tell, it looked like it consisted of three separate apartments. It had a large parking area in the rear, which backed onto a lumberyard, a large front yard with grass, and it was only a block away from the downtown strip. The only strange thing was that all of the windows were small and they seemed to be high up.

She finally showed up around fifteen minutes later, again driving home the differences between Canada and Switzerland.

"Sorry I'm late; running a bit behind today," she said.

After the introductions were over, she took me inside for the tour. There were two small bedrooms, a very small bathroom, a big kitchen, and a very large dining and living room area. The windows all seemed to start at chest height and when I asked her about this she told me that it had previously been an office complex. Not perfect, but it would be the roof we needed to start out.

Once again, I reminded her that we had a cat and a dog, which were two of the best-behaved animals in the whole wide world, and she said that wasn't a problem. Being a dog lover herself, she understood that it wasn't easy finding a place with animals, so as long as the apartment was as clean when we left it as it was now, it was ours for the taking. *Bonus!*

Right there on the spot I gave her the first month's rent as well as a damage deposit. Since it was sitting empty, she said I could move in whenever I wanted. After filling out the rental agreement she handed the keys over to me and left.

Standing there in the empty apartment, I couldn't help breaking into a big smile. The first part of my solo-scouting mission in Canada was complete. I'd found a place that Franzi and the little furry ones could come home to. It wasn't paradise, but it was a start.

Fast food hadn't yet caught on in Switzerland, though they were in the process of building a McDonald's in Interlaken, and when I left the apartment it was getting close to dinnertime and I just had a wicked urge for a big fat greasy cheeseburger – something I hadn't had in years. I knew that Chris wouldn't be back at the trailer for dinner because he'd said earlier that morning that it was every man for himself, so I hopped in the pickup truck and drove down the road to the Dairy Queen, ordering the biggest burger they had, as well as a side of fries. *Welcome back to North American nutrition.*

Sitting there, looking out the window with my burger, feeling pretty good about the world, with mustard and ketchup dripping down my chin and all over my hands, my mind drifted to the next problem: finding a car.

The classifieds hadn't turned up anything appealing and even the used car dealership in town had nothing that I viewed as practical, or for that matter, affordable. The car I wanted was something with front wheel drive, which was good for winter driving; standard transmission, because I knew Franzi wouldn't drive anything else; and it had to be a hatchback of sorts so we could load Butch in without a problem. If there weren't any hatchbacks, a four door would have to do.

My entire knowledge of cars was mediocre at best. I could change a tire, jump-start a battery, and fill up the fluids, but that was about it. If someone were to ask me how an engine operated, they could have just as easily asked me how to split an atom.

It was as I was hopping back into the pickup to leave the restaurant that I saw it. "It," being just what I was looking for, kind of. Parked way over in the corner of the lot, standing there with all its majestic rust spots, was an extremely ugly orange Volkswagen Rabbit with a "For Sale" sign in the back window; no price, just a phone number. After giving it the "walk-around" I could see that it still had good rubber on the tires, had standard transmission (which was good), but it also had end-stage skin cancer. The bright orange body was covered in rust spots that resembled a teenager's face (if they indulged in every single meal at the place I'd just eaten). Still, despite the fact that it was an eyesore and had seen better days, I felt an attachment to it. *"Why not?"* I asked myself. It wasn't like we were going to grow old with this car. It would serve its purpose until we could find something better, but right now I needed my own wheels. It didn't sit well with me having to borrow Chris's truck all the time.

The pay phone in the restaurant was out of order so I walked across the street to the gas station and gave the number a call; no answer.

Later that night when Chris came home, I shared with him the events of the day. He seemed surprised that I was able to find a place to live so quickly, because it was a tight housing market in town, and he told me he'd give me a hand the next day moving all of our stuff from the crate into the new place.

When I told him about the car, he knew right away which one I was talking about and even knew the owner. He said to me, "Dave, it's seen better years, but as you've probably noticed by now, my vehicles aren't prized possessions either. If it runs and the price is right, what do you have to lose?"

So, with those words of wisdom dancing through my head, I gave the number another call. This time the owner was home. Five hundred dollars was what he wanted for it – not a penny less – and I could take it out for a test drive the next day. And yes, it would be fine if Chris came along. Chris was the farm machinery mechanic on the cattle ranch, and could split automotive atoms.

As we pulled up to the Dairy Queen where it was still sitting, Chris turned to me and said that it was the same colour as a pumpkin and that if I bought it and it died right away thereafter, I could put some candles in its windows and use it in six weeks for Halloween. "Good idea," I thought.

The test drive was a strenuous one, with me babying the poor old thing and Chris driving it like he was in the Paris-Dakar rally. It actually came as a surprise to me that he didn't manage to get all four wheels airborne like in the *Blues Brother* film. Overall, he said it was mechanically sound, but with any sixteen-year-old car you had to expect things to break down left and right. So it was with that sound advice that I bought what would forever become known as the Pumpkin.

Without consulting Franzi on this purchase, I soon after began to have feelings of dread. I already had visions of her shaking her head and saying "what the heck were you thinking?" After getting rid of our nearly new Fiat just two months earlier, this would definitely be seen as a step backwards.

After Chris's help with the automotive transaction and insurance, which turned out to be more than the price of the car, we set about moving our crate to the new domicile. It was only a matter of taking the crate apart, moving all the boxes inside, and locking the place back up. My sleeping bag was still at the trailer so I spent one last night at the ranch, determined to unpack everything the next day and spend the night in the new place.

The next morning, after thanking Chris for all the help he'd given me over the last few days, I jumped into the Pumpkin ready to tackle the task at hand: turning a bunch of cardboard boxes in a bare apartment into a warm and cosy home.

After the third straight night of sleeping on the floor, the first stop was going to be at the furniture store. We didn't bring our bed over with us, nor our sofa, so I wanted to get something to sleep on that didn't feel like plywood.

Buying a bed is a very personal choice and it's something that has to feel comfortable to those who will be sleeping on it, so for this reason, I decided against looking into beds. That was something Franzi and I had to do together, and there was no way I was just going to buy one blindly because I already had the feeling that I might have shot myself in the foot with the Pumpkin purchase.

A sofa bed was what I ended up with. They said they would deliver it later that afternoon, so I was looking forward to a soft night.

In the early afternoon I phoned Franzi who was on her way to bed after a fight with Butch during his nightcap walk. She let him off the leash to go and do his thing in the bush and he decided to take off for half an hour and go exploring. When he eventually came back to her, he knew that he was in trouble. However, he also knew that Franzi could never stay upset with him for very long, so he went through the motions of looking like he was really sorry, in the hope that Franzi would forgive his behavioural brain fart before bed so that he could still score a bedtime treat. Labs are so clever.

She listened intently as I described the apartment, the location, the new sofa and the Volkswagen. I didn't get too descriptive about the car, figuring I'd just surprise her with it when I picked her up in Calgary, because she'd have so much on her mind then that the state of the Pumpkin might not fully register. That would be a good thing.

I was missing her and the little campers immensely. She was missing me too, she said, and was very happy that I'd taken care of everything on my side of the pond so that when she got here, she could just settle right in.

When she asked me what I was going to do with myself for the next eight days until she arrived, my answer was simply, "Look for a job."

Six hours later, with pretty much everything unpacked, the sofa delivered, and the apartment looking like someone actually lived there, my belly was rumbling with hunger pangs like a grizzly waking up from hibernation. With not a single morsel of food in the refrigerator, it was definitely time to go grocery shopping.

Starting off new like this meant that we had absolutely nothing in the kitchen. There was no salt, no paper towels, no tin foil, no dish soap, nothing! A list seemed like the logical thing to make, but due to time constraints, meaning the grocery store wasn't open that much longer, I just decided to wing it.

I hopped in the Pumpkin, mentally preparing myself for the shopping frenzy that was going to fill this little rust bucket, and turned the key. It fired right up on the first try, which gave me a good feeling about the purchase. But then again, why wouldn't it fire right up? Everything else had gone super smoothly that day. I'd bought a car, moved into an apartment, was getting ready to welcome my wife in a week's time, and our whole lives were taking a brand new direction on a different horizon. And the real added bonus was that I wasn't sleeping on the floor that night.

It really was a shopping frenzy. A list would have been useless because it would have taken about three days to write the fifteen pages of things that a kitchen requires. The best approach, or at least the one that I took, was to walk up and down the aisles slowly, picking out anything that we had had in our kitchen back in Switzerland. If we didn't have it back there, then we didn't need it here, either.

A good feeling of exhaustion was creeping up on me as I drove home from the grocery store in the fading daylight with what seemed like seventy grocery bags in the back. Seeing a couple of deer grazing in someone's flower bed reminded me that I had to be extra alert for the wildlife that inhabited the area, and that Butch would have to be walked on his leash until we discovered a good and safe area for him to roam freely.

When I got back to the apartment, I turned the key off in the Pumpkin, the exact same way that I'd done it the previous four times since taking owner-ship, and lo and behold, the whole ignition cylinder decided it would come out of the steering column with the key, drop onto the floor, and then get lost under the seat. The gizmo I'd once put the key into was now replaced by an empty hole. I couldn't help but laugh.

Buying a flashlight was one of the things I hadn't done at the grocery store, so there was no sense looking for the cylinder under the seat that night. The groceries and my dinner took priority and the rest I could worry about the next day. The groceries took an eternity to put away and my day ended with a peanut butter sandwich before dozing off on the sofa.

The next morning, under the seat, I found the cylinder. In what seemed like a previous lifetime, that toy known as a Rubik's Cube fascinated me, and this little cylinder that wouldn't let me put the key back into it presented a similar challenge. An hour of screwing around with it and playing with the teeth got me nowhere, and by a stroke of luck (or at least I thought), Chris came by to see how the moving-in process was going.

"Dave, it's right messed up. You're going to have to take it to a locksmith which will probably run you about one hundred dollars. Or, there's another way to start your car which you won't find in any owner's manual."

The decision seemed pretty straightforward, and soon thereafter I was back behind the wheel, cruising around town, with a screwdriver sticking out of the steering column. It was actually easier than using a key. Franzi was going to just love this.

The job search started in earnest that same afternoon. Invermere, a town of about three thousand people, is basically a tourist-oriented town, which comes as no surprise since it's situated on a lake, surrounded by beautiful mountains, and is only a twenty-minute drive from Panorama – a world-class ski hill. The jobs that were to be had were mainly in the service industry, with the exception of logging, trucking, or working at the lumber mill, none of which I was too interested in.

What I saw myself going for was something with a little familiarity, which translated into either the food and beverage industry or the hotel business. Ultimately, the ski hill was were I wanted to work, but since it was only mid-September, any jobs up there were still a few months away, so that meant finding something to bridge the two-month gap.

There was a small employment office, where I first went to get the pulse of the situation in town, but food and beverage jobs, as well as hotel industry jobs, were very scarce at the moment due to the fact that the summer season was winding down. The lady at the office did happen to know one place where they desperately needed someone, and within the hour I'd become a hardware store sales clerk – and a very poorly paid one at that.

In no way could I imagine it being a dream job, and my biggest worry was that I'd have to start thinking in imperial measures again after living in a country for over ten years that only dealt in the metric system, but I figured I'd just bite the bullet, knowing in the back of my mind that it was only a temporary gig.

The scouting mission was now complete. I'd found a car, an apartment, and a job. It felt good, and all I had to do now was wait another week for my life to be whole again.

Chapter 8
A Year in Canada

*T*his was the day there would be no selling of 19/32 sockets, 3 1/4 inch spiral nails, or R20 pink insulation. This was the day I would not be at the job that I absolutely hated. This was Thursday, September 25th, 1997; the day that Franzi, Butch, and Maenam crossed the Atlantic to start their new lives.

It was also the day that I prayed to God that the Pumpkin would actually be able to make the three-hour trip to Calgary and then back again without a problem. The previous evening, while on the way home from work, the clamp holding the muffler and tailpipe to the chassis had broken off, leaving a trail of sparks behind as I drove down the main drag in town. So before heading off to Calgary I had to do some coat hanger repairs.

The drive to Calgary passed without a problem, much to my delight, and at no point was the Pumpkin ever in danger of being pulled over for speeding.

Franzi had seemed quite nervous and emotional when I'd talked to her the day before, which was understandable. She'd just finished a final dinner with her parents and her two brothers, and all of the good-byes had been said. All that was left for her to do was to get the animals and their kennels to Zurich, give them their sleeping pills, get the whole gang on the plane, then sit back and relax – if that was possible.

It goes without saying that her flight had been delayed for an hour. It could very well have been that my flight was the only one that actually left on time that year. Luckily, I knew that she was on board because I phoned her friend who'd taken her to the airport and he confirmed that she'd gotten on the flight, but this was a delay I didn't want. Butch and Maenam had to be in their travel boxes for twelve hours, which I knew was an incredibly long time, so the sooner they got on the ground, the better.

Finally, the plane touched down. They were at least somewhere on the other side of the wall I found myself staring at, and the wait seemed endless. Everyone and their brother seemed to be coming out of the doors from the Customs Station, but still no Franzi. *Why was it taking so long? Did something happen to one of the campers? Was there a problem with her immigration papers? Why wasn't she out here with me?* Panic was starting to set in as I stared up at the clock and saw that the plane had already been on the ground for over an hour.

But then the double doors slid open, exposing a luggage trolley carrying a big beige animal crate with a smaller one sitting on top, being pushed by the very tired- and haggard-looking love of my life.

With tears in our eyes, we embraced for what seemed like an eternity. Oh, it was so good to have her in my arms again.

The sound of a very deep "woof" shook us out of our reverie. "Hey, I'm here too!" was probably what Butch was saying in his doggie lingo, so I bent down, opened the door on his box just enough so that he couldn't come bounding out, and received the biggest, wettest lick on my face, one that not even Franzi could top. Maenam was still sleeping, just like cats seem to do ninety percent of the time. Life was whole again.

"Dave, it was an absolute nightmare," she said during the five-minute walk back to the car. "I gave them both the sleeping pills when we left Muerren, and they zonked Maenam out almost immediately, but Butch was still wide-awake when we got to the airport two hours later. I gave him another two sleeping pills, then took him out for a pee and stayed with him as long as I could before I had to check him in. At that point he'd at least lie down and seemed to be looking a bit drowsy. When the customs people came to take him away, he managed to sit up and gave me a very puzzled look. It broke my heart to watch him being wheeled away like that.

"When we were taxiing out to the runway," she continued, "I could actually hear him barking down below. You know Butch's bark. The poor little guy had to be just terrified. After we'd taken off I didn't hear him anymore thank God, which was such a relief. I guess the tablets either settled him down or there was just too much noise from the engines and the forced air conditioning in the plane. Maenam, on the other hand, was an absolute star. She spent the whole time in her little cage down by my feet, and only had one little pee. I changed the towel she was lying on and then she just went right back to sleep. The people at the immigration desk said that all of my papers were in order, gave me a few rubber stamps, and then wished me all the best for my new life in Canada. They were really nice.

"I didn't care about my luggage or even whether it had arrived or not, I just wanted to find Butch. He was nowhere to be found and I was starting to freak out. 'Where do the animals come out?' I asked an official looking guy, and then he took me around the corner to another room where Butch's box was sitting on a conveyor belt that wasn't moving and all I could see was this motionless dog inside. Dave, I thought he was dead! I ran over to him and wanted to open the box but a customs guy stopped me. It was the government veterinarian I guess, because he told me that he had to check over both animals and all their paperwork before I could take them through customs and out the door. I just wanted to make sure Butch was okay, so I called his name and set Maenam's cage right in front of him so he knew that everything was okay too. He sat up then and whined, and then I knew he was alright.

"The paperwork was all in order and the vet just gave them a quick check-over, and then he said I was good to go. I grabbed my backpack, cleared customs, and here I am."

She'd been through one heck of a day, and just before we were at the car, I turned to her and again told her how much I loved her.

To my absolute amazement, the sight of the Pumpkin didn't seem to faze her. Her only comment was, "Will it get us home? I'd really like to get home tonight." I believed her.

With Butch and his box safely secured in the back where I'd taken the rear seat out and Maenam on Franzi's lap, I reached into the glove compartment, grabbed the screwdriver, and started up the car.

After her long day of fear, nervousness, and anxiety, I was more than a little apprehensive about how she'd react to this sight, but it was almost like the she'd let her emotions go; that nothing really mattered anymore. She and the animals had made it safely and they were all starting fresh in a new land. All she could do was laugh, long and hard.

"You've got to be kidding me! If only my parents could see me now."

We made a quick stop at Jurg's house, where, on leashes, we let Maenam and Butch out to do their business. Butch seemed to be over the whole ordeal and set about to smelling everything he could and marking every tree in Jurg's backyard, but Maenam wasn't quite recovered yet. When we opened the door to her cage she took about two steps and then fell over like she was drunk. But after a few minutes and a few more falls, she got her legs back, and then headed right over to schmooze with her big brother.

Half an hour later, leaving the outskirts of Calgary and heading west towards the Rockies, Franzi was out like a light. It was two hours later, when I had to come to a quick stop in the national park for a herd of elk crossing the highway, that she opened her eyes again, saw the herd about fifteen feet in front of us, and just said, "Wow."

Butch decided there was no better time to introduce himself to the new world of Canadian wildlife than the present, so he broke into a series of barks, perhaps just saying hello to these strange creatures that he'd never encountered before, which sent the dozen or so elk scattering for safety into the forest.

It was dark when we arrived back in Invermere, so Franzi didn't get to see any of the town which we had said we could both handle living in, some four years previously. The only interest that she had was to connect her head to the pillow on the sofa. She didn't even comment on the place except about the walls, which were all the same colour – a boring, light shade of pink. Within five minutes of entering the apartment, she had her teeth cleaned and was sound asleep. It was only 9:00 at night but for her, with the time change, it was 5:00 A.M. the next day.

Maenam found her new litter box right away, as well as the cat food, which she devoured, and then showed me, by scratching at the window that she'd jumped up to, that she wanted to go outside. There was no way I was letting her out of the place in the dark on her first night. It wasn't the same as in Switzerland. There were different smells and different predators, but she wasn't aware of that yet. It was house arrest for Maenam, at least for the night.

Butch, on the other hand, had to go out, so I grabbed his leash and took him for a tour of his new neighbourhood. This was the first time I'd been able to take the little guy for a walk in almost three weeks, and even though we had only the light given off from the streetlights to guide us, it felt wonderful. There wasn't a post he didn't stop at to mark, and he pulled me all over the place while he tried to check out each new smell. His tail was going like crazy and I was just letting him lead. He deserved that after being drugged and cooped up in the underbelly of an airplane all day.

The lake was only a few blocks from our new place, and Butch somehow seemed to know that already. His wanderings, although appearing very haphazard, led us directly to the beach, which had a big sign that read "No Dogs Allowed."

I had to agree with the sign that dogs should not be allowed on the beach where people swim and sunbathe, but this was the end of September. The swimming season was finished and soon people would be ice-skating and playing hockey here, so I decided that the rule didn't apply on this evening.

The minute I let him off his leash he bounded for the water, running as far as he could and then, when the ground under his feet was no longer there, swimming. He swam out, and then back and forth, amusing himself for a good ten minutes, before deciding that I, too, should get in on the action. With a few loud barks, Butch told me that it was time to play stick, or rock, or any other projectile I could get my hands on. And we played, with Butch bounding into the water, bringing back whatever I'd found to amuse him. It was so good to be with him again, and he was showing no signs of a hard day of travel.

The following morning I had to return to the job that I disliked, a lot, and was surprised to see that the other side of the sofa bed was empty when I awoke. Franzi and Butch were gone, for a walk I had to assume, and when she returned fifteen minutes later, with fresh croissants and a waterlogged dog, I knew that she too had found the lake, or rather, Butch had found it for her.

Jet lag can really screw up your internal clock and Franzi was no exception. She'd been up for three hours already, just waiting for daylight to arrive, and in that time she'd checked out the whole apartment and found where I'd put everything away. When I asked her what she thought of the place, all she could say was, "I don't want to get old here." That said it all. Having to stand up to look out the windows was the big turn-off.

When my workday finished we went and bought a new bed together, and then started down the road to officialdom. She had to change her driving license as well as register for health insurance. With these tasks out of the way, we settled in for the night and had our first dinner together in a long time, before going for an evening stroll with Butch.

It was during that evening stroll, after passing so many homes with "For Sale" signs on them, that Franzi presented the idea that we, too, should look into buying a house. *"Not bad"* I thought. She was only in the country for a day, and already she's talking about a house purchase. We'd always rented in Switzerland because the housing prices were about four times what they were in Canada, but buying a house was always part of our master plan, and one of the main reasons we decided to move after saving like crazy for the previous four years. I just wasn't expecting it on Day One.

So the house hunt started in earnest. After work, armed with real estate guides, we'd drive around the different neighbourhoods, visually dissecting the houses on the market. *Were they too big or too small? Did they have a good-sized yard? Would the neighbours be right on top of us?* These were all factors to be considered. Ultimately, what we really wanted was a house on a small acreage. There were a few on the market but they were all too far away from town, which was a red light for us, because we wanted to be close to the hospital for when the next colic attack overtook Franzi.

The days turned into weeks and we'd all adjusted pretty well. Butch was getting his three walks a day and I'd made a little cat entrance so Maenam could come and go as she pleased. Franzi would drop me off at work in the morning and pick me up afterwards, using the Pumpkin to take Butch exploring outside of town. She was even getting comfortable with the novelty of using a screwdriver instead of a key to start the little rust bucket. But, unfortunately, our house hunting wasn't turning up anything we felt was worthwhile.

After about a month in Invermere, Franzi came to pick me up one afternoon, and she didn't seem herself.

"Dave," she said hesitantly, "you're probably going to think I'm crazy, but is it possible that there are bears that actually come into town?"

It was an ironic question, really, because earlier that day, I'd heard about a black one that was hanging around by the school a few blocks away, but the people talking in the hardware store acted like it was the most normal thing in the world. Not wanting to look like an idiot, I played along like I saw a bear in town everyday.

"Why? Did you see one?" I asked.

"Yeah, I did, actually, right outside of our kitchen window. At first I thought it was a big dog because it was facing away from me, but I've watched enough nature shows to know a bear when I see one. And Maenam was even outside."

"You're not crazy." I told her about what I'd heard at work, and that the reason they're coming into town now was because all the fruit was falling off the trees in people's gardens and they're just getting a few final good meals in their bellies before they go into hibernation. I thought it best not to tell her that once in a while cougars also come into town.

"I sure as heck won't be walking with Butch in the woods anymore until I know that they're sleeping for the winter!" she blurted.

That same day, we picked up a copy of the weekly local newspaper, just to see what was going on in the valley, and while glancing through the classifieds, I noticed that there was a house for private sale (meaning no realtors and their big commissions), and it was only a block away from the lake. It had three bedrooms, was situated on a large double lot, and the price looked reasonable compared to some of the other places we'd looked at, so we figured, why not? Looking doesn't cost us anything. If it turned out to be a dump, then we'd only lost an hour or so of our time.

A dump it wasn't, but it did fall into the category of a "Fixer-Upper." The interior took me back to our panelled TV room in the mid-70's. Lime green shag carpeting covered the L-shaped bench where the dining table was, but at least it matched the linoleum. The chandelier was an old wagon wheel with six old-style fuel lanterns adorning it. Yes, it needed some work, but it was structurally very well built, had a lot of big windows, and a good-sized yard. "Butch would like the house," we said to each other on the way home, "because it's only one block from the water."

Like many of our decisions, this one involved a bottle of wine. It seemed pointless to pay rent every month, putting the money into someone else's pocket, when it could be going towards our own equity, and this was one of the reasons we came to Canada, so why put off the inevitable? Therefore, that night, we decided to become homeowners.

In mid-November we took possession of the house and moved in – less than two months from the time Franzi had arrived. She had a way of making things happen, whereas I was a bit of a procrastinator when it came to such monster decisions as buying a house.

Not having a whole bunch of household items to move, it only took us a couple of hours. We loaded up the back of the Chris's pickup, because he was our moving helper, with Butch in the middle of the front seat, and after four trips the move was complete. We were in our new, middle-aged house: something that we actually owned ourselves. What an amazing feeling that was after so many years of renting!

Mid-November was also a time of change on the professional front. After two whole months of selling nuts and bolts, my career as a hardware store sales clerk came to an end. I already had another job lined up at the ski hill as the food and beverage manager in their fine dining restaurant, which was a bit more up my alley than selling hammers and lumber. It was an afternoon and evening job, which was something that I wanted to get away from when we were still back in Switzerland, but Franzi and I could have our mornings and lunch together, and we could still take Butch for a good morning walk. We both agreed that it was an opportunity that I shouldn't pass up. Franzi wasn't that keen on jumping into the work force, but rather wanted to wait and see how we could make out on one income, so she was able to spend the whole day with the animals.

She really did enjoy that first month in the house, not having to go to a job, being able to set up the household how she liked it, and taking Butch for walks, though I think it started to wear a little thin on her. She wasn't getting the interaction with other people that you get when you go to work. Maybe it was boredom setting in, or just a feeling of isolation, but soon after Christmas, Franzi was itching to join the labour force again.

Due to the fact that she was fluent in five languages, finding a job in a tourist-orientated area such as Invermere wasn't much of a problem. Within a couple of days of making her decision, she was employed at the local Heli-skiing company as the front desk representative, as well as a sales person in the gift shop. The large majority of the clientele were Europeans, so it was the perfect fit for her since she was the only person who could speak anything other than English.

We both worked our schedules around Butch, making sure that he always had his two or three walks, and that he was never left alone at home for more than just a couple of hours. He used those few hours of solitude to catch up on his sleep, which was quite evident by the sleepy look he had on his face and the yawning ceremony that took place whenever one of us came home.

Franzi seemed to really enjoy her new job. She was meeting a lot of new people, making some friends and learning about working life in Canada. The added bonus of her job was that she could go heli-skiing for free, whenever there was an opening on one of the choppers.

What she didn't enjoy, however, was the three-week period in January when our temperatures seldom rose above −40 degrees Fahrenheit. The walks with Butch were very short during this spell, with the two of us bundled up like the Michelin Man, with full-face masks as well as goggles against the cold. It was even a bit chilly for Butch, as we had to put Vaseline on the pads of his paws to keep them from splitting open. Twenty minutes in these temperatures was the limit, and then a couple of hours were spent in front of the fireplace, de-thawing.

The heli-ski gig was only a seasonal job, as was my own, so when spring rolled around, Franzi again had the chance to enjoy her seasonal retirement with Butch, and I went about the semi-annual migration that most people in the valley did. That meant I went to work at a golf course, doing the exact same job, just for a different employer. With a population of 3000 people and over 15 golf courses within a half-hour drive, the golf industry is easily the largest employer over the spring, summer, and autumn months.

The purchase of a second vehicle in the spring meant that Franzi could take off with Butch for the whole day. She'd go hiking, swimming, and exploring the different back roads and wooded areas while I was at work, as well as look after the household. Butch would meet other dogs on a daily basis, and with the great big heart that he had, there was never any friction. Every encounter turned into the ultimate play round.

There are many different kinds of animals to be found in the Rocky Mountains, ones which are native to North America, and although Butch didn't bother with the elk or moose, there was a much smaller one that he just had to introduce himself to: the dreaded skunk.

One warm afternoon, when I was able to leave work early, I arrived home to an empty house. Maenam was outside doing her mouse-hunting thing, and Franzi and Butch, I assumed, were out walking. As I was standing in the kitchen making a sandwich, I suddenly caught a small whiff of skunk scent. When I looked out the kitchen window, the Pumpkin was just pulling into the driveway, with all four windows rolled down, and Butch's head hanging out the front passenger side window with a really happy look on his face.

It didn't take Sherlock Holmes to figure out what had transpired, because that rancid smell that I'd first noticed when the Pumpkin was still down the street was now just ten feet away from me. You're always aware that something like this can happen because skunks are just a fact of life, but you can never be really prepared for when it does. Franzi was shaking her head as she got out of the car, and her eyes were very red and watery from the overpowering stench.

"Butch," she hollered. "You get out of the car right now!" He complied immediately, and then started to search for the nearest play toy he could find out in the yard. "Forget it, this isn't playtime!"she yelled. Butch didn't seem the least bit bothered by his new cologne, but his mom looked more than a bit distressed.

Men are not always the most perceptive creatures when it comes to the needs of their wives, but my survival instinct told me that if I didn't want to be locked in the garden shed with Butch for the next seventy-two hours, I'd better get out there and give her a hand instead of just standing in the kitchen and chuckling. If she saw that, I'd be dead meat.

Out I went, almost gagging at the smell coming from the Pumpkin, Butch, and even Franzi. She stunk terribly.

"Dave, we've had an adventure, as you've probably figured out by now. How do I get rid of this bloody smell?"

Good question. Apparently, tomato juice is supposed to work well if you bathe in it, but who in their right mind is going to go out and buy fifty cans of tomato juice, pour it in a bathtub and then bathe in it?

"I'll phone the vet and see what I can find out," I said.

After a quick call to the vet I learned that there is a special shampoo called "Skunk Off," which neutralizes the majority of the odour, but not all of it. Still, anything was better than the way the two of them smelt out in the driveway, so I hopped in the other car and went to pick up vast quantities of the stuff.

New air fresheners were all we could do for the stinky Pumpkin, and Butch had a very long garden hose shower out in the yard. Franzi also used the animal skunk shampoo and it worked pretty well. When Butch was dried off we let him in the house, despite the lingering odour, where he went right to his bed and fell asleep as if he didn't have a care in the world.

There were no ground-breaking decisions to be made here, but a bottle of wine still seemed like a good idea, so as we were sitting out on our deck, I asked her, "Now how did *this* happen?"

"Dave, it's probably going to sound unbelievable, but when it comes to Butch, the word unbelievable ceases to exist, as you well know. We were up at Chris's cattle ranch, just walking through the bush on a small path when I saw this black movement out of the corner of my eye. At first I thought it was just a crow because they're often on the ground and they're enormous, so I didn't really pay any attention to it until Butch darted after it like it was the last piece of meat on earth.

"It was some ways away so I chased after him, and when it didn't fly away, I thought it might be a cat. When I caught up I saw him down in a ravine and then I knew that we weren't dealing with any cat here. The animal was cornered and when the little thing turned around, I saw the big white stripe on his back and my heart just sank. Butch on the other hand, who was about four feet away from it, had his tail just wagging like crazy. He wanted to play with it. Can you believe that? I called him and called him but I wasn't nearly as interesting as his new friend, and that's when it happened. The skunk sprayed him dead on. I don't think it's what Butch expected because he backed up a few feet shaking his head and licking his lips like he had some extremely rotten taste in his mouth.

"At this point I could smell it pretty strongly, but Sir Butch had it in his head that he still wanted to get this little friend of his to play, so back he went with the tail still wagging. There was no way I was going anywhere near that thing, and just then Butch got sprayed for a second time. It didn't seem to bother him that much this time because he went right up to it and tried to give the skunk a whack with his paw; bad move. Spray number three happened, and then number four. He just didn't get it, or he liked the smell or something. I don't know.

"After the fourth time I think the skunk was really getting angry with him. I was still yelling at Butch like crazy but he just wasn't hearing me at all. I actually felt sorry for the little thing, because here was this big dog standing in front of him, looking down and batting him with his paw. He was using the only defences he knew and it wasn't enough. Then, when I guess he couldn't spray anymore, he turned around to face Butch, stood up on his back legs a bit, and made what sounded like a hissing noise.

"I've got no idea what that little thing said to him, but Butch came running back in my direction like he'd seen a ghost. Oh, Dave, he stunk so badly. He had this yellow stuff dripping off his head and chest, but his tail was still going. I used my sweater to wipe him off the best I could and just left it there. When we drove back into town I had all the windows down and was trying my best not to throw up from the smell. People stopped in their tracks when I drove by, thinking there was a skunk right beside them, but I just waved and yelled, 'It's only me. No worries!'

The interior of the Pumpkin never did lose that smell.

Chapter 9

And Sammy Makes Five

*I*t was only a matter of time before curiosity got the better of Franzi's family in Switzerland. Naturally, the phone was ringing all the time and I swear she talked to her parents twice as much as when she was living just an hour away. Telephone calls are great but verbal descriptions can never do justice when it comes to explaining where we were living, or the surrounding environment, or what kind of new lives we had begun to scratch out for ourselves. These things had to be seen firsthand. Franzi is, after all, the youngest child of three, and the only daughter. The concern for her well-being was very understandable.

Rudi and Suzi had previously been to Canada in the early seventies with a group of friends who all rented campers and toured around on the west coast. Back in Switzerland they had a butcher shop and worked very hard all their lives, so when holidays did present themselves, they were never very long ones. Their previous camping trip was only two weeks long, and for such a vast country as Canada, that's like visiting the Smithsonian Institute but only having fifteen minutes to spend inside.

Now they were retired, with Franzi's oldest brother, Rudi Jr., running the family business, but they could still only manage a three-week visit with us. The reason was they had to get back to Europe for a Mediterranean cruise that they had booked. Tough life, but they definitely deserved it.

We were looking forward to seeing them again, but I was a bit disappointed that I wouldn't have more free time. My job was still going strong in mid-September with yet another full month before the golf course closed, and there was absolutely no way of getting any extra time off, so that made Franzi the official tour guide for their visit.

I picked them up from the airport in Calgary, choosing to take the four-wheel drive instead of the Pumpkin, and was quite amazed to see that they'd aged in just a year's time. When you see someone everyday or every once in a while you don't notice the changes, but after longer periods of time, the changes become pronounced.

Franzi's parents, or the "in-laws," are great people. In a country that has very few foreigners compared to North America, the norm is that Swiss marry Swiss. When I came on the scene wanting to take their only daughter as my wife, I would have understood if they had had some misgivings, but they welcomed me with open arms, even in the beginning when I could barely speak Swiss German.

That was definitely one of the driving factors for my wanting to learn the language. I wanted to be able to speak to them and let them know in my own words how I felt about their daughter, and to tell them what I was all about. Even when I went to ask Rudi for his permission to marry his daughter, I wanted it to be all in Swiss German, and I spent hours memorizing the few sentences that I would say to him.

"Rudi, with your blessings, I would be honoured to take your daughter's hand in marriage. I will love, honour, and cherish her forever." When I got him alone in his apartment, my knees were trembling with nervousness, and all that I'd managed to memorize was gone. "Can I, your daughter, my wife?" is what actually tumbled forth out of my mouth.

He grinned the broadest grin, and said, "Are you sure you know what you're getting yourself into with this one?" Then he shook my hand and wished us good luck. That's what I loved about her parents. In such a structured society as Switzerland, where most people believed that you're only as good as your educational degree or the job that you hold, they just accepted me for who I was.

They really liked where we lived and Suzi fell in love with Butch all over again. He would stick on her wherever she went in the house because he knew she was a softy for treats and table scraps. Butch could always tell who the dog people were, and he knew how to work them for all it was worth.

Franzi, armed with a map of British Columbia, set forth with her parents on what was to be a two-week tour, visiting many of the same sights that we'd seen back in 1993, leaving me to look after Butch and Maenam. It was quite the daily battle walking him in the morning, going to work, and then skipping out of work for a few hours to walk him again, before going back to the golf course. Butch was alone a large portion of those days, but he seemed to understand that I was doing the best I could. Franzi's side of the bed wasn't even empty at night, with Butch thinking that he'd better keep it warm for her in case she just happened to come home.

During the time they were gone, on one of my days off, the inevitable happened. The trusty Pumpkin took its last breath. The mechanic read me off the long list of illnesses that its motor had suffered, most of which sounded Greek to me, but all that really mattered was that it was dead, and I was without wheels.

Chris came down to the garage and towed the Pumpkin back up to his ranch, parking it in an open field with the full intention of one day getting it up and running, but in my heart, I knew that it would never see the road again. It had a great view of the Rocky Mountains and the valley and as far as cars go, the Pumpkin had one of the best final resting places imaginable. And it still smelled from the skunk.

Having the next day off work was a blessing because it gave me the chance to mourn, as well as find another vehicle. Things were looking up because this time we ended up with a Toyota 4Runner that was only thirteen years old with an odometer that read only 200,000 miles. *What a deal!*

Franzi and the in-laws arrived home a few days early, due to her father catching a stomach bug. They didn't get to see everything that they wanted to, but I could tell that Franzi was happy to be home with us again. Being the tour guide, chauffeur, and translator can get a little tiring after a few days. She didn't even seem bothered that the Pumpkin was no longer with us.

Butch was also ecstatic to have her back. As soon as the car came up the road, he could tell by the sound that it was ours and his mom was back. He went absolutely bonkers when he first saw Franzi again, jumping in the vehicle and showering her with licks. He'd missed her and the long daily walks the two of them undertook together. When she was gone, the walks were more rushed and a lot shorter because I'd be either going to work, or just home on a short break.

We had a good couple of days together and when I had another day off we decided to make a really nice dinner, which we could all sit down and enjoy as a family. My work at the golf course prevented me from being home for the evening meal, so it was going to be a real treat.

Franzi sent me with a long list to do the grocery shopping, which I didn't mind doing, while she and her parents chilled out at home. Most guys hated doing the grocery shopping, but I actually enjoyed it. It meant that I always got what I wanted. Chips and cookies always found their way into the cart when I was driving it.

When I was sure that I had everything on the list, plus a few extras, I made the usual pilgrimage over to the notice board, where you could always find what people were trying to sell, or what was happening in the valley. This notice board was responsible for me finding the Toyota that I'd bought just a few days before.

As I was glancing at all the ads, a picture caught my eye – a picture of puppies, Lab puppies. They were ready to go, six males and three females, in all different colours: yellow, brown, and black. And they were only $250, which seemed like a bargain considering Butch cost us eight times more than that. It also said that they were purebred but without papers. Being a real sucker for the cuteness of puppies, I tore off one of the strips at the bottom of the page with a telephone number on it and stuck it in my pocket.

We'd never talked about getting another dog (seeming to already have a full plate on the go with Butch), but you never know. It wasn't like we didn't have the room in the house, and we had a very large yard so that wouldn't be a problem, and if you have to feed one dog, what's one more? Although I didn't realize it at the time, I was already rationalizing another family member in my head, and working on the sales pitch that I'd be presenting to Franzi in five minutes' time.

When I got back to the house and had all the groceries unloaded, Franzi and her parents were already enjoying a glass of white wine, which I viewed as a positive, and as I poured one for myself and sat down at the table, I turned to Franzi and jokingly asked her, "Would you like your Christmas present now, or later?"

Franzi was a firm believer in the "now," because the "later" meant that it might never happen, and if you had that something now, it was yours and no one could take it away.

"What did you get me?" she asked excitedly.

"Nothing yet, but you could very well have it shortly," I teased.

"Come on, spill it."

"Okay, okay," I said reaching into my pocket and pulling out the stub of paper with the phone number on it, and handed it to her.

She looked at me quizzically and said, "Dave, if this little piece of paper is all you got me, then you're cheap. A little explanation about this phone number would be a big help in determining whether it's going to be a warm and happy evening, or a cold and frosty one."

"Just relax," I said to her. Rudi and Suzi seemed to be enjoying the whole exchange in German, waiting to see how it would all play out. "This little tab of paper has the phone number of a house here in town that has nine little Lab puppies that need a good home. How do you think Butch would feel about being a big brother?"

It was obvious that I'd caught her off guard because she was speechless – something that doesn't happen very often – and the wheels in her mind were racing. She kept trying to say something, and would stop herself, starting again with the next thought, and then stopping again. This was definitely not what she had expected at all. Still speechless, I decided that now was the time for the sales pitch.

"It's not like you're not the perfect mom to Butch, but don't you think that his life would be a lot more complete if he had a little play partner? Butch loves every dog, and when he's together with other dogs he's the happiest camper in the world. We could make him a happy camper 24 hours a day! Just think of the fantastic shape he'd be in from all that action all the time. He's only three years old, but having a little brother or sister would keep him young for a long time."

"It wouldn't hurt to go and have a look," she said, and that's when I knew that the deal was as good as done. Rudi and Suzi where just chuckling to themselves because they knew how their animal-lover daughter was going to react when she laid eyes on the little puppies.

After phoning to make sure that these people would be home, and that all of the puppies weren't already taken, we hopped in the car and drove the three blocks to their house. The house was abuzz with activity. Six cars were parked outside, and I thought to myself that they couldn't all be here for the dogs, but they were. It seems Labs were in high demand because the ad in the grocery store had just been posted earlier that day.

When we went down to the basement there were about ten people milling around the kennel they had set up, and I was wondering if we'd even be able to get close to check them out. Finally, a few people left without taking one, and it was our chance to get in there and see them for ourselves.

"Cute" doesn't begin to describe them. Three males and two females were all that were left and there were no more yellow ones, which I knew both of us would have preferred, but that wasn't a big deal. One little guy – a black one – came bounding over towards Franzi before tripping on his new feet and rolling, and then stood up against the cage, as if to say, "take me!"

Franzi picked him up and it took only a look into her eyes to see that the decision had already been made.

"Dave, this little sweetheart wants to come home with us. He picked us." And so he did.

On the way back to the house we had to stop and pick up some puppy food, a collar and a food bowl, and the whole time he was nestled inside of Franzi's jacket, which, she reasoned, would protect him from the cold. The only thing sticking out of her jacket was his little tiny head.

"You know Dave, we have to be careful now. We don't want Butch to be jealous so we have to treat them both equally. If we fawn over one, then we have to fawn over the other also. Butch was our first dog and there's no way I want him to feel like he's being neglected just because we've got a new one now."

I couldn't have agreed more. Butch was a very special dog and I, too, didn't want him to get the feeling that he was being traded in on a newer model. So with that thought in our minds, we took the little guy home to meet his new older brother and sister, if Maenam could be called a sister.

Upon entering the house, Suzi asked me right away if our family had grown and I just nodded. Franzi followed me in, with the puppy still inside her jacket, and went right over to the sofa, where Butch was relaxing and watching TV.

"Butch, I want you to meet your little brother," Franzi told him. "Be nice now," and then she set the little black one down on the sofa, right beside Butch.

Lifting his head slowly from the sleepy state that he was in, the nose came up and the sniffing of the air started. His eyes weren't really open yet, but they quickly followed the nose, and then they bulged, wide open...shocked!

Quickly trying to back away from the little black one, Butch looked like he would have been happier being anywhere but on the sofa, and that turned into his mission with his facial expression clearly showing what he was thinking.

"Get off the sofa, now! What is this thing that so resembles a guinea pig and why did they bring it to me? I've already had my dinner."

Once he'd made it to the floor, with the safety and security of a coffee table in between him and this little ball of fur, he gave the famous head tilt, a short but deep bark, and then went around the table to check this new creature out.

Butch walked right up to him, with his tail hanging straight down, and gave him a few cursory sniffs before backing away again. What happened next was not what we were expecting: Butch, who had a look of disdain on his face, sneezed a few times and then started foaming at the mouth.

In the three years since we'd had Butch, he'd never foamed at the mouth and we were shocked. The little black one wasn't looking all that happy either. He crawled up on Franzi's lap on the sofa and snuggled against her, somehow knowing that there was safety in her arms.

Butch seemed right choked at this point. He wasn't having any of this scenario, which he made very clear to us when he went downstairs and laid down behind the door in our laundry room, still foaming as if he'd just gotten into my shaving cream. He was panting like he'd run non-stop for a couple of miles, and his back legs were trembling. There was no way he could be sick because he had been absolutely fine just a short time before, and the only other explanation was that he was terrified – terrified of a tiny little puppy. If a tiny mouse could have the same effect on an elephant, I guess anything was possible.

When I made it back upstairs, Butch still hadn't settled down and Franzi was on the phone to the vet named Mark. He was the brother of Chris the cattle rancher, and had the only veterinarian practice in town.

After talking for what seemed like fifteen minutes or longer, explaining everything down to the last minuscule detail, she finally hung up with a look of relief on her face.

"Why's he foaming? What did he say?" I asked, but just then the little black one was busy relieving himself in one of my shoes on the boot tray so I had to wait on the explanation, snatching him up in my arms and running outside in case he decided to release a sequel right after the original. Over the last three years, I'd forgotten about the pee training part of puppyhood, and silently prayed that he figured it out a little faster than Butch had.

When I came back in, Franzi had made up a little bed for him, once again with a hot water bottle in it, just as she had done for Butch, and he went right to sleep within a minute.

"Come on now, Franzi, what did Mark say?"

"It's his smell that Butch doesn't like. Puppies sometimes have a certain smell from their litter which they can lose as young as six-weeks-old or up to 12 weeks. There aren't any hard and fast rules, but he said that he's seen it happen many times. With time it'll go away and everything will be fine. Don't worry about Butch, he said."

"Hopefully he'll come around," I thought to myself. Butch always had his own way of doing things and he was showing no sign that he didn't want to spend the rest of his life behind the door in the laundry room being a grumpy old foam face.

"Just let him be," Franzi said. "He'll be okay sooner or later, but for the time being, we have something else to think about. This little guy is in desperate need of a name. What are we going to call him?"

Two hours earlier I had just been walking down the aisles of the grocery store, squeezing avocadoes to check on their ripeness and now I had a shoe filled with pee and was being asked for dog name suggestions. There was no one to blame but myself, and even though Butch wasn't embracing the situation like we were, he would eventually. In my heart, I was truly happy to give him a little brother.

"Shadow," I said, after the name of the dog in Muerren whom Franzi walked every day after her surgery.

"No, we can't call him 'Shadow.' Our little guy's name has to be original. There's already a Shadow out there. What about 'Midnight'?"

"Definitely a negative," I responded.

So after sitting there for some time, looking at the new pup, Franzi said that his little black face looked a lot like the baby sea lions that we'd encountered during our trip to the Galapagos Islands; I had to agree. We'd be sitting on the sailboat watching these marvellous creatures swimming effortlessly through the water, and when one of them jumped into our dinghy, being towed behind the boat, and decided to stay there for an hour, Franzi got a little tired of calling him "the Sea Lion" and started calling him "Sammy the Seal." The name stuck after that and whenever we saw a sea lion, we'd just say to each other, "look, there's a Sammy."

Sammy it would be. Sundance had crossed through my mind, but that was a bit corny, even by my standards, and it would just end up being shortened to Sunny anyways, so why bother?

The day after Franzi's parents left to go back to Switzerland, I started building a fence around our yard. It would be perfect for the two of them to be able to be outside, playing with each other eventually, and not having to worry about them running away or taking off. Butch, for the most part, tended to stay in the yard without having to be tied up, but on occasion he would take himself for a walk around the neighbourhood.

The street we lived on was a dead end, but with the beach just a block away, he often tended to gravitate to that area. This little wandering involved crossing a set of railway tracks and a fairly well-travelled beach road. To see him or Sammy come to some terrible fate from a train or car would be something that we'd never be able to forgive ourselves for, knowing that we could've prevented it. So, after two days of sawing and hammering and digging, I'd created what was to be their own private playpen.

It was simply posts with four boards running across, and three-foot-high chicken wire all the way around so they couldn't slink through, and when the job was finished, I was sure it was impenetrable. Little did I know at the time that Sammy was in some way a direct descendant of the late Harry Houdini.

Another winter was on the way, and little Sammy grew quickly during his first month with us. It took Butch about ten days before he started to come around and warm up to the little black menace. Sammy would constantly go to him, just looking for this big guy to be his friend, and in the beginning, that just wasn't happening. Perhaps Butch still smelled the scent of his litter on him or maybe it was that Sammy was just too small for him, but eventually Sammy's persistence paid off. First it was tug of war with the toys, which Butch could have won in a nanosecond but didn't, and it worked its way up to sharing the same water bowl, and then finally, sleeping side by side, snuggled up to one another on the couch.

The big brother instinct really kicked in for Butch when other dogs would get too close to Sammy. Butch would be right beside him, making sure that no harm came his way, and if another dog did get too close or was playing a little too rough, a piece of that dog's fur usually ended up hanging out of Butch's mouth.

Chapter 10
Dreams Do Come True

*B*y the time the winter had come to an end, Sammy had grown past the puppy stage and now, in his seventh month, he was a full-blown adolescent, with the entire attitude that goes along with this phase. My electric razor, Franzi's prescription sunglasses, and even a hundred-dollar ballpoint pen that a friend had forgotten at our house all met their gnarly deaths in Sammy's mouth. We couldn't figure it out, but it seemed he only liked to destroy expensive things.

His favourite game was finding new ways to escape from our yard. What I thought was a very securely fenced-in yard turned out to be a porous, minimum-security institute for the little Houdini. The chicken wire, which was supposed to stop the dogs from going under the fence, was easy to dig up and tunnel under as Sammy so often demonstrated. The amazing thing was that when he managed a great escape, Butch wouldn't go with him. He would just sit by the place where Sammy had left and wait.

When we finally noticed that he was missing, all we had to do was put Butch on his leash and ask him, "Where's Sammy?" Sure enough, he'd lead us in the exact direction of where Sammy had taken off to. When we finally did catch up to him, the look of absolute guilt on Sammy's face was priceless. He knew what he was doing was wrong and he knew when he was busted. The moment we found him and yelled, "Sammy, get over here!" he'd come right to us and lie down, looking up with that sad face, as if throwing himself at the mercy of the court and begging the judge for leniency.

Leniency was usually what he received, too. It was too hard to get angry with him, unless of course the neighbours were looking. In those circumstances we really had to make it look like we were taking the escape artist situation seriously. Even if we knew it was all show, as did Sammy, it still looked good for the neighbours. Butch was probably sitting back and thinking to himself, "just you wait, little one. You're going to have to go to the obedience school to be set straight, just like I was. It's a blast."

Throughout the summer, we went away whenever I had time off. We'd pack up the tent and sleeping bags and head out into the woods. There were a lot of recreational camping sites on small lakes just an hour north of us, run by the British Columbia Forestry Services, and these sites were free for people to use. On some of the smaller lakes there was often only one camping site, so it was like having our own private lake. The sites normally only consisted of a fire pit and an outhouse, but the dogs didn't have to be tied up and were free to roam around and play.

It's not that we didn't like being at home, but the neighbourhood thing was getting a bit old. It felt somewhat like what we'd just left behind in Switzerland. If the dogs were outside and they started barking, sure enough, one of our neighbours would be on the phone within five minutes asking us if we, too, could hear the noise outside. Or if Maenam went next door to do her business in their garden, we would definitely hear about it. These people actually told us that we should train our cat to stay in the yard. This was a cat we were talking about here. You can't train cats, absolute insanity!

Camping was simply our way of relaxing for a few days, without a care, and without having to worry about being dirty or smelling like a campfire. The boys enjoyed it too, and Sammy was quite the professional cat burglar when it came to stealing food from the grill. It didn't matter if he burnt his mouth; as long as he got some people food, he was happy. Butch and Sammy would go exploring together, which was normally my time to try my hand at fishing, but Butch seemed to always know when I pulled the rod and reel out. He could be half a mile away chewing on a bone somewhere, but as soon as I made the first cast he'd come running, thinking that this was a game that he definitely should be involved in. I'd cast the line and he'd watch the lure land in the water; he figured it was his mission to go and retrieve that little object and bring it back to me. It was his version of playing fetch. If there ever were any fish around in those small lakes, I sure as heck didn't see them. As soon as the yellow colossal fur ball hit the water, they were gone.

What I found most unbelievable was that it didn't even matter what the water temperature was. If it was wet, Butch was in it. Lake Louise was only a two-hour drive from Invermere, and during the visit the previous fall with Franzi's parents, I took them there while Franzi was at home with the new puppy. Butch didn't seem at all bothered by the fact that ice had started to form on some parts of the lake, he just wanted to swim. And swim he did, for close to an hour.

There are probably two thousand households in Japan that all have a photograph of Butch swimming in Lake Louise. He was quite the sensation that day, even though he spent the same amount of time shivering afterwards as he did swimming.

The other extreme didn't seem to faze him either. If we went to the wild hot springs that are so plentiful in this part of the world, Butch would be the first one in, even with the water temperature at around 102 degrees Fahrenheit. He'd just lay in the hot water floating around with his head under the surface, and then about every fifteen seconds he'd come up for a breath. Afterwards, he'd sleep for about two days.

Sammy, on the other hand, was not a fan of the water at all. He'd go in, sure, but only up to his chest. Normally when I'd throw a stick, Butch would dive in and bring it back while Sammy stood there with just his feet in the water and then grab the stick from

Butch. Butch always gave it to him without a struggle, figuring that I'd just throw him another one. On the occasions that Sammy did manage to submerge himself, he often misjudged the depth, and had to jump out as fast as he went in, look around for a good patch of dirt, and finally roll in it like his life depended upon it. When he finished we'd be left looking at a four-legged mud pie with eyes. And the worst part was that you couldn't just send him back into the water to clean up, either. People never understood this when we'd tell them. Labs are supposed to just love water; it's in their breed. "Sammy must have been a little short-changed at birth" was the only explanation we could come up with.

The one aspect of life where Sammy was not short-changed was with his libido. If there was a female dog in heat within a two mile radius, he would smell it, and be gone like a bullet. No amount of hollering or calling would stop him. It's only instinct and I can't fault the little guy for wanting to spread his seeds, but we'd get really worried when after an hour or so he still hadn't returned. Butch never behaved this way when other dogs were in heat, and the only explanation we had for that was we just got lucky, and so did Butch. He got to keep his testicles, whereas Sammy was a little less fortunate.

These little weekend excursions were relaxing and what we enjoyed most was the privacy. There was never anyone else around and it felt like we were the only people on earth. This was how we wanted to live; privately and out-of-town, without a neighbour in sight. Then again, we didn't want to be *too* far away from town or the hospital.

Franzi had become kind of a fixture at the local hospital. After only two years in the valley, the staff knew exactly what to do whenever she came in with one of her colic attacks. These attacks started happening in the last year with a greater frequency than when we were in Switzerland, and they had us both a little worried. We talked about getting further tests done, but she said that it was probably being caused by all the scar tissue from the surgeries she'd had. Not being too keen on going under the knife again, Franzi developed a very high tolerance for pain, and when these attacks took place, there was only one thing you could count on: Butch would always be at her side, and when the pain had subsided and she was feeling alright again, it was pretty much a given that he'd end up getting sick. His health was almost a mirror image of Franzi's health; very bizarre.

You never know what kind of twists life will throw your way, so if you really want to do or get something, you have to make the effort. Good things just don't fall into your hands, and it was for this reason that we tried our hardest not to give up on our search for the magical small acreage, close to town. It wasn't an easy task to stay optimistic.

Every week when the real estate guide came out, we'd sit down together and study it from cover to cover; a circle here, a question mark there, or a big

X through some of them. By the time we'd finished with the real estate guide it looked more like a horse racing program from the track. Probably around a dozen times, we phoned up a realtor and went with him or her to check out a property, only to have our hopes crushed by the various flaws and untold down-sides of the piece of land in question. It was getting frustrating after two years, and although neither of us ever admitted it to the other, we were slowly starting to wonder if our dream of finding a little piece of paradise was ever going to materialize.

House hunting seems to be one of those things that you do during the spring, summer and fall seasons. Houses don't look that appealing in winter. They're covered in snow, making the roofs and land virtually invisible – just as if a blanket covered them. If you're going to fork over major cash, you want to see, in its entirety, what you're getting for your money. What the realtor or seller might be calling a wonderfully manicured lawn could turn out to be a dirt covered, grassless piece of turf. The shingles on the roof might be frayed and tattered, but you would never know because it's all covered in snow.

Throughout the next year, we still picked up the real estate brochures, glanced through them, but nothing really caught our eye. It could be that we were just going through the motions, not wanting to give up, but we were getting pretty dejected.

During the summer of 2000, Franzi's brother Beat, along with his wife and my godson, finally made it over to visit us. Being both a chiropractor and an orthopaedic surgeon, Beat is one smart cookie who worked extremely hard to get where he is today. As a family, they managed to get away for a vacation about four times a year, and after doing his four-year chiropractic school in Toronto and a Heli-skiing trip to British Columbia a few years back, Beat was quite a big fan of Canada.

It was Beat, on a hot afternoon after coming back from the beach, who revitalized our interest in our small acreage quest. Sitting out on our covered deck, he asked Franzi, "What are the houses going for around here?"

"Why, are you thinking of packing up your place in Zurich and starting up a new practice here in Invermere?"

Chuckling to himself he said, "No, I've got a pretty good set-up in Zurich and I would be a fool to leave the practice I've built up over the years. I was thinking more along the lines of a little holiday place that we could come to a couple times a year. This area that you found seems to have everything: skiing, the lake, hiking, lots of tennis courts, and even plenty of golf courses."

Franzi and I were both thrilled that he was even entertaining the idea of a holiday place in or near Invermere, because it would be a dream come true for us to be able to see them a little more than once every couple of years, so I ran to the store and grabbed the latest, most up-to-date real estate guides that they had available.

Beat was pretty amazed at how inexpensive the houses and condos were in comparison to Zurich, but this was small-town Canada, and not the banking capital of the world we were talking about. A house that we would pay $200,000 for would cost at least a million in his neighbourhood.

When he finished browsing, he tossed the guide over to me and said, "There are a lot of properties and houses in here, but very few condos. That's what we would need; a maintenance-free place, where all we have to do is turn the key and it's ready to go. I don't want to be bothered with hiring someone to cut the grass or shovel the snow. Keep an eye out for me and if something should come along, fax it to me."

Franzi and I were hoping he'd see something and just jump on it. She'd be in seventh heaven if her brother had a holiday place here, and I would too, because I'd get to see my godson a lot more, and watch him grow up a bit.

After dinner that evening I was flipping through the properties, trying to find something for them that Beat may have missed, and when I came to the section with acreages, I was surprised to see that there were about ten new listings that hadn't been in there a month previously.

Three of the acreages were within a fifteen-minute drive to town and they all had houses on them. One was twenty acres, one was eighteen and the third one was just over five acres. With my heart beating just a few beats faster than a couple of minutes before, I said to Franzi, "Hey, you won't believe this, but there's a few places here that kind of fit the description of what we're looking for."

"Yeah, right!" she said.

"No really, check them out! I've circled them," I tossed her the open booklets, which she began to examine in earnest.

"Dave," she said excitedly, "we've got to go look at these places. They're not too far from here."

Franzi and I were pumped up to go and look at these properties, so the following day I phoned one of the realtors and asked if it would be possible to view all three in the same afternoon, and if we could bring Franzi's family along with us.

"Not a problem," he said. "The more sets of eyes you have looking at it, the better perspective you get." He probably would have said that we could bring the whole high school football team if we wanted, because at that moment the real estate market was fairly slow, and a property viewing with a lot of people was better than no viewing at all.

"Franzi, don't go getting yourself too excited," I said to her as the realtor pulled into our driveway with his van. "We've been here before and things have looked great on paper, but remember, they're trying to make these places look great in the ads. They don't tell you that it needs a new roof, or that the septic field backs up every spring."

"I know, but I can't help thinking that today might, just might, be the day that we find what we're looking for. I promised Butch that one day he would be totally free, and I've never lost sight of that promise."

So off we went – the realtor and the five of us packed into the minivan. Butch and Sammy watched us leave from the fenced yard, and I'm sure they were wishing us luck, because neither of them was too fond of being fenced in the yard whenever we left. They, too, wanted room to roam.

The first place we looked at, the twenty-acre one, turned out to be about twenty-five minutes from town with the house nestled in against the east side of a mountain. That meant that for about four months of the year, we would never see sunshine, only continual shade. Winter is cold enough, but not having any sun shining through the windows during those cold months was just unimaginable. The house itself didn't even appeal to any of us either, except my godson, who was seven years old at the time. He seemed to like the seventy-five different kinds of mounted animal heads that adorned every room in the house, including the bathrooms. All those dead animals on the walls, even though they'd be gone if we were to buy the place, made us feel a little queasy. I'm sure there are such things as animal ghosts too.

The second place, which was eighteen acres, wasn't as far out of town as the first one, but was still on the same side of the valley, meaning that there was a little bit of sunshine allowed in during the winter months, but not much. The house had a European flair too, with a lot of custom woodwork, but it was more of a ranch. Two barns, horse stables, and riding areas surrounded the house.

Franzi had a healthy fear of any animal that was bigger than her, and we had tried horseback riding in the past, but the up and down motion caused her a tremendous amount of stomach pain, so we knew that we would never be horse people. We didn't actually come out and say that we couldn't live there; there'd just be a lot of outbuildings that wouldn't have horses in them.

The third and last place on our itinerary that afternoon was a property on the other side of the valley, situated on the western side of a mountain range, meaning that there'd be lots of winter and evening sun. The drive there took about half an hour because it meant coming back to town and then going out the other side, and none of us in the minivan said very much during the drive. Franzi and I had been down this road before and it always seemed to end the same. We'd get our hopes up, thinking this will be the one, only to have them crashing back down again once we actually saw the place. Beat and his family weren't very impressed by the first two either.

The horse ranch place hadn't been too bad, but when you have a vision in your head of what your own little paradise should look like, you don't want to have to settle for something that you might grow to like. It has to feel good right from the outset.

Ten minutes outside of Invermere, as we pulled off the highway and headed down a winding gravel road towards the wetlands, the song streaming out of the minivan's radio was the 1969 Rolling Stones classic, "You Can't Always Get What You Want." *"That's just great!"* I muttered to myself. Up until this point, Mick and the boys had been spot on as far as our paradise search had gone, but negative thoughts seem to attract negative results so I blocked the song out, replacing it in my mind with Katrina and the Waves' "Walking on Sunshine."

Katrina must have come through for us, because as soon as we turned into the driveway with the real estate sign on it, the house came into view. And in unison, our mouths dropped open.

Even before we had moved to Canada and were just in the planning stages, the vision that we'd always had in our minds was to live somewhere secluded in a nice big log home. We even went so far as to subscribe to *Log Homes Magazine,* and had them sent over every three months so that we could dream and plan how we would like our log place to look, but we didn't have to do that any longer because it was standing right in front of us.

It only took one look at Franzi to know she was thinking exactly what I was: this *had to be ours.* Even Beat and his wife Kathi both had bulging eyes. Dominic, my godson, just said, "Cool!"

Doing our utmost to stay calm and collected in front of the realtor, we got out of the van and did a walk around the outside of the house before going in. Even with only seeing it from the outside, in my mind, it was already sold. The five-acre parcel was shaped like a stop sign, with the log house, a large vegetable garden and a huge grassy yard right in the middle of it. The house and yard were surrounded by thick, dense forest and it had a great view of the mountains. The land even bordered on a brook. *Total privacy! Total paradise!*

Just before we went inside, Franzi turned to me and said in German, "Dave, this is it. Whatever the inside looks like, it doesn't matter. We can change it."

Being almost too good to be true, the inside was even nicer-looking than the outside, with a large open concept kitchen-living-dining area, and big picture windows all over the place. The log work was all customized and you could tell that the people who built the home had put a lot of hard work into it. The basement was unfinished, which was perfect because it would give us a chance to put our signature on the house.

When the realtor went back to the van to gave us some time to talk amongst ourselves, the consensus amongst the five of us was unanimous: we had to buy this house. There was no question – we had to! After looking for close to three years, we'd finally stumbled upon the diamond in the rough, and if we passed it up, it might never come along again.

Butch, Sammy, and Maenam were going to have a blast living out here. They could be outside all day long, playing in the grass or in the forest, drinking in the little stream, or going down to the wetlands, which were only a few hundred yards away, for a swim whenever they wanted. The promise that Franzi made to Butch back in Switzerland was looking like it was about to become a reality. No more walks on leashes, being fenced in, or having neighbours complaining every time one of them showed an emotion.

Back at the house over dinner, the conversation was almost solely about this log house we'd found on the wonderful little acreage. The first two properties were basically forgotten about as we deemed them to be too large. Twenty acres would be nice, but all that land has to be looked after, meaning fenced in, unless you wanted cattle coming right up to your door and leaving their patties right beside your car. Both of these properties were in cattle grazing country, where all the local ranches would let the cows roam and graze for the whole summer and then gather them up in the fall. The last place had only a few cattle in the area, and they were fenced in, so that wouldn't be an issue.

Thanks to Beat's desire to see what our housing market looked like, we had stumbled upon our dream place. Had they not been there visiting us, we might have missed the opportunity altogether.

After the give and take involved in the buying process, and the arrangement of financing, we moved in at the beginning of October, just three short years after setting foot in British Columbia. Sitting at our dining room table the first night, munching on a store-bought pizza (which is the standard moving fare), and surrounded by unpacked boxcs, we just looked at each other and smiled. We'd found it, finally. The boys and the cat now had a new lifestyle – one they deserved and one they would never want to give up.

Chapter 11
Tests

*T*he first winter in the house was quite a learning experience for the two of us. We learned that the driveway out to the road took two hours to shovel by hand, that the wood-burning oven down in the basement devoured up logs faster than a pack of wild dogs on a three-legged cat, and that a log house can be a wind tunnel when the wind outside decides to howl.

None of this mattered though. We were in heaven, and there wasn't a day that went by when we didn't say to each other, "We've finally found Paradise." Butch, Sammy, and Maenam were of the same opinion. After we rigged up a little cat door, Maenam could come and go as she pleased, and Butch and Sammy had a great time exploring the woods and just playing outside with each other the whole day. We'd take them on long walks right from our front door, exploring the hills and ravines of the nature reserve just a few hundred yards away that overlooked the wetlands, and every day would be a new adventure. There were so many different trails up there that we hardly ever walked the same one twice. The promise had come true, and the two leashes that we used to have to use to take the boys for a walk in town were now hanging up on a hook, collecting dust. Life was good, and we appreciated every moment of it.

As we were to find out from some of our distant neighbours, the couple that had built the house and cleared the land some seven years before ended up getting a divorce, and neither of them could afford to keep the place on their own. When we found this out, we both had a somewhat heavy feeling in our hearts, because we were already more than in love with the house after just a few months, and we could only imagine how heartbreaking it must have been for them to give up what they had built with their own hands. Franzi, one evening at dinner, said to me, "we are so lucky to have found this place, but I hope that we don't end up having to pay some terrible cosmic price because our good fortune was built on someone else's misfortune." I didn't answer her, but I was thinking the exact same thing.

With Franzi back for another season at the heli-skiing company, and the restaurant still going strong at the golf course, we had to schedule our lives around the dogs. The most important thing to both of us was that they never missed a walk. They didn't ask to have us as their humans. That was a responsibility that we took on ourselves, and by making that commitment, we were bound to make sure they had the best possible lives they could have. There were, of course, times when we'd have to leave them alone for a few hours, but we always saw to it that they'd had a good walk beforehand and that they were good and tired so that they would sleep until one of us came home. They were, after all, our children.

We went through more firewood that first winter than either of us could have imagined and it seemed like every couple weeks I was out in the bush cutting up another pick-up truck full. Firewood gives off more heat than any other fuel source. It heats you up when you cut it, when you load it in the truck, when you unload it and bring it in the house, and when you actually get around to burning it. Sammy wasn't so interested in gathering wood, preferring for the most part to just meander around the truck, but Butch loved it. He'd try to rip the branches off the fallen trees, and when I'd get a few stacked up and ready to load, he took it upon himself to pull them off the pile and drag them back into the bush. Even after I explained the whole concept to him, he still just wanted to grab them from the pile and transport them to another location that only he seemed to know the reason for. When I'd try to take one away from him, it turned into a tug of war match that I never won.

The snow slowly melted, giving way to springtime and it was only then, raking up the entire winter kill from the yard, that I realized it was going to be one heck of a job to cut all this grass with just a push mower. When I threw the idea of a riding mower out to Franzi, I was shut down almost instantly.

"Are you out of your mind? We're young. Riding mowers are for old people, and besides, you're going to be working all summer, and I won't be, so I'll do it myself. I actually like cutting the grass; it's good exercise." Since I knew that I was already in charge of the vegetable garden, she definitely wasn't going to get an argument out of me on this one.

And cut the grass she did. Like a demon, she'd be out there working up a sweat, with Sammy looking on from a safe distance and Butch walking along right beside her, throwing his rubber Kong right in front of the lawnmower so that she had to stop and throw it for him. He'd do this about fifty times throughout the two-hour lawn cutting ordeal, and when it finally came to an end, he would actually be smiling, knowing that he'd done his part to help us out with the chores.

One afternoon, as I arrived home from work, I found Franzi lying on the couch in the living room, groaning and writhing in pain. This was the third colic she'd had in about a six-week span, so I helped her to the car and we again made the ten-minute drive to the emergency room. I knew that she'd get through it after they gave her the injection and a few hours of bed rest, but it terrified me every time it happened. Although she didn't want to admit it (saying that it was just scar tissue), I think we both knew that there was something else going on.

A few hours later, after they'd released her from the emergency room and we were back at home again, all she wanted to do was go to bed. I knew that it wasn't the time to broach the subject of her stomach colic because she was pretty doped up from the medicine they'd given her, so I let her sleep. Butch, as usual when these attacks hit her, was curled up on the bed lying right beside her, guarding his mom. If Sammy or Maenam wanted to get close, he'd let out a throaty growl that told the other two, "now is not the time."

Over coffee the next morning, Franzi was still a bit out of it, and the pain was lingering, which was a new development because normally it would disappear as quickly as it came. Then, I threw it out there on the table.

"Franzi, I love you more than life itself, and I know that the last thing you want is another stomach operation, but you can't keep going on like this. It isn't normal and it's affecting your quality of life. Please, for all of us here, let's get you to a specialist and see what's going on."

I don't know if my argument was that convincing, or if she just knew it deep down within herself, but a tear welled up in her eye and she said, "I know. Something's not right." And then the tears flowed from her: scared tears.

The province of British Columbia had just been through an election which had brought about a change of power, and the new ruling party had set about to revamp our provincial health care system with sweeping changes. These changes were quite major and had thrown the whole public health care system into turmoil with a large number of bugs that still needed to be ironed out. The one disastrous affect that these times of change had brought upon the general public was that wait times, to see both general practitioners and specialists, had gone up dramatically. There was even talk of closing many hospitals across the province.

Luckily for us, Franzi was able to see her regular doctor in early May and got a referral to see the stomach specialist. Her doctor knew that the wait times in British Columbia were long, and it was for this reason that she decided to send Franzi to a specialist in Calgary, which was only three hours away, in the province of Alberta to the east of us. The appointment was for the middle of June so we still had a good six weeks to wait for an initial consultation.

We both wanted to know what was going on inside of her tummy, but she had lived with these colic attacks and the pain for so long that neither of us saw a six-week waiting period as a big deal. Summer was here and it was time to have some fun.

Our tent and sleeping bags were relegated to the storage room in the basement, as there was no longer a need to have to get away and search for a little privacy whenever we had some days off together. We had a veggie garden that had to be tended to, flower beds to be planted, lawn to be mowed, and although these things sounded like work, we just loved doing them because we could be together. Butch and

Sammy could be outside with us all day, doing their best to con us into a play round, or making sure that we didn't forget about their dinner. Maenam would also help out by digging up whatever I'd just managed to plant in the garden. I think she viewed it as the world's largest litter box.

The middle of June finally did roll around and her appointment was for 1:00 P.M. so we decided to make a day out of it. Shopping is a lot cheaper in the big city than in a rural small town, so with a lengthy list, we left early, hoping to get it all out of the way before she had to see the doctor. Butch and Sammy were along for the ride because we never left them at home unless we absolutely had to. If we were going to see the skyscrapers and hustle and bustle of the big city, they were too. Sammy would always sit in the back of the truck with his eyes bulging out from the array of things he'd never seen before, like his first trip through an automated carwash. We don't have one of those in Invermere, and we honestly thought he was going to have an accident in the truck, just out of sheer fear. Butch was the exact opposite. He was the cool, older brother, who nothing seemed to faze. It was only because he'd seen it all before in Switzerland that he was able to act as cool as he did, but I could tell what he was thinking: "Sammy doesn't have to know that."

When the shopping was finished and the boys had been taken for a walk in an off-leash park we'd found, it was time for the doctor. Franzi spoke very good English, but at times, when the conversation got technical or medical, there were some words that she didn't know. I was the same way in German, and because of this, whenever she had a consultation with a doctor, she insisted I be with her. Two sets of ears were better than one, and if there was something she didn't understand that well, there was a good chance that I could clarify it in German.

The doctor (Internist, I believe, was his official doctor title) was a few years older than we were and he asked question after question about her health history and all the operations she'd been through.

"How often do these attacks occur? How long do they last? Are they getting worse in severity?" Lots and lots and lots of questions flew our way. I found it a little strange that he wasn't taking any notes, but then again, I could take a dinner order for ten people including drinks without writing anything down either. He probably just had a good memory.

The verbal history questionnaire came to an end, which meant that it was now time for the finger-poking section of the examination. The poking, pressing, probing, and pushing went on for about fifteen minutes, all concentrated around her lower stomach area, and she was having a difficult time describing where the pain was or how it affected other areas simply because she wasn't having an attack at the moment. It was like trying to describe to your mechanic the grinding noise that you'd been hearing coming from your engine all week and then suddenly it's not making the noise anymore when he's looking at it.

After getting up off the table and getting dressed again, Franzi was very anxious to know what he thought it might be, but he was playing his cards pretty close to his chest. If he had any suspicions or ideas, he wasn't sharing them with us. What he wanted was for Franzi to go to his lab, which was in the same building, in two days time to get a full ultrasound done.

"Okay," she said dejectedly. "We'll just have to come back to Calgary again."

The doctor must not have realized that we were from out of town, but when I told him that we had a three-hour drive each way, he called his secretary and saw to it that we could get the ultrasound in an hour's time, and then return to see him for the results at 4:00 P.M. We were so thankful to him for squeezing everything into the same afternoon for us, because having to come back another time wasn't something either of us was excited about.

We had an hour to kill so we went back to the truck, grabbed the boys, and did a little window-shopping in downtown Calgary. Sammy was definitely not used to having so many people around him and he was constantly shying away from anyone who got too close. Butch, on the other hand, saw it as an opportunity to make new human friends. The minute we turned our heads away from him, he had his nose stuck in someone's crotch or rear end. Franzi kept scolding him, because we knew from experience that's what was expected from us, but it brought us a light moment during an anxious wait.

The ultrasound was finished quickly, which was no surprise because it's just a little jelly on the belly and then running a small machine over the area to get a visual picture of what's on the inside, and then with yet another hour to occupy ourselves before we had to be back at the specialist's office, we did the same routine all over again.

"Dave, do you think he's going to find anything?" Franzi asked. It had taken a lot of courage on her part to actually get to the point of having her stomach checked out. I knew she had a natural dislike of doctors, after having seen so many and none of them really helping her, so I said, "I don't know Franzi, but if they do, at least that'll be a start. Then we can concentrate on getting it fixed so that you don't have to end up in the emergency room every month."

"I know. I just can't get my head around another surgery. I'm always so terrified when they put me out that I'll never wake up again."

"If it comes to that, I'll be right there beside you, but let's not even go there. All he's doing is the standard tests. Maybe it's something that can be taken care of with just a little pill," I said, not really believing it myself, but trying my best to give her something positive to hold onto.

While sitting in the doctor's waiting room once again, mindlessly flipping through old *National Geographic* magazines, Franzi's name was called.

"You're coming in with me, right?" she asked.

"Absolutely, honey."

The specialist, who had now changed out of his white coat, was clad in a casual golf shirt and slacks and looked like he was ready to hit the links right after our appointment. I was a bit surprised not to see a golf glove on his hand.

"Have a seat," he said. "Mrs. Cassidy, have you ever had any problems with your kidneys before?"

"No, not that I'm aware of."

"How about when you urinate: do you ever have any pain then, and do you have to go to the bathroom more frequently than what you feel is normal?"

"No."

"Perhaps, when you were only a child, was there an infection or anything else that you might not be aware of, but your parents might remember: an illness or an injury, maybe?"

"I'd have to call them and ask, but I really don't know of anything," Franzi replied.

"The reason I'm asking these questions is because the pictures from the ultrasound, as you can see here, are showing an anomaly between the two kidneys. If you look at the left kidney here, and then at the right kidney, over here, it's a lot more defined."

Yes, he was right. There was a definite difference when you compared the two kidneys – two organs doing the same function – that normally looked very much alike.

"Well, what does that mean?" Franzi asked, in a low-level state of panic.

"That means that there's something there that isn't right. We're going to have to do a Computerized Tomography or CT scan, which will give us a much better idea of what's going on in your stomach. Talk to the receptionist on your way out to set up an appointment for the scan, and give your parents a call. Find out if you had any childhood illnesses or infections. If you did, I want to know about them, please."

With those muddy waters, we left his office. The first available CT scan wasn't until mid-October, but we took it anyway. *What other options did we have, really?* The wait would be interminable, with countless mind games sure to be played out, but we'd just have to be strong and stay positive.

As soon as we left his office, Franzi and I found the first pay phone available and gave her parents a call. It was 1:00 A.M. back in Switzerland, but this was one of those situations where you just had to have an answer now. After apologizing for waking her mom up, Franzi explained what the doctor had told her, and sure enough, Suzi knew of no such illnesses or infections from Franzi's childhood.

"I don't feel sick or have any pain at the moment," she said during the ride back to Invermere. "If it was something serious, I'd be sick and have pain all the time, right?"

Franzi was nervous, as was I. The fact that the doctor couldn't give us any answers, except for more tests, seemed to be playing on both our minds.

Again that night, Butch crawled into bed with Franzi. He only did this when he knew that something just wasn't right.

The summer wore on, with no shortage of work to do around the new house, as well as the other work, which paid the bills, and after a two-month period when Franzi had absolutely no problems with her stomach, we'd begun to put the worries of the coming CT scan behind us. She was feeling good and that was a positive sign.

There were other things to look forward to, like Franzi's parents (who hadn't seen Sammy since he was about 8 inches long), coming for a visit in early September, and a short two-week holiday to Switzerland in late October to celebrate Rudi and Suzi's seventieth birthdays. They had organized a big party for the whole family – about 70 people in total – and we told them that there was no way we'd be able to attend because I was working, but we wanted to surprise them. They wouldn't expect to see the two of us at the birthday party when we'd seen them just five weeks before on this side of the pond.

We'd be leaving just two days after the CT scan, and my mother would be coming to stay at our place to look after the house, as well as Butch, Sammy, and Maenam. She always spoiled them rotten and whenever she left after a visit, the boys ended up on a diet. It was very similar to humans and how they dealt with the Christmas and New Year holiday season. Humans tend to go on their diets voluntarily, whereas Butch and Sammy have no choice when we cut out all their treats after a Mom Visit.

She'd feed them a lot more than we did, and walk them a lot less than we did, so simple arithmetic meant that they would turn into little butterballs. It wasn't only when my mother was here that they'd get round in the belly. On occasion (and thankfully not very often), they'd go off in the woods for a cruise, following the different scents, and stumble upon a fresh kill. The kill could be from nature or from hunters who would skin and gut the animal, leaving all the entrails for whatever hungry animal happened to come along.

Normally when this happened, it wasn't a very pretty sight – or smell. With Butch it was a lot more visible than with Sammy because of his yellow fur, but they would both come home with blood all over their faces, waddling like little penguins more than walking like dogs, because they'd both eaten a two-week portion of fresh meat. And then the real fun would start. First would come the vomiting, followed by the constant diarrhoea and then finishing with the worst farts imaginable. These were toxic – chem-ical warfare toxic. These symptoms often lasted for a couple of days, and when we let them out of the house, we really had to keep an eye on them that they didn't take off and repeat the whole "all-you-can-eat" buffet process again.

Suzi and Rudi stayed with us for three weeks, doing a lot of little day tours with their daughter and the boys while I was at work. It was a relaxing visit and near the end of it Rudi told us that now that he had seen our new home, he was very happy for us, but that it would be his last visit to Canada. He's a big man with some knee and back problems, and he didn't want to fly that far anymore. Depending on the flight pattern, Zurich to Calgary can be anywhere from ten to twelve hours, so it was easy to understand his reasoning.

We were going to stay with Franzi's brother Beat and his family when we went back to surprise her parents, and Franzi had filled him in on what was happening with her stomach. When he found out that she was having a CT scan, he immediately said that we should get extra copies of the X-rays and bring them over with us so he could have a look at them with his fellow doctors at the university hospital in Zurich.

"Not a problem," she said.

With the final preparations being made for our trip, picking up my mother and trying not to neglect the boys in any way, we didn't have a lot of time to think about the CT scan. Before we knew it, we were sitting in the waiting room again. The specialist reassured us that it wouldn't be a problem to get extra copies of the X-rays to take with us, and told us that as soon as we got back we should give his office a call to find out the results of the scan.

Franzi, who hadn't eaten or drunk anything the whole day (with the exception of the X-ray dye that they make you swallow to get a better visual of your organs), wasn't saying very much as we waited there. Her thoughts were of just getting it all over with and getting back home. She still hadn't had a colic attack since we'd seen the doctor back in June, which was a nice wave to be riding, and she was more and more convinced that the ultrasound wasn't anything to be worried about. In five days' time we'd be sitting in a big room, with her whole extended family around us, shocking her parents with our appearance. That was what we were trying to focus on.

The lab technicians that actually did the scan were not allowed to make any comments on the X-rays, so when we left the lab after the scan was finished, we knew nothing more than when we had arrived. With the extra copy of the CT scan X-rays we headed home again, where all the campers and my mom were waiting to greet us.

The next day we pulled out the suitcases and started packing. Sammy doesn't really care when he sees a suitcase, but for Butch it's a very different story. He knows right away what a suitcase means. This was when the sulking started. From the living room floor, all he would do was follow us with his eyes, not even lifting his head. If you gave him a treat, he wouldn't take it. His dinner was only nibbled at, and you could forget about calling him and telling him to come; it just wasn't going to happen. He was sad, very sad. His humans were leaving him, and whether it was only for a day or for a month, it didn't matter. He was being abandoned.

I knew my mother would look after them like they were her own, so that wasn't a worry, but as we were ready to leave; the goodbyes were still very emotional. Sammy had his tail wagging and wanted to jump in the car with us, but Butch, still in his pouting mood, just sat there on the deck looking disconsolate. It was very heart-wrenching for both of us.

With uncomfortable seats, a few crying babies, and a movie playing that we'd both already seen, the flight was destined to be a crummy one. I guess that's the reason they serve alcohol.

Chapter 12
Serious Times

With the long, overnight flight under our belts, we had a whole day to recuperate with Beat and Kathi before the birthday celebrations were set to commence. Naturally, the first thing that Franzi did was phone my mother to make sure that the boys were doing well, and sure enough, they were really down in the dumps. She said that Butch waited by the door for three hours after we'd left, hoping that it was only a quick shopping trip that we'd gone for. When she took the two of them for a walk, neither one of them was interested in playing or running, preferring to just saunter along beside her.

This wasn't the news that Franzi wanted to hear, but it was, basically, what she'd expected. She spent the most time with them; she fed them and she cared for them like no other pet-mom I know. It wasn't a surprise that they were missing us, especially her.

"The two weeks will pass quickly," I told her, "and then we'll be back in the bush having a good, long walk with the campers. They don't hold grudges and

I'm sure that when we walk through our door, they'll be all over us." But she wasn't so easily convinced.

"Sammy maybe, but I don't know about Butch. He's very headstrong and he won't forget so quickly that we left him alone for so long."

Before we left for the birthday celebrations the next day, Franzi gave the CT scan results to her brother, but he didn't open them up.

"I'll give them to one of my colleagues at the hospital to look at," he told us. "Besides, I'm not your doctor so even if I was to see something on the X-rays, ethically, I wouldn't be allowed to say anything. That's up to your doctor to tell you. I'm just curious though."

The drive to Solothurn from Zurich took just over an hour, and we'd both forgotten how crowded the highways of Switzerland were. Beat and Kathi said that the traffic was really good on this particular Sunday morning, but to us it felt like we were in the middle of the pack during the first lap of the Daytona 500. Tailgating was the norm at seventy-five miles an hour, because if you tried to leave a space between you and the car in front, someone would just pull in there; no point.

The celebrations were held in the big banquet room of one of the finer restaurants in Solothurn, and Franzi and I had to hide out across the street in a little coffee shop until someone came to get us and we were told it was time to make an appearance. That time arrived shortly thereafter, and as the string of waiters and waitresses made their way to the head table where her parents were seated, we walked right along with them, carrying their salads.

Franzi's father was so shocked that for the first time in my life, I saw him speechless and with tears in his eyes. Her mother cries at everything, so there was no real surprise there. After the initial shock had worn off, a few more seats were brought to the head table for us, and we enjoyed a wonderful day and a six-course meal fit for a king and queen.

We spent a couple of days in Solothurn with her parents, and then went to Interlaken and Muerren to catch up with old friends before heading back to Zurich to spend the last days with Beat, Kathi, and Dominic.

When Beat picked us up at the train station, he seemed rather subdued, and we both took this to mean that he was just sad that we'd be leaving, and that it would be another year or two before we saw one another again. Distance is hard when you're away from the people you care about, but we had a new home in another country, and although she missed her family and friends, Franzi always said that she couldn't go back to Switzerland to live.

"Butch, Sammy, and Maenam could never get used to all the rules and restrictions of living here, especially after having so much freedom. It just wouldn't be fair to them."

As we were sitting at the table that evening enjoying our coffee and Schnapps after dinner, Beat asked Franzi if she was going to see the specialist when she got home, to which Franzi answered, "Eventually I'll probably see him. It just takes so long to get an appointment; the Heli-ski season will more than likely be over before I get to see him."

"Promise me," he said, "that you'll phone him as soon as you get home."

"Yes brother, I promise," she said.

Before bed that night, Beat took me aside and made me also promise, with an extreme sense of urgency, that she really would get in contact with the specialist when we got home. He'd had the X-rays for close to two weeks, had obviously seen them with his colleagues, but wasn't allowed to comment on them. That was a little unsettling, to say the least.

The flight back to Canada went off without a hitch, having to change planes in Frankfurt, and our luggage even managed to arrive with us back in Calgary, which was a balmy minus thirty degrees Fahrenheit when we stepped out of the airport. Neither of us were bothered by the cold temperatures, because the only thing we had on our minds was to make it home as quickly as possible and give the boys – and my mom, of course – a big hug.

Pulling into the driveway we could hear the barks coming from inside. No one could ever sneak up on our house; it just wasn't humanly possible. As soon as the car was parked and we'd gotten out, my mother opened the door and out came a yellow and a black blur. Franzi had to actually jump out of the way because they were coming so fast. The two of them were wagging their tails so quickly that if you were to harness the energy, like a windmill, you could have powered a small village.

They were both ecstatic to have us back home again, as were we. The first fifteen minutes that we were in the house was solely devoted to scratches, pets, and hugs. Even Maenam came upstairs, from the warmth of her blanket down by the furnace room, to welcome us back and, coincidentally, to use her litter box.

The boys didn't appear to have put on too much weight, probably because I asked my mom to go easy on their treats, and they had behaved beautifully, she said. During the walks, they never took off on her, and they even let her sleep until seven in the morning before barking for breakfast. *How considerate!*

After about a half hour of being home, Butch seemed to have remembered that we left him for two weeks. It was as if suddenly he thought to himself, "Oh yeah, I'm supposed to be a little upset with these humans for abandoning me for so long." And with this sudden brain flash, he turned his tail towards us and went downstairs for the evening. His entire display of disapproval only lasted for a few hours and when he figured that he'd made his point, he came back upstairs and headed to the pantry where the treats were hidden, knowing that he wouldn't be denied.

The following morning, after laying awake in bed with jet lag for a couple hours, Franzi made good on her promise to Beat and phoned the specialist in Calgary who had ordered the CT scan for her, hoping that she could just find out the results over the phone and not have to make another trip back to the big city. But as luck would have it, that wasn't meant to be.

The internist doctor wasn't in on that particular morning, but it wouldn't have made any difference even if he were. The receptionist told Franzi that her files had been sent on to a new specialist – a urologist – and that she also had an appointment with him on the following Monday, November 12th. He'd be able to answer all of her questions.

Not knowing what we should be feeling, the week dragged on very slowly. *Was it a good sign that we had this appointment with the urologist in such a short time period, or did that mean that there was something wrong?* I couldn't help but think about Beat's final little talk, and how urgent he seemed about his sister getting in contact with the specialist as soon as possible. On the other hand, it could all just be a coincidence. Perhaps the urologist had a cancellation for the next week and nothing more. *Were we reading too much into it?*

Either way, during that cold and blustery week, we made our best attempts to not think about the situation, choosing to distract ourselves with long, snowy walks with the boys. If there was ever a sight that could bring a smile to our faces, it was Butch diving and digging in the snow. We called his approach to finding sticks "the submarine."

"Check it out! He's doing the submarine again." This entailed walking along with practically his whole head under the snow until he found a stick, which he would then surface with, bringing it to us to play fetch with. Sammy was about as into playing with sticks as he was into swimming.

Dogs are like people. No two are alike, and ours were definitely like night and day – and not only with the colours. Where Butch could chase a tennis ball or stick for hours on end, Sammy would chase it once and then take off with it so that what he deemed to be a senseless exercise would come to an end, with the minimum amount of effort expended. This probably had something to do with his physique. Butch was the muscular athlete and Sammy, although not overweight, had nowhere near the stamina or muscle tone of his older brother. If we were comparing them to humans, he might've been called a couch potato.

Monday finally rolled around, and with my mother having already left to go home, we arranged to have a good friend of ours come over for the day and look after the boys and take them for a walk. She had a couple of dogs also, so it would be a real doggy party at our house. We didn't want to take them with us for yet another trip to Calgary, even though they travelled well in the car. They never complained or got unruly as long as we would stop for ten minutes each way so they could get out and stretch their legs and take care of business. It was just not a very nice day for them, being cooped up in the car. Therefore, if they could be home having some fun, we felt a lot better for them.

We almost missed the appointment in Calgary, getting stuck in rerouted traffic due to construction and then not being able to find a place to park. So when we finally ran into the doctor's office with a minute to spare and slightly out of breath, we were whisked right into one of his exam rooms, where we were told that he'd be with us shortly.

The exam room had a lot of diagrams and medical posters on the walls of kidneys, urethras, and bladders, as well as little scale-size models of the organs on the shelves. There were three chairs and an exam table with stirrups. Other than that, it was just a small and plain-looking room.

Neither of us said much to each other as we sat there waiting to hear about the next step we'd have to take, or the magical pill that would cure her of her ongoing stomach problems. Up until this point, we'd received no answers, or even hints with the exception of the kidney anomaly, and a little information would be a welcome thing.

The wait seemed like an hour but it was actually only ten minutes before the door opened and the urologist walked in. He was roughly our age (give or take a couple years), and had the appearance of someone who spent his free time outdoors.

We'd stood up to introduce ourselves, so after the pleasantries were out of the way, we sat back down. He flipped open Franzi's file and said to her, very understatedly, "So, we're dealing with cancer here, and we're going to have to operate on you as soon as possible." *Whoa!*

I don't think my mind registered anything after the "cancer" word, because someone had basically just punched me in the face with a cinderblock.

What? Did he just say what I thought he said? Why is Franzi's hand suddenly gripping mine like a vice? Why are Franzi and I both shaking? Why is this guy staring at us so quizzically? Tears are running down her cheeks. Buddy, you've got the wrong chart there. What kind of a sick joke is this, if it's actually even happening? Dave, you can wake up now. It's just a dream. God, please make this dream end.

Something was definitely wrong here and the urologist picked up on it right away as he looked across at these two people who had suddenly turned grey.

"Cancer?" was all Franzi could manage to say.

"What exactly did the internist tell you about your condition, Mrs. Cassidy?" he asked.

"Nothing, we didn't even see him after the CT scan. He just sent us here to see you," Franzi said, functioning much better than I was at the moment. I don't recall even saying a word. This was my wife. We're going to grow old together. *No, this can't be right. This can't be happening.*

"Oh no, I thought you knew. I thought he'd gone over the results with you already. Oh, I'm so sorry. I'm really sorry."

At this point I caught onto a small mental thread that seemed to be leading me back to reality, but speech was still elusive. Franzi, who was the one who actually had the cancer, had done her switch to autopilot, which she is so gifted at doing in times of crisis (as I learned back in Ecuador), had started talking again.

"No, no one told us it was cancer. Where exactly is it and what can we do about it?" Franzi asked the doctor.

"Well," he replied, "from what I've seen, there's a fairly large tumour in your left kidney, and I don't know if it's grown so I want to run another CT scan because these X-rays are close to a month old."

"How large?" was the next question she put forth.

"It looks like it's about five centimetres in diameter, but I'll know more when we can get a new set of X-rays."

"That's almost the size of a tennis ball," she commented.

"Yes, pretty close. It'll definitely have to be operated on, and there's a good chance that you will lose your kidney. I know it's not any great consolation but people can live long and full lives with only one kidney." He was right; it was a very small consolation.

After finding my voice again, still gripping tightly onto Franzi's hand, I voiced my first words since the introductions were done.

"Is it only the kidney or has it spread around inside of her?"

"Again, the CT scan that we have to work from right now shows that the tumour is only inside the kidney, which is a very positive sign, but there's always a chance – and you have to be prepared for it – that we might find it has grown through the wall of the kidney. We'll know more after the next scan. I'll be right back, I just want to go out front and make a few calls." And then he left.

We just sat there holding each other in our arms, dumbstruck. Words didn't have to be said because we were both thinking the same things as the tears started to flow down both of our cheeks.

"I love you, honey," was all I could manage to say, meaning it more so than any time I'd ever said it before.

"I know. We're going to get through this. We have to stay positive. You heard what he said about people living a long time with only one kidney," she said, a bit more collected now than five minutes before.

When the urologist returned, he said straight out, "We've booked you in for the first slot tomorrow morning for the CT scan, and I'm going to go ahead and book the operating theatre for the first available time for the surgery. 9:00 A.M. for the scan and the same rules about food and drink beforehand apply this time also. Please believe me when I say that I am truly sorry that you had to hear about it from me the way you did. We're going to do the best we possibly can for you."

After filling out a few forms with the receptionist for the scan, she told us to check in with her for the surgery time the next morning.

Judy, our friend who was staying at the house and looking after the dogs, agreed right away to spend the night and stay as long as she was needed after she heard about our disheartening news, and it was a blessing not to have to go home that night and come right back the next morning. The distraction of finding a hotel, buying toiletries, and going out for a meal, which neither of us could eat, were all welcome. Anything that put the cancer word out of our minds for a few minutes was more than welcome.

Late that night, from our hotel, I phoned Franzi's parents to tell them the news, but they were too choked up to talk. Her brother knew it already, not surprisingly, having seen the scans two weeks before. I understood now why he insisted we get to the specialist as soon as possible. From a medical ethics point of view, I know he wasn't allowed to say anything to us, but I still found it hard to swallow that he knew what was going on when we didn't.

We were both still digesting the news and as we lay in bed that night Franzi said to me, "Doesn't it seem odd to you that we had to wait almost four months for the first CT scan and now we get one the next day? That can only mean that it's serious and this doctor doesn't want to screw around." She was right; that's how it looked to me too.

Neither of us managed to fall asleep that night, with our minds playing the "what if?" game, and even a cup of coffee the next morning was out of the question because I wasn't going to drink one in front of her when she couldn't have one.

We left to get the scan done and were out of the lab by 10:00 A.M., and then went back to the urologist's office a few minutes later, as we were instructed.

We didn't see the doctor during this short visit, but the receptionist told us that if he saw anything had changed with the scans, he'd be in touch. She also let us know that all of the operating theatres at the hospital were booked out and the first available time for the operation would be January 22nd of the following year.

"Would that be alright for you?" she asked.

Of course it wasn't alright for us. Here was my wife next to me, with a cancerous tumor sitting inside of her kidney – growing on a daily basis for all I knew – and this lady was asking us if two months down the road was okay.

"If it has to be, there's not much we can do about it," I said. "But if there's any humanly possible way in the world, we want to get this over with. If you phone us at six in the morning and tell us there's an opening at ten, we'll be there. Any cancellation at all, we'll take it."

On the drive home, we saw a couple of black bears and even a moose. Things that would normally have us all excited and on the edge of our seats had virtually no effect on either one of us; we didn't even comment on the sights as we drove by. Two months of waiting, with what I could only describe as a ticking time bomb in her tummy, just seemed like too much to bear.

"Remember, Dave," Franzi said to me shortly before we got home, "we said that we were going to try and stay positive. It's not going to be an easy wait, but we'll get through it the best we can; you, Butch, Sammy, Maenam, and I will. Together."

The boys were there to greet us when we got home, with Franzi in the driveway on her knees, giving them both a long hug, again with tears in her eyes. They obviously sensed that the world was out of kilter, because both of their flailing tails stopped almost instantly. Judy sat with us for a coffee and as she was about to leave, said to me, "I think there's a message on your answering machine. I heard it ring when I was playing with the boys out back."

Chapter 13
A Ray of Sunshine

*I*t seemed rather surreal to be back home again, in the house that we had planned on growing old in, the paradise that we had searched so long for, with the possibility – despite how positive we thought or remained – that the whole scenario might just not play out as planned. Neither of us had any appetite going on even though we hadn't had a bite to eat the whole day. Not even a bottle of wine was going to pull any rabbits out of the hat for this problem, so we settled on stiff vodka. Butch, who normally would show his displeasure at us for leaving him for a few days, was very different. He had settled himself in beside Franzi on the couch, and if she got up to go to the kitchen or bedroom, he was beside her every step of the way – ears down and tail down.

With a slew of messages on the answering machine, I set about playing them all back. There was one from my parents, wishing Franzi good luck with the doctor's appointment, one from her parents, wishing her the same, a free carpet shampooing if we

222

took advantage of the offer right away, and the last one, which caught me by surprise, was from the urologist's office:

"Hi, this is Jackie at the urologist's office in Calgary, and this message is for Franzi. You are presently scheduled for surgery on the 22nd of January, but there has been a cancellation and we now have an opening for the surgery on November 22nd. I know you're probably still on your way home from Calgary, but if you could give our office a call as soon as you get this message, that would be great. Thank you."

"Franzi!" I yelled excitedly from the bedroom, "They've got a surgery opening for next Thursday! We've got to call them back right away."

She didn't really smile at this news, but I could see that there was a little sign of relief on her face. The two-month wait would have made us both crazy, and now we were faced with only a nine-day wait. That was sixty-one days that the tumour in her kidney would not be growing into something larger and potentially more dangerous.

Franzi was on the phone within two minutes, accepting the new surgery appointment, and getting all the details of when she had to be at the hospital. Four o'clock in the afternoon on the 21st was when she had to be checked into her room at the hospital, and they would be doing the operation around noon the next day. They expected that the operation would take around three hours, barring any unforeseen complications, and she would be in the recovery station around 4:00 P.M.

This surgery opening was a major blessing to us and it managed to give us at least a little piece of mind, knowing that the whole thing would be over – for better or for worse – very soon. The worst part about cancer is the waiting and the uncertainty. If you have the operation behind you, then either you know that life is good again, or you know exactly where you stand and what you're still facing.

Luckily, during the month of November, I wasn't working at the golf course. November is the slowest month of the year and it was the perfect time to take a leave of absence, which meant that I could spend every waking hour with the loves of my life. We'd take the boys for long walks each day, cook good meals at night, and even with the thought of the coming event in our minds, we tried to live life as normally as possible. At times, things would downslide with just the simplest of everyday things – things that we take for granted, bringing up a fresh wave of emotions. One never knew with certainty what would happen. An operation is still an operation, with the ever-present chance of complications.

Franzi, after already having had eight operations in the last thirteen years (five of which were on her stomach), was getting extremely nervous as the day approached.

"Dave, I know it's all going to be okay and I'm going to be fine, but we have to face up to the very real possibility that something might not go as planned.

If this were to happen, you have to promise me that you'll make Butch, Sammy, and Maenam the number one priority in your life." Not wanting to think about anything even remotely resembling this scenario she had just laid out, I promised – with all my heart.

Judy had agreed to stay at our house again and look after the four-legged ones, which was a big relief, knowing that they'd be in good hands. Butch had been stuck on Franzi – much like a shadow would be – the entire week. As much as she told him that the world would be good again, he sensed her fear and shared her worry.

On Tuesday, the day before we were to head off to Calgary, we wanted to take the boys for an extra long walk, just to spend some quality time with them before leaving. I wasn't sure how long Franzi would have to stay in the hospital, and we'd already agreed that as soon as she was out of the woods, I was to return home and give the animals some normality in their daily routines. I wasn't keen on leaving her there on her own, but it was something that she insisted strongly upon.

The day, much like our moods, was cloudy and grey, with even a few sprinkles thrown in to round off the atmosphere. However, we were used to it by now, so we just bundled up and set off from our front door. Butch, who stuck on Franzi like glue at home, was a much different dog when outdoors. It was as if he could check his mood at the door, and then pick it up again when we were home. He ran and sniffed and played stick as if his whole mission was to bring a smile to our faces: the exact same behaviour as every other walk he'd ever been on. Sammy would play too, but he was more content to just do his own thing. He didn't feel the need to be entertained with sticks.

A two-hour walk was normally a long one for us, but on this day it turned into a three-hour walk, as neither of us wanted it to come to an end. *One never knew, right?* Having made it back to the house, we were all a little knackered, with Franzi heading directly to the couch, Butch and Sammy lying down on their cushions, and me hopping in the car to do the last-minute grocery shopping so that Judy had something to eat while we were gone.

The skies had grown tired of just looking grey and dreary, so as I was leaving they decided to dump a load of rain down on our valley. It was very strange weather for November – a time when we normally have snowfall. With no idea of what Judy would actually like to eat, I settled on things that were quick and easy to prepare in the oven or on the stovetop. We were probably the only people in the area that didn't have a microwave.

The shopping, which I normally enjoyed, was a tedious affair and I had to dash to the car to keep from getting soaked when I left the store. The whole way home it was drizzling and when I entered the house there was only Sammy and Maenam to greet me. *"Very strange,"* I thought. *Perhaps Butch and Franzi were out in the backyard?* But for the life of me, I couldn't figure out why they would be out in that weather and after searching the house from top to bottom, they were nowhere to be found. Even Franzi's car was still parked out front; really strange.

It wouldn't have been the first time that Butch had taken off, chasing after a coyote, and she'd gone to find him. I thought for sure that after putting the groceries away, I'd be joining the search party, but before I could even get my boots on, the door swung open and in walked a very wet Butch with muddy foot prints, followed by Franzi with a glowing ear-to-ear smile on her dripping wet face. Actually she wasn't just smiling – she was beaming.

"Dave, it's all going to be good!" she said. "Butchy told me."

"What?"

"Yeah, Butchy told me."

"Franzi, you're going to have to explain this one to me, because I'm not getting it."

"Okay. Well, after you left to go into town I was just about to doze off on the couch, which I welcomed, considering the way I've been sleeping for the past week, when suddenly I got a big wet lick across my cheek and eye. It was Butch, naturally, and when I told him to go lay down, I got another lick. He was tired also when we came home from the walk and it was way too early for his dinner, so I really had no idea of what he wanted. After a few more licks I finally sat up and then he ran over to the door and started barking. Sammy didn't even raise his head.

"I thought he probably just wanted out to take care of his business, so I sent him out and shut the door, but he just stood there, barking even louder. I couldn't have him just standing out there going berserk so I let him back in and he didn't move from the door. The little goof wouldn't stop barking! So I put my boots on and my rain jacket and followed him outside to see what was making him so crazy."

"Do you remember when we were in obedience school and we were trying to get him to walk heel with the sausages in my pocket?"

"Yeah, that's something I'll never forget. Doing quantum physics would have been easier," I replied.

"Well – and you should sit down for this one because I still can't believe it myself – Butch walked heel. I just let him lead, to go wherever he wanted and he walked, about a pace ahead, but never so far away that I couldn't reach out and touch his tail. He should have been sound asleep, but here he was, leading me on the same walk that you and I had just come back from.

"When we got up to the top of the embankment and made our way to the lookout spot where you could see over the whole valley and wetlands, it was still drizzling and he still hadn't left my side. *This is Butch we're talking about here! Butch never walks heel! Ever! Period!* He led me to the big tree where we always said it would be a great place to build a house because of the view, and then he just stopped and leaned against my leg with his head looking up at me. His face was so full of love that I just had to bend down and give him a hug even though he was soaked. At that moment, the clouds opened up, just enough to let a little ray of the sunshine through, but it was shining on us. The only sun in the whole valley and it was on me and this wonderful dog I was holding in my arms. He gave me a lick on the face, took off at a run, and the sun disappeared just as quickly as it had come.

"Dave, I don't know how or why, or anything about what just happened, but it was Butch's way of telling me not to worry and that everything would turn out alright. I feel really good now. I believe he's got a sense that knows these things and he needed to tell me, in his own way. Once he'd left me and the sun was gone, he was right back to his old self again. Heel, which he had done so well without any prompting, was forgotten, though I didn't care. He took me up there to give me this message. He knows it's going to be good. He just had to take care of my fears first."

With our luggage packed up and in the car, it was time to say goodbye to the campers. Franzi was feeling a bit better because of the sign that Butch had shown her the day before, but when it came time to say goodbye, the tears still flowed.

"I'll just be gone for a few days, guys, and when I get back I'll be as good as new," Franzi promised the boys. "We'll spend all our days together and I won't leave you anymore." Both of them gave her a lick on the face to say goodbye, and Maenam even lifted her head from the comfort of the pillow on the bed where she was sleeping.

Franzi, who'd been very strong during the whole time since the last trip to Calgary, was starting to get nervous during the drive, bringing up a few "what if?" scenarios, but I cut her off before she could get started.

"We agreed we would stay positive," I said. "It's all going to turn out good."

After arriving at the hospital and getting her unpacked and settled into the two-bedded room, we were told that it would be alright if we left the hospital as long as Franzi was back by five that afternoon. And so, leave we did. Saturday was to be our anniversary, so we decided to go out for an early celebratory dinner, without the wine.

That evening I stayed with her in her room, watching some mindless television sitcoms and we were fortunate that we could be alone. The other bed to her left had stayed empty. That was what she wanted, but there would be someone arriving the next day. I didn't want to leave that night as the 9:00 P.M. visiting time limit neared, but I promised I'd be back first thing in the morning, before the operation, and told her that the boys were counting on her. Naturally, she had their pictures on the table beside her bed.

At eight o'clock the next morning, after a terrible night of hotel sleep, I was back in her room. Breakfast, on this day, would consist of a sedative. She was very emotional and afraid. Since she had been through way too many operations before, I guess the thought of "when will my luck run out?" had to run through her head despite all the positive thinking.

The time had come and she didn't want me to leave, so I was allowed to accompany her down to the prep area. Seeing the panicky state that she was in, the nurses must have thought it better if I was to accompany her as long as possible. While waiting down in the prep area along with about four other people who were also getting set for various operations, we met the anaesthesiologist, who could obviously sense Franzi's distress. He politely introduced himself to us.

"Hello, Mrs. Cassidy, my name is Doctor Bean and I'm going to be the one who puts you to sleep today."

Having just watched the *Mr. Bean* movie a month or so before, Franzi's eyes, probably from the effects of the sedative, popped wide open.

"Mr. Bean?" she said, with a small smile on her face.

"Yes, I get that a lot," he replied.

"I love you to the moon and back," I said to Franzi, and after a kiss and a hand squeeze, they wheeled her off. It was tearing me apart inside, as I wanted to be with her throughout the whole ordeal, but it just doesn't work like that in the real world, so I had to be content with wandering the halls of the hospital, talking to the higher powers of the universe.

The wait seemed interminable, as I must have made the same loop within the hospital walls five times without registering anything mentally, before I settled into the waiting room to flip through year-old copies of *Us* and *People* magazines. The stars and all of their problems seemed so minuscule compared to

Franzi's, but they sure did get a lot of print. *Who's had breast implants? Who's sleeping with whom? Are Ben and Jennifer going to last...blah, blah, blah?* They must have served their purpose though, because when I looked at my watch, another hour had passed: only another hour to go, if all went well.

The next two hours (which should have only been one), dragged on and on, and the fact that the doctor or any of the nurses hadn't come out yet was really making me nervous. *What was happening? Where was she? Please, oh please, let everything be alright.*

Someone up there in the prayer-answering department must have heard my mental pleas because shortly thereafter, the doors to the hallway opened up, and out walked the urologist who had performed the operation. He saw me running up to him and probably had visions of being tackled because I was moving pretty quickly, and he even stepped a bit to the side as I got closer.

"Doc, how'd it go with my wife?" I managed to blurt out. "Is she okay? Is everything alright? Why'd it take so long?"

"Relax!" he said to me. "She's in the recovery room right now and in about an hour or so they'll be moving her back up to her room. The operation went well, but we had to remove part of her urinary tract as well as the whole kidney. The tumour was very close to breaking through the kidney wall, and luckily it was a very slow-growing one, which she could have had for years. The kidney had probably stopped functioning quite some time ago, but it'll have to be monitored every couple months for the foreseeable future."

"What about chemotherapy? Is she going to need that?"

"No. We got the whole tumour out. If it had broken through the kidney wall, it would've been a different story. She's very fortunate that it turned out like it did. Not everyone is so lucky. She'll be pretty much out of it for the evening, but you can be with her in her room when they bring her back."

"Doc, I don't know how to thank you enough," I said with my voice cracking.

"You're welcome. Like I said before, she was one of the fortunate ones. Not everyone comes away so lucky."

If someone had walked up to me right then and there and handed me the thirty-million-dollar winning lottery ticket, it would have been so minor in comparison to the joy and elation that was pumping through my veins at the thought of Franzi coming through the operation with the success that she had. This was damn good news, and for the next hour I made it my mission to see that good news travelled fast. I called her parents, her brothers, my parents, her friends, and anyone else that I had in my cell phone address book. I even phoned Judy, making her promise that she told Butch, Sammy, and Maenam about our good fortune.

When they finally wheeled Franzi back into her room, which now had another person in there scheduled for surgery the next day, she was really zonked out. With lots of tubes sticking out of her and machines being rolled in, I did my best to stay out of the way until they had her all settled in and gave me the green light to pull up a chair beside the bed. There I sat, just holding her hand, thanking the universe for making me the luckiest guy in the world.

An hour had passed since she'd been returned to the room and she was beginning to stir – first with her eyelids fluttering, and then a little pressure on my hand. She was coming around.

"Is it over? Dave, is it over?" she asked, trying to lift her head. "My stomach pain is gone. It's gone." And then she closed her eyes again.

"Yes, it's over. You're back in your room and everything went perfectly." I wanted to tell her everything the doctor had told me, but she had dozed off once more.

That whole evening, as I sat with her, she only opened her eyes a few more times, which I attributed to the morphine drip they had her hooked up to. After I sat with her as long as I could, the nurses finally told me, very politely, that she'd be a lot more responsive in the morning, and that I could come back at nine. I took the hint, said goodbye to my sleeping angel, and went back to the hotel, feeling a lot lighter inside than I had in weeks.

When I arrived the next morning she was sitting up with a tray of breakfast in front of her, as well as some juice and a coffee. Right outside her door in the hallway was a big poster of all the things that were supposedly bad for your kidneys. Most people would think that smoking would be at the top of the list, because smoking is just bad for everything in general, but topping the list was coffee. I was a little disturbed to see that the drink they gave her the first morning after the operation was coffee. Perhaps she had threatened them, because this was her drink of choice first thing in the morning.

"Dave, I don't remember much from last night. Were you here?"

"Of course I was here, right up until the point where they almost threw me out," I answered. "How are you feeling this morning?"

"I've got a lot of pain from the surgery which is to be expected, but my stomach pain is gone. It hasn't been gone for the last fifteen years. The urologist was just in here checking up on me and he told me everything about the operation. I think it's safe to say that I got pretty lucky. An eighth of an inch more and it would have broken through the wall, and then I would have really been screwed. He figures that I'll have to stay here for about four or five days so they can keep me under observation, and then I can go home and be with the boys and Maenam again."

It was good to see her with her senses again, even though she could push the morphine button whenever she felt the need for a little relief. She did that very sparingly because she knew that they monitor the usage at the nurses station, and her reasoning was that the less she used the button, the quicker they'd let her go home.

I'd learned from experience that when Franzi was in the hospital, she never touched the food that they gave her with the exception of yoghurt, so she'd always get me to eat it to make it look like she was playing by their rules. I didn't mind, not being very fussy, but I had to remind her that she needed her strength, too. It was always the same battle, but this time I had a feeling that it might be the last time that we had to walk this walk together. The fact that she had no more stomach pain was phenomenal, and although I'm not a doctor, a little bit of common sense told me that the kidney that was so enlarged due to the tumour must have been squeezing something in her stomach to cause the constant pain. The doctors who treated her in Switzerland never checked on the kidneys. Even the urologist had never seen this form of kidney cancer in someone so young before. He even asked Franzi if she would mind if he used her kidney (which had been removed) as a teaching tool at the medical school.

"No problem," she said. It wasn't like we wanted to take it home and put it in a jar on top of the television, anyway.

We spent the whole day in her room, counting our blessings, with me helping her to the washroom and even taking her for a walk down the hallway a couple of times. After I'd finished off her dinner and was about to head to the hotel, the topic came up about me leaving the next day. I wanted to stay and she wanted me to go back home to the boys, and then come and pick her up when they released her. As with most of these kinds of discussions, I came out on the losing end and it was agreed that after I'd eaten her breakfast the next morning, I'd be on my way.

I was happy to get out of the hotel the next morning, but didn't feel too wonderful about leaving her there by herself in the hospital room.

"I'll be fine," she said. "The most important thing is that you get home and you take the boys for a good long walk. They probably think that we've abandoned them. Give them all a hug and tell them that I'll be walking with them again in no time. And say 'thanks' to Butch for me, because he knew it would be alright, long before we did."

Four days later, we came home to the house where we were going to grow old together. That fact looked a lot more certain than a week previously. It was a very beautiful sight as we got out of the car (Franzi still with her catheter in), and I let the boys out to greet her. Normally, the two of them would be jumping all over her with excitement, but when they got up close, they both slowed right down and proceeded with caution. Dogs have amazing senses and they figured out right away that she wasn't the top fit mommy that they'd seen just a week before. They went to her slowly, so she could pet them, but their tails were wagging faster than the wings of a hummingbird.

Chapter 14
Where Did They Go?

*W*ith patience not being one of Franzi's strong points, it came as no surprise to me that she wanted to get back to a normal life as quickly as possible. It was an ongoing struggle after she arrived home to get her to rest. The catheter stayed in for a few more days, but once that was out I really had to keep an eye on her.

"You don't just heal overnight," I told her.

"Yeah, but I feel bad that you're looking after the whole household, and I'm jealous that you get to go for the dog walks while I'm stuck in here."

"Baby steps, Honey, baby steps."

The one thing that brought her great joy while she was cooped up inside was that Butch would never leave her side. He was her new guard dog, protecting her every step around the house. Day by day, as her strength returned, she would venture out into our snow-filled yard, doing what she called "mini-walks" with Butch and Sammy. These little mini-walks progressed into ten-minute, then fifteen-minute, and then half-hour walks with the boys.

There was no holding her back anymore, and after a month out of the hospital, she was pretty much back in full swing and wanting to get back to work A.S.A.P. Christmas and New Years – the busiest times of the season in the heli-ski business – were upon us, and luckily I was able to get through to her to wait until the big rush was over before heading back to work.

"The company won't fall apart without you. It'll still be there in two weeks time."

Skiing was out of the question for the winter, but we made up for that by doing a lot of snowshoeing. There was no speed involved in this sport (unlike skiing), but it was a good workout and helped her build up her strength again. The best of all was that it was a sport that Butch and Sammy could also partake in. They loved barrelling through the deep powder snow, and on a few rare occasions they would step on the backs of my shoes, causing some fantastic face plants into the white stuff. For some reason unknown to me, they only seemed to step on the backs of *my* snowshoes.

Butch was absolutely in his element in the snow. Where Sammy would get bogged down when the snow got too deep, Butch would jump and plough his way through anything. Even when we thought that there was no way he was going to get out of the snow-drift he'd just disappeared into, the black nose would somehow find a way to poke its way through. At times, all we'd see would be the snow moving, and we

239

would wonder if we should try to rig a snorkel up to him so he could stay under the snow even longer. In the deep powder, he was literally a yellow submarine.

We'd often talked about how it would be so great to have a puppy from Butch, even though he listened only selectively. What he had in the love and feelings department more than made up for his inability to follow simple commands. He was sensitive when he knew that something serious was going on, and when life was good, he'd revert back to his "Tasmanian Devil" state.

After the whole kidney ordeal, Franzi's way of thinking took a bit of a left turn. What was once "someday" quickly turned into "now." There was no longer any point of putting things off for sometime down the road, because that little scare taught her that you never know if there's going to be a "sometime down the road." It was time to live for the present, and if you wanted something, you went for it. This was the thinking of the new and improved Franzi. I liked it.

With the "let's-dive-right-into-it" gusto, we set out on a quest to find the perfect female Lab that would be a worthy recipient for Butch's manhood. He was coming up on his seventh birthday and we were pretty sure that, with the exception of cushions and stuffed animals, he was still a virgin. It was time to show off his manly European side and all we had to do was find the right partner for him. That was a lot easier said than done.

The first thing we did was simply ask around.

"Does anyone know of a female Lab available for breeding purposes?" No, no, and no. We weren't really expecting much from this approach because the vast majority of all dogs in North America are spayed or neutered, but we had a plan B: a classified advertisement to be run in about six different newspapers covering a two hundred mile radius.

"Hi, my name is Butch and I'm a gorgeous six-year-old yellow Labrador retriever. Born in Switzerland, but now residing in British Columbia, I would love to meet up with a feisty female Labrador for the purpose of producing some puppies. If you're interested in this Eurostud, please give me a call."

The first week that the ad ran in the papers, we had four phone calls. "Not a bad response," we thought. Two of the respondents gave us the slimy impression that they were running a puppy mill, which we wanted absolutely no part of. Butch's offspring were to be cared after in similar fashion as the royal family, so they just wouldn't cut it: scratched off the list. The other two respondents sounded quite a bit better and they were both from an area two hours south of us, so we agreed to drive down there on a Sunday afternoon and check out the females.

The first family that we met with at their home didn't give us the positive vibes in person as they had on the phone. Their house was run-down and the female dog was shut up in a small kennel out in the backyard that looked like it hadn't been cleaned in two weeks. The lady was about five months pregnant, with four little ones surrounding her and the two of us just had to say no. After seeing the conditions that their dog had to live in and four little kids running around with another on the way, it just didn't seem like the right surroundings for Butch's offspring. We wanted Butch's female friend to be the centre of the universe for the owners who would have to look after the mother and the puppies. We couldn't see that happening with these two people.

The other couple that we met were like night and day compared to the first ones. In their mid-fifties, they had a small hobby farm with chickens, cows, and a few goats. They were very friendly people as well as very down-to-earth. Their black Lab was named Daisy, and she was just gorgeous. She and Butch – if they hooked up – would be having the best looking puppies in the world, no doubt. They seemed very impressed with Butch, commenting on how big he was and what great muscle form he had. Although the two dogs were both on their leashes when we met, Butch was already showing some serious interest in her rear end. True love is often found in the sniff of a butt in the doggy world.

They said that Daisy was eighteen-months-old and would love to have Butch give it a try as soon as she went into heat. They seemed to know more about the breeding process than we did, and said that the bitch is the most receptive between the tenth and fifteenth day of her heat. They had a guest suite in their basement and told us that we were more than welcome to stay with them when the time arrived. We graciously accepted their offer and were quite excited about the possibility of having the pick of the litter if and when it ever happened.

Butch seemed quite excited about the whole potential hump-fest, too. When we tried to get him back into the truck, all he wanted to do was head back to Daisy. If I didn't know better, I'd say he had a crush on her.

Franzi came through her first full check-up, back at the hospital in Calgary, with flying colours. These exams were to be every three months for the first year, every six months for the next two years, and then every year for the next seven years. Ten years in total, where she'd be constantly reminded of how lucky she was. Physically, she was back to normal, but the thought of how close she had come to something a lot worse played on her mind quite strongly from time to time. She tried her best to push these thoughts away, which was her own way of dealing with it, but I wasn't so convinced that blocking it all out was the best way to get over it.

The snow turned into slush, which then turned into mud, and eventually springtime was rearing its pretty little head again. Our dream home, although very beautiful, was a heck of a lot of work to get looking good in the spring. The animals always did their best to help me with digging up the garden, but their assistance wasn't always appreciated when it came planting time. When I closed the garden gate to keep them from entering, Butch became extremely vocal about being barred from the area he had worked so hard turning over.

The log work was also one of his favourite jobs. Every couple of years the whole house had to be stained, and this spring was one of those years. With me up on the ladder, and Butch normally positioned right underneath, he often had more spots on him at the end of the day than a leopard. Sammy was the specialist for knocking over the can of stain and then walking through the puddle, leaving his footprints all over the deck. It was always frustrating when these incidents happened, but we loved them nevertheless and couldn't imagine living in this great place without them.

Six weeks later, with Franzi finished work for the winter and the golf course back in full swing, we got the call that Daisy was going into heat and it was time for Butch to dust off the tackle and start spreading his little seeds of joy. He seemed oblivious to the whole thing when Franzi told him we were going to see Daisy, but when we pulled up to their house and she was out in the front yard, he just went wild in the back of the truck. Sammy, having never seen Butch like this before, cowered in the corner. It looked like Butch was finally about to lose his virginity.

The owner said that Daisy was on day eleven as far as he could tell, and should be good to go. When we let the back gate down on the truck, Butch did his best Superman impersonation by trying to fly all the way to where Daisy was standing. With his feet eventually hitting the ground he beelined it over to her and the sniffing party started in earnest. Daisy was playing a little hard to get, constantly turning her rear end away from the big yellow humping machine who already had his rocket out and was raring to go. There would be no wining and dining before the act took place judging by the look on Butch's face. He was on a mission, with his ears back in their "excited" state, and his eyes giving her a look as if to say, "Come on now and let's get this thing going. I've waited almost seven years."

As with many first-timers – in both the human and animal world – things didn't exactly go off as planned for Butch. After circling her for about five minutes and trying to mount her but not being allowed, he just couldn't help himself anymore, as his little seeds of fertility starting spraying into the air, missing the target by a good three feet.

All that effort expended and somehow he knew it hadn't gone as it should have. The puzzled look on his face made that pretty evident. Perhaps we should have had him watch the nature channel prior to throwing him into the game.

"No big deal," we all said. He'd have plenty of time to figure it out in the next three days, after which I'd have to be back at work. If it happened, that'd be great, but if not, then it wasn't meant to be. It was our dream for a puppy from him, but maybe he had no desire to have another little one pestering him for a year.

Later that evening he tried again, but Daisy still wasn't in the mood. It could be that she had a headache; that seems to be a common deterrent to passionate romance. Another possibility was that maybe she just didn't like, or want to get intimate, with Butch. There could've been a German Shepherd just down the road that none of us knew of, whom she was wildly crazy about. Either way, as it became apparent the next morning, Butch seemed to have given up.

She would still go to him as they cruised around the farm, and they would play together, but the sexual interest, for reasons totally unknown to us, seemed to be gone – at least on Butch's part. The following day was no different and when there was still no interest on the third day, we decided it was time to head back home. Disappointment was what we should have been feeling as we made the two-hour drive, but it was actually worry that was in our heads. *Why wasn't he interested? Was there something wrong with him physically or was it a mental thing?* We both agreed that when we got home, we'd make an appointment with Mark, our vet, to have him checked out.

We hadn't thought to have Butch checked out beforehand, just assuming that he was only approaching seven years old, middle age, and it shouldn't be a problem for him whatsoever. When we saw Mark a few days later, he examined him and stated that although he could find nothing wrong with Butch, the dog world can be a little mysterious in this department. He told us that a dog that can breed, will, and that if the dog feels that he's no longer able to or that something is physically wrong with him, he won't even try. Always trying to put a positive spin on things, we took it to be a good sign that he at least tried on the first day. Maybe he was just past his prime. Not a lot more thought went into the subject until later that summer.

Maybe seven years old was just that point in his life where he knew it wouldn't work anymore. Physically it might work, but perhaps dogs can sense when the sperm count isn't up to snuff. *Who knows?* What we do know is that the summer of 2002 was the summer when we noticed that Butch had finally started to slow down, but only a bit. A three- or four-hour hike was still not a problem for him, but he seemed to have gotten quieter at home. They say that Labs normally settle down when they're three or four years old, and we were actually starting to wonder if the yellow ball of energy was ever going to slow down. Sammy was only turning four years old, but since he never really got going too fast in his life, it was hard to tell if he'd slowed down any.

Beat, Kathi and Dominic had come to spend a few weeks with us in August, which was again a pleasure. Beat was happy to see that Franzi had come through her kidney ordeal with flying colours, and we could both tell that he had some unpleasant feelings about not being able to tell us about what was going on when we were back in Switzerland the previous fall.

They loved what we had done with the house, which they were directly responsible for us purchasing, and when I wasn't working, we'd occupy our time by playing tennis, mountain biking, golfing, hiking with the boys, or just going down to the beach for a swim and some sun. We had a lot of fun together and for Franzi, these visits were always so special because she didn't see her family very often, and she and her brother were extremely close to one another.

Just before they were about to leave they told us they had planned on coming over every two years and we said that we would try to get back to Switzerland a little more often. Family is important, and just because we lived so far away, keeping in contact and visiting was a very high priority for us. Her parents weren't getting any younger, and Franzi was blessed to still have them both. Though you never know, when you're saying goodbye at the airport, if it'll be for the last time.

Labour Day weekend is the unofficial end of the summer season here in the valley. There are still a lot of tourists that come in September, but as soon as the long weekend passes, you can almost hear a collective sigh of relief from the locals. Everyone is so busy during the summer months that autumn is viewed with great anticipation. It means that people have time in their lives again; time to spend with their families and time to touch base with friends who've been just as busy over the summer months. September means that you don't have to wait in long lines at the grocery store and that you can find a parking spot in the downtown core. It is also the most beautiful time of the year for hiking, with warm sunny days and crisp mountain air that is so clear you can see for miles and miles.

On one particular hike we took up into a valley called Jumbo, we walked for close to four hours before settling down beside a glacier stream to have a picnic lunch. These lunches were always an adventure because you had to guard the backpack full of food from the prying snouts of Butch and Sammy. We'd bring all kinds of treats for them, but they felt that they should be entitled to our treats as well. Butch was constantly in the freezing glacier stream, coming out only to stand beside us as we lounged in the long grass and shake all the water from his fur, thinking that we too needed to be cooled off. If you were dozing off even a little, this whole experience was like having a bucket of ice water dumped on you.

As I sat up from the most recent spraying, reaching for my T-shirt to wipe my face off, I noticed that Butch, who was standing a few feet away with his bum towards me, seemed to have smaller testicles than the ping-pong ball-sized ones that normally adorned his caboose.

"That water must be damn cold to make his balls shrivel up like that," I said to Franzi, who had avoided most of the shower that Butch had shared with me.

"Yeah, they do look kind of small don't they?" she said. "Is that normal?"

"No idea." I replied. "Mine don't shrink like that, but then again I don't spend an hour in glacial streams either."

Later that night, totally exhausted from the hike, I was laying on the carpeted floor in the living room, with Butch beside me, and decided to have another look at his baggage to see if it really was from the water or whether our eyes were just playing tricks on us. When I lifted up his leg, he gave me the "What do you think you're doing?" look, but put his head right back down, too tired to really care. Sure enough, they were smaller – a lot smaller. Like half the size smaller. Alarm bells started to go off in my head because this just wasn't right. I grabbed his scrotum in my hand and gave it a good squeeze, which again brought his head rearing up in my direction. What used to be two healthy little egg-shaped things the size of ping-pong balls were now two mushy little things the size of marbles. "This can't be good," I thought.

"Franzi," I yelled, "get over here and look at this!"

"What?" she said, somewhat startled, as she'd been half-dozing on the sofa.

"We weren't imagining it today. His balls are shrinking!"

"Oh my God!" was all she could say, as she too grabbed them and gave them a squeeze. "We've got to phone Mark first thing in the morning. This isn't normal."

Butch, who probably thought that he was in the middle of some veterinarian examination nightmare, put his head back down and went back to sleep – something that didn't come that easily for either of us that night.

The next morning Franzi was on the phone as soon as the vet office opened, only to find out that Mark was gone for a few days. There was a replacement vet there if we wanted to see him, but neither of us trusted these replacement guys like we did Mark. We decided to wait the extra couple of days and see him when he was back.

Over the next three days we kept quite a close eye on both Butch's behaviour and on his marbles. He was acting and eating like normal, and still giving us attitude whenever he felt like it was time for a play round, but those little marbles he had were quickly downsizing to peanuts. Within a couple days' time they had visibly shrunk again. The whole sack was still there, but it was almost totally empty except for the two little peanut-sized testicles. At this pace, there'd be absolutely nothing left in two days' time!

Something was definitely not functioning properly within the inner workings of Sir Butch, and we were both counting down the hours until we could see Mark the next day. Even a day of searching on the Internet didn't shed any light on Butch's dilemma.

We took both of the boys with us to the clinic the next morning, because we knew that Sammy would panic if Butch wasn't around at home, and that didn't seem like a nice thing to do to him. What he didn't object to though, was waiting in the car while we took Butch in alone. He knew what happened within those walls, and was quite content to wait outside. It almost looked like he had a smile on his face as he watched from the car window as Butch put on his best braking manoeuvres at the front door of the clinic.

When we marched him into the examination room Mark was waiting for us, and in his cool, calm manner, asked, "Well, what seems to be the problem with Butch?"

"Mark," Franzi said, "I don't know. It seems like he's losing his testicles. They shrank to almost nothing and it's freaking me right out."

Mark checked him out, poking and prodding, the whole time with a very puzzled look on his face, and after about five minutes said, "I've been working as a vet for about ten years now, and I've honestly never seen anything like this before. I'm going to have to run a series of tests here."

And tests he ran – tons of them: blood samples, stool samples, skin samples. Test after test after test, and a month later there was still no definitive cause. Everything seemed to be normal on the little guy, and his testicles, once they had reached the soybean size, stabilized and stayed that way. The one thing that we were definitely sure about, though, was that Butch really hated going to the vet clinic.

Franzi, who would leave no stone unturned, even contacted Maya (Butch's breeder in Switzerland), to see if she'd ever heard of this happening. That was a big "N-O," but she did give us the name of a professor at the University Medical Centre for Animals just outside of Frankfurt, and after receiving Franzi's e-mail about Butch, he too was at a loss to explain what had happened.

No one could figure it out, but we knew that he wasn't in any pain or acting differently so we decided to let it go. It didn't seem right to subject him to an endless series of tests on the off-chance that maybe something would be found. What it did bring into clarity a bit more was his behaviour during the breeding time with Daisy. He must have sensed that something wasn't one hundred percent with his equipment and that was probably the reason he gave up on trying to mount her.

There was no change for the next few months and after a while we didn't think about it anymore. It didn't seem to be bothering Butch, and that was the main thing. Most dogs get neutered at the vet's office, but it looked like Butch had decided to forego the surgery and do it himself.

This was going to be Franzi's sixth season at the heli-ski company, and before it even got going, things went seriously south. The owner suffered a major heart attack and passed away on the one-year anniversary of her surgery, and this was a major blow to her morale as well as all the staff who worked for him. He was a hard but fair boss whom she really looked up to and respected. With his passing, the atmosphere changed quite a bit and most will say for the worse. Franzi had committed herself to work for the winter, and never one to go back on her word, she did, but we also knew that it would be the last season she would do. It was time for a change.

Chapter 15

A Mirror of Franzi's Health

The winter season was a long and arduous one that, with great relief, finally ended for her. Up until this point in the Canadian adventure that Franzi was on, she'd only worked winter seasons, taking the summers off, but even that was getting a little old. She wanted contact with the outside world and that was best found when working, so for this reason, the job hunt started in earnest for her.

Seasonal jobs were a dime a dozen here in the valley, so finding one wasn't a problem. Finding one that paid decently and would allow her to only work three or four days a week was a little more difficult, but with time she stumbled upon one that would eventually change her life. The job was as a front desk receptionist at a spa situated at the hot spring pools in the village of Radium Hot Springs.

It was only a ten-minute drive from our house and she could work her hours around mine so that Butch and Sammy were seldom left alone for more than an hour or two. This was a key factor and had it not worked out so well, she never would have accepted the job. The boys always came first and that would never change.

The hot springs were a bustling place in the summer months. British Columbia has incredible scenery, with the mountains and the lakes attracting tourists from all over the world, and the hot springs were a huge draw with people both young and old. I preferred them in the winter when it was cold outside and there were a lot less people around. During the summer, there were always busloads of tourists and at times you could hardly even move in the pools.

Needless to say, summer was the time when the spa also thrived. Franzi didn't get to use her five languages as much as when she was working at the heli-ski company, but she enjoyed her new job, regardless. There were different challenges and things to learn, and she also had free use of the pools as well as the steam room – which she absolutely adored.

The pace was very hectic at the spa, and even though there were four massage therapists working there, they could have easily used another one or two. People would walk in right out of the pools, wanting a quick massage or some other treatment, only to hear that there weren't any available spots for that day. Having to turn people away was the part of the job that she wasn't too crazy about. The staff on the front-line always took the brunt of people's frustrations.

Butch, who was now barrelling towards his eighth birthday, was doing alright; although his testicles were still the size of soybeans and his pace had continued to slow down around the house. Out on the daily walks, it was now Sammy who seemed to be putting on the most mileage, zigzagging all over the place. Butch would still run and play, but he just seemed to have lost a step over the last year. He was our first dog, and we accepted it as part of the aging process, thinking that at eight years old (which would translate to somewhere in his mid-fifties in people years), it was only natural that he wasn't the wild playing-machine that he had been in his youth.

Sammy and Butch would cruise around the woods surrounding our house, playing in the stream and lounging on the deck when they became tired. It was during one of these lounging times, when we had company over for a barbeque, that I noticed something that would turn our lives upside down for the next year or so.

Looking down on Butch from my comfy chair at the table, I noticed that his leg looked a little strange, like there was a big tuft of hair sticking out. While the others remained inside in the kitchen, I bent down to examine it, slowly running my hand down the inside of his back right leg until my fingers were literally stopped by a very large obstruction – or a lump. Not just any old run-of-the-mill kind of lump though, but a lump about the size of a golf ball. It was an evil looking lump – evil because it was big and evil because big lumps usually meant only one thing: the "C" word.

"No. Don't let it be true." I said to myself with closed eyes, but when I opened them again, the lump

was still there. Butch turned around and gave me a big lick on the face, and looked at me as if to say, "What are you doing? Why are you checking out my butt area again?"

My heart sank down into the bottom of my stomach as I looked at this beautiful dog who already had a brush with death under his belt, just lying there on the deck, oblivious to the world around him with the exception of the piece of steak that might happen to make its way from the picnic table down to his waiting jaws.

"What had he done to deserve this?" I wondered. He was a great dog with the perfect personality, and even though he didn't always feel like listening, his loyalty to Franzi and me never faltered. He loved children and was extremely gentle and tolerant with them when they pulled his tail or ears, and there wasn't another dog out there that he didn't get along with. It just wasn't right.

When our company left a short while later, I showed Franzi what I'd found on his leg, as much as I didn't want to. She, who'd held it together pretty well when she was told that she had cancer, didn't do so well this time around. Her tears came fast and furious as she checked the lump over, and then over again, and then over yet again.

"Dave," she said after regaining her composure, "we have to get this checked out right away. Waiting won't help here – it has to be now."

And there wouldn't be any waiting. It was a Saturday evening and the vet clinic was now closed, but all forms of correctness seemed unimportant at this point so Franzi phoned Mark at his home, and it was a good thing that she did. The next morning he was leaving with his family for two weeks of summer holidays and would be unable to meet her at the clinic. But he could, however, meet her at the grocery store parking lot as they were on their way out of town. It didn't matter where he saw Butch, as long as he saw him and could give us an idea of what we were dealing with.

The next morning we both woke up early and quickly checked out the lump again. Unfortunately, we both swore that it had gotten bigger overnight. Maybe it was our imagination, but it really seemed to have grown.

With a big golf tournament going on that day and 200 people to feed, I had to leave for work, but I promised Franzi that I wouldn't hang around and would come straight home as soon as the luncheon was finished. Butch, who normally liked to sleep in a bit in the morning, was very restless this particular morning – probably due to his sensing that our world was not in order. When something was bothering us, it had a major impact on his behaviour. Nervous and clingy would probably be the two best words to describe how he acted when we were worried or panicked.

Franzi was supposed to be at the parking lot of the grocery store by nine, but I know she was there and waiting at eight-thirty, just in case Mark happened to be early, but with four little kids in tow, early didn't happen. Mark knew that we were both stressed out, which he'd heard the night before on the phone, and when he did finally show up he did a quick examination of the leg with Franzi keeping Butch calm in the back of the truck.

She knew right away, just from the look on his face, that it wasn't good. Mark is a very good-natured guy, who has the special talent of making you feel like your animal is the most important animal in the world when he's working on him or examining him, and he always had a good rapport going with us, as well as with many other animal owners that we know. But on this morning, he was quiet. Not a word was said as he checked our friend over.

"I'm sorry, Franzi, but it definitely looks like a tumour. What kind of a tumour is hard to say without doing a biopsy on it, but I'm going to send you to a place in Calgary – an animal veterinary hospital that specializes in cancer – because I know how much you and Dave love this dog, and I, too, want to see him get the best treatment possible. This hospital is certainly one of the best in Canada." His voice was reassuring.

"I know in my heart that it's cancer, because Butch ends up getting everything bad that I've had. What I don't understand is why we didn't see it before yesterday? Just look at it; it's huge. I even think that it's grown since yesterday. Mark, is that possible?" Franzi asked, puzzled.

"Yes, it's very possible. Some tumours grow very slowly, much like what you had in your kidney, and some you can almost watch grow. What I want you to do, though it won't be cheap, is get on this right away if Butch is to have any kind of a chance."

"Believe me; we will do whatever it takes to save our friend. He's too special."

"Okay, I'll phone them right now. There probably won't be any doctors on, but I know the head surgeon and I'll leave him a message explaining what I think Butch has, and I'm going to stress the urgency with him. I'll tell him that you'll give him a call first thing tomorrow morning and that you would like to set up the first available appointment for Butch. Is that alright with you, Franzi?"

"Yes, thanks so much, Mark," she said.

Sitting on the sofa when I came home in the early afternoon, Franzi had Butch in her arms, and she'd been crying.

"It's so unfair, Dave. Why does this little guy have to go through the same crap that I had to?"

Just that sentence told me everything I needed to know about his outlook and the tumour. I was asking myself the exact same question. It wasn't fair that this little guy, who was supposed to grow old with us too, was now facing a very uncertain future.

"He was fine when I took him for a walk this morning; running and playing like normal. If this tumour is giving him problems, he sure isn't showing it by favouring the leg or anything like that. If it's bothering him, well then at least he doesn't know what it is, which is to his advantage. Humans aren't so lucky."

"So, Mark obviously thinks it's a cancer tumour then?" I asked.

"Yes, and he couldn't even be optimistic about it. I could see in his face that it's serious, and we have to phone the animal hospital in Calgary tomorrow morning. That's what Mark arranged for us, and he thinks that is where Butch will have his best chance. They're supposed to be really good, but Dave, just like we always talked about – I don't want him to have to suffer. We owe him that and he can't speak for himself, so no matter how hard it might be, we have to do the right thing for him if it comes to that point."

As much as I didn't want to go there or to even think about that possibility, I knew she was right, and all I could do was nod my head, while putting up one hell of a fight to hold back my own tears. The last thing in the world I wanted to imagine was a life without Butch. Once again, just like a year and a half previously, it was time to think positive, and remain that way.

The next morning we were on the phone. *"Please God. Please let us be able to get him in there as soon as possible"* was the only thought running through my head. We wanted to know what we were dealing with – simple as that. It was the uncertainty of not knowing what was going on that was so hard on both of us.

The receptionist, it seemed, had already checked the messages and told us that Doctor Dave (the doggy cancer doctor), would be able to see Butch on Wednesday at 10:00 A.M. *"Perfect,"* we thought. Only two days to wait. That wasn't so long. *We could handle that right?* Or so we thought. It turned out to be the longest two days that I can remember, as we both tried our hardest to not let our worry show to our little friend.

Butch didn't seem to catch onto our worry, but Sammy sure did. He was always a little more receptive to our moods and this was certainly no exception. Wherever Butch went, Sammy was right there with him, imitating his shadow, virtually. On the walks, the two of them normally went their own separate ways exploring the woods, but for those two days Sammy didn't let Butch out of his sight, sticking with him every single step of the way.

When Wednesday finally arrived, we packed up their blankets, a couple of portions of food, and their leashes, and loaded the boys in the back of the truck. Even Maenam, who normally couldn't care less what the dogs were up to, came out to the truck to say goodbye. At six-thirty we were on the road, not wanting to be late, and after a few stops for nature calls, we arrived with fifteen minutes to spare.

We left Sammy in the truck with a bowl of water, under a nice shady tree because it was going to be a very hot day, and in we went with Butch, who was looking a bit confused at not having his brother with him. The waiting room was large, with a few other dog owners – pets in tow, sitting there all looking as dejected as we probably were. One lady was talking to the receptionist about procedures for getting her animal cremated and we knew that could easily be us. Needless to say, the waiting room was not a very happy place.

Doctor Dave was a tall, athletic-looking man, who introduced himself to us in his green scrubs, and then to Butch, who he referred to as "Sunshine."

"Hi, Sunshine. Aren't you a beautiful dog? Let's see what we can do for you."

Like any surgeon, he was faced with heart-wrenching decisions on a daily basis. *Which patient has a chance? Which patient is going to suffer if we prolong the inevitable? Which one will have some quality of life if we perform the surgery?* There were a whole pile of hard questions that he had to deal with as part of his everyday job. I didn't envy him, but I did admire how he treated Butch and the other animals. If you didn't know any better, you would think they were all his pets.

Lifting Butch up on to the examination table didn't go over too well. He'd seen enough examination tables and started trembling and panting and even tried to jump down a couple of times. With Franzi holding his head and me taking over the hind end, we managed to get him on his side, while Franzi whispered soothing words into his ear and scratched and petted him non-stop.

After some poking, prodding, and measuring, Dr. Dave looked up and said straight out that it didn't look good.

"The tumour is right on the joint, and that's always a bad sign. Has it gotten any bigger since you first noticed it?"

"Yes," we both said in unison. "We only saw it on Saturday for the first time, but it's definitely grown since then."

"I can't know for sure what kind of a tumour it is until I do the biopsy and send that away, but my biggest worry is that the cancer might have spread to his organs. Although the odds are in our favour that it hasn't spread, there's always a chance and we won't know for sure until we do the whole series of X-rays. Are you folks alright with staying around here for a few hours?"

"Absolutely," I answered. "We want to know what Butch's dealing with here. Oh, and another question – do you think that this tumour has anything to do with Butch losing his testicles?"

"He lost his testicles? I just assumed that he was neutered because there's really nothing there except skin," he said.

"If you feel for them, they're there. They're just the size of soybeans. That happened about eight months ago."

Sure enough, his hand was down there checking them out and he too was quite shocked.

"I've never seen or heard of that happening before. I'll see if I can find some information on that."

One of the nurses came in after we got our trembling friend down off the table and led him away to the X-ray room.

"C'mon Sunshine, were going to go get some pictures taken of you."

Dr. Dave told us that it would probably take about an hour, so if we wanted to go and get a bite for lunch, now was the time. With food being the farthest thing from our minds, we just wandered outside to the truck, and got our other little friend out so he could stretch his legs. Sammy started sniffing the hospital smells on our clothing and then looked up and made a whining sound as if to ask us, "Why didn't you bring my brother back?"

"Sorry Sammy, Butch will be back with us soon. Now we just have to wait and go for a little walk." Neither Franzi nor I spoke very much during that half-hour walk, both caught up in our own thoughts, and without any real answers other than he had a cancerous tumour, any words would just be speculation. I think we were both simply too busy praying that the disease hadn't spread to any of his organs to make conversation.

When we went back inside we decided to bring Sammy in with us. He had that look on his face that told us he didn't want to be left alone; that he wanted to wait for his brother with us. It took about fifteen minutes and then Butch, stopping to sniff as many crotches as he could along the way, was brought back out to us.

"I'm sorry, but Dr. Dave just got called into an emergency surgery, and it's going to be a few hours before he can talk to you about the X-ray results. Do you mind waiting?"

Every minute that we waited was torturous, but what were we going to say, really?

"No, of course not," we replied. At least Sammy was a happy camper again as the two of them traded licks. The next couple of hours were spent with either Franzi or me walking the two boys while one of us waited to see if the doctor had finished up with the surgery and had some results for us. It was while I was on doctor-duty and Franzi was out, that I started wandering around the waiting room, looking at the paintings and plaques on the walls – having already flipped through every magazine they had. On one wall I came across a printed page that had been framed, and after reading it, I could feel the tears running down my cheeks. It was called "Rainbow Bridge – Author Unknown."

Just this side of heaven is a place called Rainbow Bridge.

When an animal dies that has been especially close to someone here that pet goes to Rainbow Bridge.

There are meadows and hills for all of our special friends so they can run and play together.

There is plenty of food, water and sunshine, and our friends are warm and comfortable.

All the animals who had been ill and old are restored to health and vigour; those who were hurt or maimed are made whole and strong again, just as we remember them in our dreams of days and times gone by.

The animals are happy and content, except for one small thing; they each miss someone very special to them, who had to be left behind.

They all run and play together, but the day comes when one suddenly stops and looks into the distance.

His bright eyes are intent; his eager body quivers.

Suddenly he begins to run from the group, flying over the green grass, his legs carrying him faster and faster.

You have been spotted, and when you and your special friend finally meet, you cling together in joyous reunion, never to be parted again.

The happy kisses rain upon your face; your hands again caress the beloved head, and you look once more into the trusting eyes of your pet, so long gone from your life but never absent from your heart.

Then you cross Rainbow Bridge together.....

I just knew that if I was to show Franzi this little piece of literature, she'd lose it for sure. I just asked for a copy – like so many people do who have to sit in that waiting room – folded it up, and put it in my pocket.

Franzi returned with the two boys and it was now getting close to 3:00 P.M. We just sat there looking down at the two campers when, finally, Dr. Dave came out and invited us back into his exam room – this time with Sammy tagging along. He had a whole series of X-rays up on the lighted panels and was just about to start explaining them all when Franzi, who couldn't wait anymore, came right out and asked, "has the cancer spread to the organs?"

"No. In all these pictures you see here, I couldn't find any. That's the good news. The bad news is two-fold. First, if you look at this one here, you can see that the tumour is almost wrapped around the joint, meaning that parts of it will be intertwined. The removal of the tumour, which I want to do a biopsy on, is extremely difficult, and it will be hard to get all of it out without serious damage to the leg. Normally, in these kinds of situations, we amputate the whole leg to be sure that we get it all."

Not thinking too straight at all, I thought to myself, "That's great. They can get rid of the cancer." Then the consequences of what he'd said set in. Butch was an active eight-year-old dog. The people who lived down the road from us had a three-legged dog that was known as "Tripod," and he couldn't run at all. All he did was lie around or hop from place to place. He'd been like that from the time he was a pup, after being run over, so he really knew nothing else. For Butch, who's known only wild activity, that would be a crushing blow to his whole quality of life. *What a dilemma; save his life so he can spend his remaining time hopping around, or put him down?* But then again, I told myself, he's not that old, and maybe he'd surprise us and adjust quite well with only three legs. Looking into Franzi's eyes, I could clearly see that having a "Tripod" wasn't an option.

Not letting us dwell on the negative tumour news for too long, Dr. Dave then hit us with the knockout punch.

"Has Butch had any trouble breathing, or shortness of breath? Does he sometimes cough a lot?"

"No, he doesn't have any of that." Franzi replied. "He goes for at least a two-hour walk everyday, and for most of that walk he's running and playing. And when he's in the water, he can swim for an hour. Why do you ask us this? What else is wrong with him?"

"Well, if you look at this picture here, it's the chest X-ray of a Golden Retriever that we took yesterday.

He's the same size as Butch and also very active. This area here," which he pointed to with a pencil, "is his heart. It's a healthy and strong heart: nothing wrong with it at all. This picture over here, which you can see is taken from the same distance, is Butch's heart." Again he outlined the heart with the pencil. "As you can clearly see, Butch's heart is roughly twice the size of that of the golden retriever's. That's not good. It's extremely enlarged and I'm really surprised that he can run at all. If you look at the ribs here in the breast cage, you can even see that it's pushing against them."

It was hard to not go numb from what appeared to be an unending series of crushing news, and the room seemed to have suddenly gotten a lot smaller. What he was saying was true. The pictures weren't lying, as much as I'd wished they were. Butch's heart was shot and his leg had to come off. I was really starting to wonder if he'd even be coming home with us again.

"What I want to do is get a full ultrasound of his heart, which will give me an idea if he's even strong enough to survive a surgery should you decide to go that route, but our radiologist is away at a conference and won't be back until next week. So if it's okay, I'd like to go ahead and schedule that for next Tuesday. I can see that you're undecided about the leg and I still want to do a biopsy before you leave today. It'll show me what kind of cancer we're dealing with here and what kind of follow-up treatment may or may not be needed."

"Sure," was all I could mutter.

"We're going to have to put him out for the biopsy, so it'll be another three to four hours before you'll be able to take him home with you. We'll get started on it right away, if that's what you want."

Franzi and I talked in tones normally reserved for viewing areas in funeral homes, and it was obvious that she was thinking more clearly than I was. Her autopilot had again been turned on, and I was at least a bit relieved to see it.

"This is un-flippin'-believable. A week ago we had one of the happiest dogs in the world, and now it feels like we're getting ready to bury him. Dave, I want the biopsy done. I want to know as much as there is to know about what's wrong with him. Also the ultrasound – we're going to do that next week also. I'm not going to lose this dog without a fight. He's not suffering right now and that's the main thing. He helped me through the toughest time of my life, and I owe him. I owe him big, and I'll do whatever I can for him." And I knew she would.

"Okay," we said, "let's do the biopsy."

Butch was again led away from us, this time to a room in the back, which I could only assume was the surgery room. Before he turned the corner he looked back at us with a look on his face that just screamed out "What the hell is going on?"

Absolutely dazed, we walked out of that place for the umpteenth time that day, not saying a word. With Sammy at our side, we just walked and walked and walked. And then we ate: a couple of fast food sandwiches, which Sammy benefited the most from due to our less than ferocious appetites.

"You know Franzi, he could still be okay with only three legs. He's not that old and he can still learn to adapt. He definitely won't be as mobile, but he'll still be with us." I really didn't want to face up to the fact that we might have to put him down. Cancer on the leg and a heart that was about to explode didn't bode well at all for the prospect of a long and healthy life.

"Dave, I don't want to see him hobbling around trying to keep up with Sammy, because he knows nothing else. We didn't even know about this heart thing. Did you see the size of that? Even Dr. Dave was shocked by it. In German, we call that a "*sportler*" heart. A lot of the top athletes have hearts that are bigger than the average person's heart. We always knew that he had a big heart, but that wasn't the picture that I wanted to see. Do you think that it's so big because he's a top athlete in the dog world?"

"Oh honey, I would love nothing more than for that to be true, but I think we're looking at something here that goes beyond a highly athletic, over-walked, dog's heart. He doesn't show the signs that Dr. Dave described but he has slowed down in the last year or so, and you can't deny that."

"Yeah, I know – I just don't want to admit it. I really don't know what I'm more afraid of: his heart that's pushing on his rib cage, or the cancer. I just can't see him with three legs. That's not Butch. Butch is majestic, and should remain so.

When we went back to the clinic around six, most of the staff were at the front desk eating pizza. Normally the hospital would close its doors at this time, but as they explained to us, life happened, and it wasn't unusual for them to be there until nine or ten at night, a few nights a week.

Dr. Dave came over to us with a slice in his hands and told us that the biopsy went alright and that Butch should be coming around any moment. When we came back the next week for the ultrasound, he should have the results and then we could decide on a course of action. It was then, from the bowels of the hospital, that we heard a long, pitiful howl.

"That would be your Butch coming around. He's having the flight of his life right now."

We'd never heard Butch howling before, but he was sure doing his best wolf impersonation now. Sammy, who'd been very quiet all day through the whole ordeal, just nestled up against Franzi's leg and started shaking. He couldn't understand what was happening with his big brother and he wanted him back. Except for when Sammy was neutered, they'd never been separated from one another, and he was more than scared, obviously.

At around seven-thirty, one of the nurses brought an extremely groggy looking Butch out to the waiting room area. With Dr. Dave's instructions to keep him warm, and only minimum exercise, he was given the "okay" to go home.

We settled up the hefty bill from the ten-hour hospital day, and I remember thinking that this was an awful way to earn air miles. Butch was still pretty much out of it; so putting him in the cab of the pickup truck wasn't an option. Franzi wanted to keep him as warm as possible, and with a three-hour drive ahead of us, through the mountains at night, she decided that she would ride in the back of the truck with him, and Sammy would be my co-pilot in the front. Even with the canopy on the back of the truck, it could still get pretty chilly at night, so she wanted to stay back there with him and make sure that he didn't throw off his blankets. It was illegal to ride in the back, but neither of us cared about that at the moment. We just wanted our friend to be comfortable.

The ride was uneventful, and my co-pilot was extremely nervous in the front. He didn't like being separated from Butch, and this, along with Butch's state of health, totally overwhelmed my thoughts. There were thirty-mile stretches that I didn't even remember driving. I was just suddenly there and couldn't remember any of the roads we'd covered.

It was a relief to finally be home at eleven that night, and even Butch had recovered from the anaesthesia as he showed by jumping out of the truck and running inside to see if there was anything in his food bowl. Franzi took a little longer to recover from the cold and bumpy ride, but after half an hour with the electric heating blanket wrapped around her, she, too, was better.

Chapter 16
From Bad to Worse

*O*ver the next few days, we spent as much time with Butch as we possibly could, walking, swimming, and playing stick. These were the joys of his life, and as long as he still could, we wanted him to have quality of life. Dr. Dave told us to go easy on the exercise, but Butch would never have understood that. If we even tried to walk him for only half an hour he would surely take off on his own and turn it into an hour and a half.

Our jobs were probably the only things that kept us sane. If it weren't for having to go to work, interact with other people, and perform different tasks, we probably would have made each other crazy. At night, when we were home alone, Butch was the only topic that was ever brought up.

I was getting my head around the idea that he could adjust to three-legged life and still have some quality, but Franzi was going in the exact opposite direction. The whole monster heart thing was another factor that she used in her arguments.

"He's going to have to work so much harder to get around on three legs, and we don't know if his heart can take that."

The truth is, we didn't know very much at all at that point, and after about three days of non-stop deliberations we decided to stop making ourselves crazy, and just wait and see what they said the following Tuesday. The one positive thing during those difficult days was that Butch's tumour had ceased its rapid growth pattern. It grew a tiny bit, which we knew from measuring it twice a day, but nothing like it had grown before we saw Dr. Dave.

When we made the trip back the following Tuesday, we were both on pins and needles as to what the radiologist was going to tell us about his ticker. Sammy again was in distress when we left him in the truck, but we were hoping that on this day it would be a quicker visit than the marathon of a few days previous. Butch, who had a great memory, didn't want to go back inside, as he made obvious to us with his full braking position by the door. Even the sight of other dogs in the waiting area just inside the door wasn't enough to change his thinking, so with all ninety pounds in my arms, Butch made his entrance. Once he was inside and took in a few crotches, he seemed to settle down a bit. Or maybe it was just resignation.

"They carried me in here and the door is closed, so what's the point of fighting it?" At least he was a logical dog.

Dr. Sue, the radiologist, came out to meet us and Butch seemed to like her right off the bat. She had a very soothing voice, which must have put him at ease, or maybe it was the pile of treats she had in her hand. Either way, he followed her willingly. She told us that she was just taking him in the back room to shave his belly and get him ready for the ultrasound, and that she'd come out and get us both before she started the tests.

A short while later, we were greeted in the hallway by a very different, and what I could only guess would be an embarrassed-looking dog. His entire belly had been shaved, as well as his chest and some of his sides. He didn't have a happy look on his face, and he actually reminded me of one of those poor little kids who has to go back to school and face the ridicule of the others after their mother had given them a haircut using the dreaded bowl. It was almost like he was looking around for something to cover himself up with before any of the other dogs saw him. Butch would have warmly welcomed even one of those stupid doggy sweaters, usually worn by handbag dogs. Franzi bent down with a smile on her face, gave him a big hug, and that was all the medicine he needed to get his tail in motion again. With his best brave face, we headed into the ultrasound room together.

Getting Butch up on the table was again the same battle, with the extreme shaking and the terrified look on his face, but I couldn't blame the poor little guy. The last time he was put on a table like this, he woke up stoned out of his mind. When he was settled into the right position, again with Franzi holding his head and whispering soothing words in his ear while I held down the rear end of the bargain, Dr. Sue got started. First he had to have some kind of jelly smeared on his belly, and then she ran the little machine over different areas.

She said very little during the whole process, concentrating on the lines and numbers showing up on the computer screen as she went along. When she was finally finished thirty minutes later and we'd gotten Butch back on all fours and off the table, she had a rather grim look on her face. *"This can't be good,"* I thought.

"Your little friend here is suffering from dilated cardiomyopathy."

"Cardio what?" I asked, having never heard the term in my life before.

"Cardiomyopathy. Let me explain. Dilated cardiomyopathy is a disease of the heart muscle, which makes the heart get bigger and not function properly. It's commonly found in the larger breeds of dogs like the Doberman, Newfoundland, Irish Wolfhound, Boxer, Golden Retrievers and Labrador Retrievers. DCM, as it is known for short, can start anywhere from four to ten years of age in a dog and the cause isn't known. Some researchers think that it's genetic.

"It usually affects both the right and left sides of the heart, and normally both the ventricle, which is the lower chamber, and the atrium, which is the upper chamber, get bigger. The lower chamber loses the ability to contract and pump the blood out into the body or out into the lungs. It's very similar to when your basement floods and you're pumping out the water with a sump pump. If that pump breaks down, the water will back up into the basement. If the right heart fails, then the fluid will back up into his abdomen or the area surrounding his lungs. If the left heart fails, the fluid will back up right into his lungs. With the information from the ultrasound, it looks as if your Butch is somewhat progressed in his state. His heart is extremely large, and the disease normally progresses to the point of congestive heart failure. What I could call a positive is the fact that the fluids haven't started accumulating in the lungs or abdomen."

"Yeah, but what does this mean for Butch? Can we treat it somehow?" I asked. As if cancer wasn't enough, the Gods of misfortune were now dumping a failing heart on our friend.

"There are a series of drugs we can use to slow down the whole process, which are targeted at improving the functioning of the heart and controlling the signs of congestive heart failure."

"Please," Franzi said, "just tell us what drugs we have to give him to keep him alive."

"I'll write it all down for you, and the prescription will be ready for you after you've seen Dr. Dave across the hall. I have to talk to him first about the ultrasound results, but you're welcome to wait here until he's available."

As she left the room, Franzi and I just sat there with our heads in our hands, thinking that the odds for Butchy were getting even more insurmountable. Staying positive had just been dealt another major blow.

Dr. Dave saw us all a short while later, and after measuring the tumour again, he seemed pleased that it had only grown a bit. What he said though, was basically what we'd been expecting. The biopsy results showed that the tumour was a malignant fibrosarcoma grade 2 and if we wanted to keep Butch, the best chance we had was to remove the whole leg. Even then, he said, the cancer could return in a year or two in another part of the body.

The other concern was whether Butch's heart could withstand the major surgery that it would be subjected to. Dr. Sue seemed to think that the odds were favourable, but there were no guarantees that he would survive.

This was a little too much to digest all at once, as Franzi and I sat there just staring at one another, each hoping that the other one would say something. Dr. Dave must have sensed this, having been in similar situations hundreds of times, and it was he who broke the silence.

"You have to feel that it's the right choice, for both yourself and for Butch, whatever you decide to do. I'd like to have another ultrasound done in about four weeks' time if you think that's alright and then we can make the decision about surgery. The tumour's not progressing as quickly as I'd expected, but it will spread – don't get me wrong about that."

Feeling like we'd just received a reprieve from the governor, we agreed that we'd be back in four weeks for the next ultrasound. Whether we would go ahead with the surgery or not would be our three-hour-drive home discussion.

Nothing at all was decided upon during the drive home. If his heart was even strong enough to survive the surgery, there was the chance that the cancer could return in just another year. Then we'd have a three-legged Butch facing the same fate again with, as we understood the radiologist, a much weaker heart. We both had real problems with the thought of the little guy making it through the operation, learning how to walk again minus a post, and then being right back in the same position. If it went like that, it would be like watching someone you really loved wither away in a long-term care facility. An operation here and there, and at the end of the day we'd be asking ourselves whether we had we just prolonged his existence or was there actually some quality of life in the whole exercise.

That evening and over the course of the next day our thinking seemed to be heading in the direction of not going through the surgery, making his remaining time with us the most extraordinary that it possibly could, and when the time came that we saw he was in trouble, we would let him go with dignity – as difficult as that would be. Butch had always been a majestic creature and he didn't deserve to leave this world in misery and suffering.

Franzi went back to work at the spa and I at the restaurant, but every single moment we were home was spent with Butch. Sammy, who didn't like to be left out and would often include himself when he wasn't involved in the activities, seemed to understand what was going on. He didn't get jealous when we played with Butch more than with him, and when Butch was at rest, Sammy would even walk up to him and give him a face-licking bath, something he'd never done before.

Three days after the last trip to the hospital, Franzi came home from the spa quite excited, and that was an emotion that we hadn't seen in our household for some time. She had a positive energy about her and I could see that she was just buzzing to tell me something good. "What's up?' I asked.

"Dave, you remember Ian, right?"

"Ian who?"

"Ian – the massage therapist who works at the spa." Franzi said, giving me a look like I was a space cadet. I'd only met the guy once and I'm terrible with remembering names.

"Oh, that Ian. Yes of course I remember him," I lied.

"Well, today he had an hour break because one of his clients didn't show up for his appointment, so he hung out at the front desk with me. We got to talking and eventually the whole story of Butch came up and everything we've been through for the past month or so. He knows of a woman – a friend of his – who might be able to help us with Butch."

"What do you mean by 'she might be able to help'?" I asked with my interest piqued despite my scepticism level being set on high.

"Well, this lady works with people who have all sorts of illnesses, including cancer, and apparently, according to Ian, she has a pretty good success rate. She's not a doctor in the western medical sense, but has a vast medical knowledge. She is a healer who works with diet, herbs, essential oils, and all kinds of other things that you probably think is hocus-pocus voodoo stuff, but the truth, Dave, is that I want to see her. Butch will die, sooner rather than later as it looks now, and I don't want that to happen knowing that we didn't exhaust every avenue to help him. You do remember Frau K. back in Switzerland, don't you?"

"Yeah, I'll never forget that."

"Neither will I, and that showed us that you can't always count on regular medicine. There are alternatives out there, and in Butch's case, I really think we have to explore them."

Once again, she was right. I didn't make any comment on her last statement, instead choosing to watch Butch out in the back playing tug o' war with Sammy. The poor stuffed animal that was substituting for the rope didn't last long, with the final result being a tie, as it always was. They both celebrated their victory by prancing around the yard, each with his own half of the stuffy in their mouths. Butch was just beautiful to watch and still so full of life. We had nothing to lose by contacting this mystery lady and everything to gain, so my mind was made up right there.

Fifteen minutes later, Franzi was on the phone with this lady who was named Stancia. Franzi went through the whole story of what Butch had been through, answering all of Stancia's questions as they came up: he is eight-years-old, he doesn't have a cough, his energy level is still high, they say the best thing is to take the whole leg, his heart is double the size of what it should be, and so on, and so on, and so on.

Stancia didn't normally work with animals, but hearing the desperation and pleading in Franzi's voice must have convinced her to at least take a look at Butch. So when Franzi turned to me with the phone still at her ear and asked, "Can we be there at two in the afternoon the day after tomorrow?" I instantly said yes. It was a workday for me, but I'd figure that out somehow. My co-workers had been very helpful during the last month with all of Butch's appointments and I was hoping they would be again. If not, there were plenty of other jobs out there.

When Franzi had hung up the phone, my first question was, "Does she think she can help him?"

"She said that first she has to see him. The telephone is a great medium for general information, but until she lays her hands upon him, she can't tell. One thing she did say and was very firm about, was that if she thought Butch had a chance, we'd have to follow her instructions to the letter. No deviations whatsoever."

"Well, where exactly are we going, and can we bring Sammy along?" I asked.

"No problem with Sammy. He'll just have to stay out of the way while she's examining Butch. As to where we're going, it's a little summer town on Upper Arrow Lake about five to six hours from here, depending how often the ferry runs, because we have to cross a lake."

Being the former world traveller that I was, I immediately pulled out the map of British Columbia and found the place. As the crow flies it was only about seventy-five miles away, but this was the Rocky Mountains. The route there would take us two-and-a-half hours northwest and then another two-and-a-half hours southwest. *Whatever.* We would have driven Butch to Florida if we thought there was a chance someone there could help him.

I'd managed to swing two days off of work so we left early in the morning to make sure we wouldn't be late due to the ferry schedule, with our tent and camping gear stored behind the seats of the truck. It was mid-summer and we hadn't been camping in three years, so we thought it would be a nice treat for the four-legged ones.

Arriving in town about an hour-and-a-half early, we took the boys for a walk so they could stretch their legs, and then we grabbed a quick bite to eat, having forsaken breakfast so we could get off to an early start. We didn't want to show up at her house early in case she had other clients or patients. Two dogs barking their heads off outside her door wouldn't be the best way to introduce ourselves.

As soon as two o'clock rolled around, we were standing on her doorstep, ready to knock, but the door opened before my knuckles hit the wood. Standing there was a little lady, probably in her mid-fifties, with reddish hair and a welcoming smile that could melt your heart. It was genuine.

"Well, hello there. You must be Franzi and Dave. Where's Butch?"

There are times in your life when you know that things are just right, and this was one of them. She'd only said three short sentences, but just the tone of her voice put me at ease. She had this aura about her that I can't put into words, and Franzi said the exact same thing later that night when we were lying in our tent.

"He's out in the back of the truck with his brother Sammy," Franzi said. "They're not the best behaved and we didn't want them running you over."

"Sammy is a black lab," she said. "I had a vision in my mind about him. Let's go see them."

Franzi had not mentioned on the phone that Sammy was either black or a Labrador, and we both stole a glance at each other in disbelief as we followed her to the truck. Lifting the canopy window, both of the boys greeted her with wild exuberance, like they'd known her all of their lives.

"Should we let them out?" I asked.

"Not yet, I can check out Butch just fine right here."

She spoke soothingly to both of them, telling them that they were beauties and soon they were both sitting back down as if they were posing for a picture. She started off by petting Butch and then just held her hands above his head, moving them ever so slowly in different directions but not touching him. She did this in total silence with a very far-away look on her face for what seemed like an eternity but was only a couple of minutes. Finally, she broke into a little smile and gave Butch some big-time scratches behind his ears. He got up with his tail just flying back and forth, followed by Sammy.

"He's going to be okay," she stated.

"He's going to be okay," I thought to myself. *How could she tell he was going to be okay just by holding her hands over his head?* She hadn't even asked about or looked at the golf ball–sized tumour on his back leg. This was weird – really weird – but then I thought back to what Ian had told Franzi about Stancia.

"She works in some very strange ways; ways that I don't even bother to try and understand. Just trust me; she knows what she's doing. She's been doing it for years."

"Really?" was all Franzi could manage to say.

"Yes, really. He's just not ready to go yet," She said, nonchalantly. "If he was ready to let go, I would have seen the black shadow or ball above his head. It's not there. I didn't see anything. If you take care of him like I tell you to and follow my instructions exactly, then you're going to have Butch for quite some time yet. Sammy, on the other hand, is one of the most sensitive dogs I've seen and he would have real troubles if he were ever alone without his brother."

Well, that was definitely a whole headful to digest. As strange as it all seemed at the moment, I was feeling a great sense of relief because finally someone had told us that there was hope, and that we had a chance to save our friend.

"You can't always listen to doctors. They're trained in Western medicine and know nothing else. Chinese medicine has been around for five thousand years, and many ancient civilizations have used herbs and oils for hundreds of years or longer to treat many ailments. Western medicine is still in its infancy stages and many professionals are simply not willing to look at alternatives. They'd rather cut and radiate than look at the root of the illness. You can take out a lump, but that lump is only the end result of an illness that is within the body. The lump is how the illness manifests itself.

"The root of the cancer," she continued as she ran her hand over Butch's back, "is right here. Touch it."

I felt through Butch's fur, down to the skin, and sure enough there was something there on the rear part of the back, on the right side close to where his tail started. It was only a small area, about half the size of a dime, but the little area felt rough, like there were crystals attached to the skin, or sand.

"Yeah, I can feel it!" I said, excitedly.

"That is the root area. If you were to go straight down with a long needle, you would come out very close to the tumour on his upper joint. This illness is also the reason that his testicles have shrunken to the point they're at. His body is trying to fight this illness."

Logically, it all kind of made sense, which surprised even me. *"Could it really all be so simple?"* I pondered.

Franzi checked out the spot on his back as well, feeling it almost instantly, and then asked Stancia straight out, "How do we fix him?"

She gave a little chuckle and said, "Let's go inside, have a cup of tea, and we'll talk about that. Oh, and by the way, you should let those guys out so they can cruise around here. They can't get into any trouble."

So, in we went, stopping briefly to introduce ourselves to Paul (her partner), who was busy fixing some fencing in their garden. The house was filled with books – lots of books. Not novels or fiction, but books about anatomy, plants, herbs, oils, biology, medicine; all the kinds of books you would expect to find in some professor's office. So yes, as Ian had said, I guess she did know her stuff.

We sat there for a little while, reliving the last month of our lives and the whole ordeal at the hospital in Calgary, and all she said was, "You can't blame them because that's what they've been taught. Western medicine is useful, because it can show you the illnesses which you wouldn't be able to detect if you weren't in tune with your own body, but there are other solutions out there, also. My doctor told me many years ago that the tumours in my stomach would have to be operated on and I just said 'no way!' I started doing some research and got rid of them with essential oils. The problem is that although there are so many natural remedies out there, people are always looking for the easy way. With many illnesses, curing them naturally involves a total lifestyle change. Diet is the key here.

"I want Butch to get a good portion of real salmon – and not the fish-farmed stuff – in his diet everyday. For breakfast he's to get a cup of fresh goat milk. You'll have to find someone in your area that raises and milks goats. The next big one is no more carbs for him, whether they are dog cookies, table scraps, whatever. Wolves never eat carbs in their natural diet and your dogs shouldn't either. And absolutely no pork – that's the worst you can give them. If you really want to give them red meat, make sure they're organs; and only organic organs. There's too much garbage in regular meat. What you will also do is give him a capsule of Frankincense oil; fifteen drops, three times a day, as well as putting five drops on the spot on his back that I showed you. Frankincense was one of the gifts that the three Wise Men brought the baby Jesus, so they knew of its value even thousands of years ago. Aloe Vera powder will also be a large part of his diet and I want you to begin this now. I've got a supply of oil and powder here to get you started but you'll have to get a lot more for this treatment to be successful. Here are the companies that you can order the Frankincense and the powder from; order *only* from them. I've researched and tested many, but these companies have the best products. Don't delay, because it's really important that he doesn't miss even one round of these natural medications.

"If you have any questions, phone me or e-mail me. I probably won't answer the phone, but leave a message. I'm extremely busy with clients and I'll do my absolute best to get back to you as soon as possible."

We left after big hugs, feeling better than we had in weeks and ready to dive into our new treatment with Butch. It was late in the afternoon and the thought of driving back on unfamiliar roads, through the mountains and half in the dark, wasn't the most appealing thought. We'd promised the boys we'd go camping, so that's exactly what we did. We found a nice secluded lake, with just one camping site on it, and the water, which Butch so enjoyed, was as blue as the sky. After getting the tent set up, the dogs fed, and our dinner prepared, we started on the new treatment for Butch.

Chapter 17
To Better

*W*ith our obsession to get started on the new mission we spent the whole afternoon the next day playing around on the Internet, ordering all the Frankincense and Aloe Vera powder that we would need. As Stancia had said, "you can't miss even a single treatment." And we had no intention of doing so.

The few people that we told about our new treatment method were sceptical even though they tried to hide it, knowing that we were grasping at straws. But at least they didn't come right out and tell us we were crazy, and we appreciated their attempts at concealing these oh-so-obviously doubtful thoughts. We both told ourselves with our heads that it would work, and with our hearts we just hoped; that was all we could do.

Sir Butch, on the other hand, seemed somewhat bothered by the natural medicine route. He absolutely hated the taste of the Frankincense oil, which, even though it was put into capsules, he could still taste, and he wasn't nuts about the Aloe Vera powder either.

He probably would have preferred Tabasco over the oil, which really *did* taste bad as I sampled a drop myself just to see what I was putting him through. He would spit those capsules out quicker than we could shove them in his mouth, and it was starting to turn into a struggle until we figured out that if we stuffed them into a piece of salmon, they then went down a lot easier. It's pretty easy to fool a dog, but it doesn't say a lot about us humans because it took us a few days to figure it out.

Franzi would put the oil three times a day on the small spot on his lower back and even though the Frankincense is a very gentle oil, the spot soon started to get red, and then it crusted over. We weren't sure if this was a good sign or a bad sign, but after a quick e-mail to Stancia, she assured us that things were progressing just fine.

On about the sixth day of our unorthodox treatment, after coming home from a very nasty rain-soaked walk, our first tiny little miracle happened, or at least we saw it as a miracle. Franzi was drying Sammy and Butch off with a towel, which was the normal soaking wet dog procedure before letting them in the house, when she looked up at me and said, "Dave, check out the tumour. Maybe it's just me, but I think it's gotten a little smaller. Or maybe it just looks like that because his fur is wet. Check it out."

And so I did. It was hard for me to say whether it had shrunk or not, wanting so much to believe that it had, but it definitely hadn't gotten any larger – that I was sure of. Franzi was pretty positive that it had gone down in size "just a little, tiny bit" as she finished drying him off and gave him a big hug. "You see, Butch, you're getting better already!" she said to him.

I hoped so much that she was right, but just her assuredness was infectious. We decided that night that a bottle of wine was in order, and as we sat out on the deck with our good friend between us, Franzi raised her glass and said, "*Gesundheit* Butch; to your health." I was still not certain about the seemingly smaller tumour, but soaking up the joy in Franzi's face made that night one of the best in a long time.

"You know, Dave, a few weeks ago when I was sitting out here, looking at our yard and forest, the thought I had that day was, where are we going to bury Butch? What would be a nice spot for him?"

"I know, Franzi; I asked myself those exact same questions. I just didn't tell you because we agreed to stay positive, and I thought it would be a bad omen."

"Yeah, but we don't have to think about those things anymore. I know he's going to get better."

The following morning I was up bright and early getting ready for work, and after tricking Butch into yet another round of awful-tasting oil I decided to check his tumour again. He had settled back on the sofa for another forty winks, so it seemed like no better time. With my coffee in hand, I knelt down on the floor beside the sofa, and he didn't even stir. Perfect. When Butch was asleep you could pretty much do whatever you wanted to him within reason, and lifting up one of his legs was definitely within reason.

He had never shown that he was in any pain when we touched the tumour and I took this to be a good sign. With every light in the living room turned on, it kind of resembled a night game at Wrigley Field. I ran my hand along the leg and over the bump, examining it from about six inches away, and I swear my heart skipped a beat. It was smaller! Not a lot, but at least today I could see it with my own eyes. It had definitely gotten smaller.

"Franzi," I yelled, "get out of bed. Get out here, now!"

"What?" she mumbled as she stumbled from the bedroom. "What is it?"

"It did get smaller; the tumour's getting smaller!"

"I told you!" she blurted excitedly.

"Yeah, I didn't really see it last night, but today I can definitely see it."

It was going to be a good day. As positive as I'd tried to be, and as hard as I had hoped for something good, it caught me off guard when it actually happened. The little sucker was really getting smaller. The only one who wasn't excited by the whole thing was Butch himself. He just looked at us as if we'd lost our marbles, and then went back to sleep.

The following week was a virtual whirlwind of emotion and excitement. Everyday we jumped out of bed, woke Butch out of his slumber on the sofa with our callipers in hand to measure the progress of the tumour, and everyday except one, we were greeted with a tumour that had gotten smaller in size. It was unbelievable how it had shrunk so fast, and by the end of the week it was about a third of the size as when we started the treatment.

We phoned Stancia one evening and told her all about the progress that Butch was making and how happy and excited we were with the results, but she didn't seem surprised at all.

"Oh, that thing. You mean it's not gone yet? I'd almost forgotten about it. Right now I'm working on some research to see what kind of herbs will fix his heart. Gotta run – very busy schedule." And that was that. With what we were seeing happening to Butch's leg, the worry over his heart had suddenly gotten a little smaller.

The third week of treatment came to an end and the tumour had vanished. All that was left was a little tiny bump where the skin hadn't healed evenly from the biopsy, but other than that, his right leg looked and felt the exact same as the left one. And as if this wasn't enough, his testicles had started down the comeback trail from their soybean state. They weren't fully back yet, but with the way things were going for our dear friend, there wasn't a doubt in our minds that they'd be fully back soon and bigger than ever. Christmas had come to our house five months early this year.

It's not often that you take your animal to the vet or the hospital and actually feel good about it, but this was what we were experiencing when the calendar told us it was time to go back for another ultrasound and to make the decision on the course of action that we'd follow with Butch. I almost had a giddy feeling inside of me as I wondered how Dr. Dave was going to react at seeing that the tumour was gone. *Would he be happy, or shocked, or puzzled?* Time would tell, but first we had to see Dr. Sue for another round of ultrasound tests.

After a full month of growth, Butch had to be taken back into the shaving room once more and out he came with a smooth chest and belly, again looking not too happy about it. He had definitely not forgotten what had gone on within these walls just a few short weeks ago.

Dr. Sue ran him through the whole series of scans once again, very quietly and concentrated, not even noticing (or if she did, not saying anything about) the lack of a tumour on the back leg. She would have been a good person to have at a poker table, because you could pretty much read from her facial expressions how Butch's ticker was doing. Not well by the looks of it.

Our bubble of jubilation at ridding Butch of his tumour was burst quickly as she pulled the printouts from the machine and announced that our friend's heart had gotten worse. Not monstrously worse, but there was a progressive downslide.

"There's a new drug out on the market, which apparently has shown some good results in slowing down the progression of cardiomyopathy in dogs, and I'd really like to try it on Butch. I'm very concerned about some of the readings that have turned up today."

"Do you think it'll help? You do know that he's going to live to the ripe old age of thirty, right?" Franzi stated. Despite her bravado, I could see that she was a bit crushed by this latest news in the ongoing saga.

"It's hard to say if it'll help. He is getting worse and I really have some optimism for this new medicine that should slow down his symptoms. What we're trying to do is lengthen the period of time before congestive heart failure sets in. It's a great dream to think that he'll make it to thirty but it's not going to happen. I know that's not what you want to hear, but that's always the way that cardiomyopathy goes."

"We'll try the new drug," Franzi said.

"Good. I know that these ultrasounds are quite expensive, but I'd like to see him again in three months' time to see if the new medicine is helping. You won't have to pay because we'll call this research."

Now that his leg was better and his testicles had almost grown back to the healthy state that we remembered, we had to concentrate on his heart, and once again, we were willing to try anything.

"If worse comes to worse, at least he'll be standing on all fours when his time comes." That was the thought that went through my head as we walked Butch down the hallway towards Dr. Dave's exam room, but then I had to give myself a mental kick in the ass, because it was a negative thought and there was no room for those in the treatment of Sir Butch Cassidy.

When we entered the exam room, Dr. Dave was leaning against the examination table in his green operating scrubs, reading over what I could only assume was Butch's file.

"Good morning," he said. "How's our little Sunshine doing today?"

"Extremely well in some departments; not so well in other departments," Franzi answered.

"It says in the files that the leg would have to come off, but that all depended upon whether the operation was viable with his heart condition, and whether or not that was what the two of you decided on. I just talked with Dr. Sue, and she filled me in on the worsening condition of his heart, which I see as a real dilemma because the fibrosarcoma will just get bigger and spread throughout his body. I've even booked the operating room for early this afternoon in the event that we could actually do the surgery today."

Butch had curled up in a ball on the floor as far away from the exam table as possible, hoping that it would save him from having to once again go through the examination ordeal. You could just see his "Don't even think of touching me" face. His leg, where the tumour had been, wasn't visible because of the way he was lying, and when Dr. Dave asked us to help him get Butch up on the table, Franzi just couldn't hold it in any longer, and I was really surprised that she'd held out this long.

"Dr. Dave," she said excitedly, "the tumour is gone."

"Pardon me?" he responded.

"It's gone."

"No, that can't be. Fibrosarcomas don't just go away," he said, with a detectable note of sarcasm in his voice.

"Dr. Dave," Franzi started again, "read my lips. It's gone."

Where she'd picked up the George H. W. Bush line was a total mystery to me, but it seemed to get Dr. Dave's attention. He had a really quizzical look on his face, and while I was struggling with our ninety-pound friend who was resisting the best he could, Dr. Dave was flipping through his charts again. The puzzled look hadn't subsided. With Butch finally up on the table, he set his charts down and immediately started examining the back right leg. Not saying a word, he switched over and started examining the left leg, probably thinking that he'd gotten the wrong one; still no lumps. At this point, he was noticeably shaking his head back and forth, muttering words that weren't forming sentences. *"But...where...how...?"*

"It's not there," he stated, still with a look of disbelief on his face.

"Yeah, we know," I chirped in.

"Fibrosarcomas don't just disappear though."

Butch had noticed that we'd all let our guard down, so he took this opportunity to lunge off the table and head back over to the corner of the room.

"Testicles don't just disappear either, but his did." I countered. "Now they're back too."

The next scene brought watery eyes to both Franzi and me. Dr. Dave walked over to Butch who was standing in the corner doing his best to shield his back legs from any further observation, squeezed in behind him, and squatted down to do some further checking.

"Yeah, his testicles did come back. That's really strange. In all my years I've never seen anything like this. I was dead certain that when you came back today, I'd be looking at a tumour that had grown to the size of a baseball. Medically speaking, I can't explain the tumour or the testicles, but whatever you two did to him, you did a damn good job. It's just unbelievable."

He then went from his squatting position, down onto his rear end on the floor with his legs out-stretched on both sides of Butch, and gave him a very long embrace, filled with scratches and pets, the whole time shaking his head with a monster smile plastered across his face. It was like he had just witnessed a miracle.

By the time he'd pulled himself away from Butch, some five minutes later, the smile was still stuck on his face. He was like a six-year-old on Christmas morning who had just gotten the puppy he had hoped for. He quickly excused himself, darting out of the exam room, and two minutes later returned with what looked like three quarters of the staff who worked at the hospital, showing them all our Butch – the miracle dog. Butch's tail was going like crazy at all the attention that was being showered down on him. He could tell that they weren't in the room to examine him, so he just soaked it all in.

When the mayhem had subsided and it was just the four of us in the room again, the natural question arose from Dr. Dave.

"How did you do it?!"

Franzi went into the long story about Stancia, the oils, the new diet, and the powders without missing any details, especially the part where Stancia had said, "we can fix that."

The whole time she was telling the story, he'd stop her with questions; some, which we could answer, and some, which we couldn't, but he never gave us the feeling of disbelief or doubt. In fact, he was totally fixated on every oil or powder that Franzi described.

When she'd finished the story, Dr. Dave said, "You know, I'm still having some trouble getting my head around what I've witnessed here today, but what I've seen with my own eyes cannot be denied. I'm a surgeon. It's what I do, with the Western medicine I've learned, but you've shown me that there can be other forms of treatment. They're treatments that I can't go into because my knowledge in natural medicine is limited, but it's great to see a result like this. If someone should come in, with a seemingly hopeless case that even I don't think will have a good outcome, and elect not to do surgery, perhaps I could tell them about this woman, 'Stancia,' who did such a great job of looking after Butch. Do you think she would mind if I contacted her? I've got a few questions I'd like to ask her and I'd like to know if it would be alright to tell people about her who are looking for alternative treatments."

"I'll give her a call tonight and ask her. Give me your e-mail address so that she can get in contact with you if she so decides." Franzi said. "I really don't think that she'd mind. Although she does mainly deal with humans, she has an enormous heart for all living creatures."

The ride back home was a sweet and a sour one. On the one hand, we both loved how Dr. Dave reacted to the news, and how genuinely happy he was for Butch. However, on the other hand, there was still Dr. Sue and her less-than-positive prognosis for our little friend's heart.

When I brought up the point that we'd just have to accept the fact that Butch probably wasn't long for this world due to the whole cardiomyopathy thing, Franzi once again showed her determined and strong-willed side.

"Dave, I know what the doctors say about his heart, but I truly, and I mean truly, believe that no matter what all the tests and scientific results show or say, from the bottom of my heart I can feel, and I mean really feel, that it's not Butch's time to leave us. He is not ready to go. I can see it in his eyes. I always promised all of our animals that they will never suffer, and I can feel that it's not the time yet to say goodbye to Butch. Anybody who tries to convince me otherwise will be shut out of my life for whatever period of time is required. I will not have any negativity around me. It's all about having hope and faith."

Butch definitely had the best mom in the world.

The rest of the summer, when we weren't both hard at work, was spent walking and hiking with the two boys. Butch still ruled the roost even though he was now eight years old and Sammy never made any attempts to try and take over the alpha spot. Butch may have lost a step over the years, but physically, he was still incredibly strong, and as stubborn as when he was in obedience school.

Dr. Sue had told us that we should try to limit his exercise a bit, so as to not put too much strain on his heart, and we actually did try that, for all of one week, but Butch wasn't having any of that. If he wasn't getting his ninety-minute or two-hour walks, he was pretty unbearable to live with, standing at the door barking or bringing any toy he could find for a play round. This wasn't the picture of a dog that had a bad heart. We monitored his overall attitude and watched him closely for any of the telltale signs that he was going downhill. There was no coughing, heavy or laboured breathing or fainting spells, and he definitely wasn't lethargic. There were absolutely no signs that he was sick – nothing, except for these bloody ultrasound tests which were making us crazy.

Having ceased with the oils and the powders, we were now on the internet hunt for natural heart medicines that could possibly slow down, halt, or even reverse his condition, and with Stancia's help in telling us what ingredients to look for, we finally found a homeopathic veterinarian way down in Hawaii. After a few consultations with him by phone, we found ourselves with a yearlong supply of some tablets called "Canine Cardio Health." We couldn't tell if they helped him or not because he wasn't showing any signs of being sick, but we still kept him on the heart tablets that Dr. Sue prescribed. I think we were just trying to cover all the bases.

Dogs, like humans, will all cough at one point or another, but when Butch would let out a little one, we'd both be on high alert, packing him into the truck and heading off to see our vet. Mark, who is strictly a Western medicine veterinarian, had followed Butch's whole summer of trouble, expressing the same amazement as Dr. Dave had at our results from the rather unorthodox treatment that we'd pursued. He was happy for Butch, but kind of at a loss with things that went outside the realm of his training. None of that really mattered to Franzi and me though, because the end result was all that was important.

The three months passed rather quickly, and the day that we'd been dreading was once again upon us. The ultrasound test was a freebie this time around, but we still didn't relish the thought of putting our little buddy through another round of belly-shaving and jelly-testing. Nevertheless, we went back. With nothing but bad news from Dr. Sue up until this point, who could blame us? Maybe it was just a morbid curiosity to know, but Franzi phrased it a little better. "The more we know about his heart condition, the better we can treat it."

"Progressively worse" was the diagnosis, as we helped Butch off of the table and onto the floor where he did his utmost best to hide from anyone standing on two legs. We could both tell from the look on Dr. Sue's face that the news would be bad, as we'd come to expect, and we weren't disappointed. "I could go into all the technical terms and aspects with you, but I know from previous visits that the two of you are obviously more interested in just the bottom line, so that's how I'll put it. Butch's cardiomyopathy has again gotten worse, and I know this isn't what you want to hear, but he's probably only got about six months to live; at the outside best, a year."

Butch took this news better than Franzi and I did because he'd found an open cupboard in Dr. Sue's exam room that contained a bucket of dog treats which he was helping himself to, totally oblivious to the death sentence that had just been handed to him. Despite the mortal blow that we'd both been hit by, my heart smiled just a little bit inside because he didn't have to deal with the worry of what we'd just heard. His only concept of time was "How long until my food bowl gets filled again?" A day, a week, a month, six months or a year – they were all the same to him. He was fortunate that he didn't know what was going on. He could focus on what he did best, just being Butch, standing on all four legs until the end.

For Franzi and me, the news came a lot harder. Up until this point, the whole cardiomyopathy thing had just been some illness that he had -something that would eventually slow him down – but now this illness had taken on new dimensions with the terms, "six months to live, and at the outside best, a year."

Would he go downhill quickly? Would the symptoms start showing soon? When would we know that it was time to put him down? These were just some of the questions kicking around in my head as we made the drive home from Calgary, but I didn't voice them. They went against the positive thinking principle that the two of us were trying to stick to.

As we drove along, Sammy started barking in the back, followed shortly after by Butch. This was a common occurrence when driving through the mountains and it usually meant that there was something wild out there, and sure enough, the boys smelt it before we saw it. Just off to the side of the road, flipping over rocks and looking for food, was a mother grizzly with her two cubs. We pulled the truck off to the side of the road to watch them because it's not everyday you see a grizzly bear, but the sound of two wild dogs coming from the back of the truck caused them to bolt towards the safety of the forest.

It was still a beautiful little bonus on an otherwise crappy day, and as we sat there watching them scamper away, Franzi turned to me and said, "I don't want to take him back for any more ultrasound tests. Every time we go there it's nothing but bad news. I haven't seen any difference in his behaviour whatsoever. He still runs, he still plays, he still swims, and he still gives us major attitude. Those aren't the signs of a sick dog. We'll treat him with the medicines that we have, and just keep a very close eye on him. If we see him starting to slide, then we'll deal with it at that time, but right now I'm going to do everything in my power to make his remaining time on earth as enjoyable as possible. No more short little walks or babying him – he hates that. His big walks and hikes are what he lives for, and if someday we're out in the woods and he keels over from overexertion on his heart, then so be it. He will have had a beautiful death, living his life right to the end. He deserves that. What will be, will be."

And that was how we carried on. There was no way Franzi was going to accept this death sentence that Dr. Sue had handed down on Butch, being utterly determined, by any means possible, to keep him happy and healthy, regardless of what some test said. We were constantly searching the Internet for information and various natural medicines that might help him, and we tried quite a few, but the problem was that he still wasn't showing any signs of cardiomyopathy, so we had no idea if all these natural medicines and the few conventional ones were actually working, other than the fact that he was as lively as ever, so we just assumed they were.

Chapter 18
Continuing Education and a Chico

The snowy season had crept up on us, and that was always a welcome time. The spa had slowed right down, as had the restaurant where I was working, which meant that we both had a lot more time for each other and the boys. We'd take them snowshoeing in the bush, or out on the frozen lakes, and they'd just have a blast barrelling through the powdered snow.

It was during one of these long marches just before Christmas that Franzi sprung a good one on me. Out on the middle of the lake, watching Butch run along with a frozen fish in his mouth that he must have stolen from an ice fishing hut, she turned to me and said, "Dave, when I was younger back in Switzerland, I'd always wanted to get into massage therapy, but with my stomach problems and all, I kind of put those thoughts by the wayside, figuring that I wouldn't be able to do it because it's a very physical profession.

It's now been over two years since my cancer surgery and my stomach feels great. I haven't had a single colic during that time and I just feel a lot stronger. All summer long I had to deal with people at the spa who were quite irate about the fact that we didn't have enough massage therapists, and it's not just at the spa where I work. All of the spas in the valley seem to have a shortage of therapists. What would you think about me going back to school and studying massage?"

Caught a little off guard with this sudden goal of Franzi's, I tripped over one of my snowshoes and landed on my face in the snow. All I'd ever heard from her was how much she hated going to school when she was younger, and now here she was, twenty-five years later, telling me she wanted to study again. I was very surprised, to say the least, but we'd always said that we should follow our dreams and pursue that which made us happy. If this was really what she wanted to try, then I would back her one hundred percent.

"Are you sure?" I asked, wiping the snow from my face.

"Of course I'm sure. I've given this a lot of thought. There's a program starting just after New Year's at the University of Calgary, which goes through to the end of April. It'll mean staying in a hotel a lot of the time, but I'd really like to give it a try."

"Okay then, let's get you enrolled. I'm not crazy about having only Butch and Sammy to keep the bed warm at night, but four months will go by quickly; or at least I hope so."

"You just have to promise me that when I'm gone you'll keep a good eye on Butch. If you can't promise me that, then I won't even bother going."

"Done deal," I said.

And so it was. The new year rolled around and off she went to Calgary on a weekly basis, studying what she hoped would be her new profession come summertime. It was hard for her at first because she wasn't used to dealing with all of the medical terminology in English, and although she spoke it fluently, writing it was another matter. At the end of the day when the other students would be leaving to go home, she'd still be there, making sure that she got everything just right. I was extremely proud of her for taking on this new venture, but I really missed her that winter. The boys did their best to keep me company and keep me distracted; they were always great at distraction.

Butch was going strong all winter long, showing no signs of his ticker failing as the six-month death sentence date quickly approached, and Franzi was just loving her new university experience. When she'd come home filled with knowledge from the previous week, she needed a victim to try out all of the techniques she'd just learned, and there was no way I was going to turn down all those free massages. I looked upon it as helping her with her studies.

She seemed to have a natural knack for massage, being able to find all the trouble spots on my body just by feeling around. She'd find spots where I didn't even know that I was aching, running her hands over my back or legs, and saying, "That hurts there, doesn't it?" All the other people that she practiced on said the same. She was a natural, and when the end of April rolled around and I went to her graduation ceremony in Calgary, she'd managed to finish first in her class of thirty people. She was just ecstatic about that, and I was one very proud hubby.

It took only one massage on her boss at the spa, and she was hired on as a full-time massage therapist, leaving the world of receptionist and front desk employee behind. It was again the perfect set-up for her because she worked afternoons and evenings, allowing her to spend the mornings walking with Butch and Sammy, and when I came home from work in the afternoon, I could take them out again for another tour. They didn't seem to mind being alone for a few hours, as it gave them a chance to catch up on their sleep after the morning hike.

We were still watching Butch like a hawk, monitoring his breathing when he was asleep, as Dr. Sue had instructed us to do. "Count the number of breaths he takes when he's sound asleep. It should be between thirteen and seventeen. When you see that those numbers are starting to go up, that means that fluid is starting to build up in either his lungs or abdomen or both. These will be the signs that he's starting to fail," she had told us.

For the six-month period after the last ultrasound, we'd been counting his breathing on a daily basis and that monster ticker of his had shown no change at all. When Butch slept, he consistently had between ten and twelve breaths, lower than that which Dr. Sue had said would be the norm. This was a good sign and when the sixth month anniversary came, Butch was treated to a steak, as was Sammy. We couldn't just give to one and not the other. Sammy never would have understood that one. We, in turn, celebrated with champagne.

Sammy, who was a very sensitive dog, had also been playing on our minds over the last nine months. He and Butch had never really been separated from one another, except for the many times when we had to leave him in the truck while Butch was in with the doctors, and he didn't react well to being separated from his older brother. Whenever they were apart, even for just a couple of hours, his whole demeanour would change afterwards. He'd barely eat, and if he did, he'd often throw it back up, and he wasn't his usual happy self. We could see it on his face and in his eyes. Sure, he was happy when we'd bring Butch back to the truck, but then his version of doggy depression would set in, sometimes lasting for two or three days.

It worried us, because Butch was three years his senior, and as much as we didn't want to admit it, there would come a day when Sammy would be on his own, with no big brother to play with or to go cruising with. It was a sad thought but a very realistic one. Dogs are pack animals, not meant to live solitary lives, although so many of them do.

For this reason, we started kicking around the idea of getting another four-legged friend for our family. We were afraid that if Butch were no longer with us, it would be really devastating for Sammy. Butch was still healthy enough to deal with the rigors of having a young puppy running around the house, and who knew, maybe he could even teach the little one a thing or two. We tried not to think of the new puppy as a replacement for Butch, because to do so was to accept the fact that he was leaving us, so we justified it by saying that a new pup would add some spice to both their lives and keep them active and younger in mind and spirit. *Well why not?* We had the space for three dogs on an open acreage and there wasn't much difference preparing two bowls of food or three, so the search began.

It only made sense that with a yellow and a black Lab already a part of our family, the next one would be a brown or chocolate-coloured one. A little bit of asking around was all it took to find the name of a breeder who had chocolate Labs, and she was only two hours south of us.

Not wanting to grab just any dog, we made a trip down to see her because she'd told us that her bitch was expecting in about three weeks' time. Franzi and I both wanted to see what kind of an operation she had going on. There are puppy mills out there and they are plentiful, so we paid her a surprise visit. If you let them know you're coming in advance, it gives the puppy mill people a chance to clean up their act before you get there, and we didn't want that.

When we got there, the house and yard looked very tidy from the outside, and the big male dog that was out of his kennel, just roaming free, greeted us. This was nice to see because normally in puppy mills, the dogs never see the outside of their cages. We heard some barking from the side of the house, where the female emerged, looking very pregnant and somewhat suspicious of the intruders. Our boys were in the back of the truck, expressing their verbal desire to get out and introduce themselves, so we let them out and the four of them had a great little play round while they were getting to know one another.

The lady of the house heard the commotion outside, and came out with a big smile on her face. She didn't look like a puppy-miller, and after the introductions were made, she invited us in for a coffee. Not wanting it to look like we were checking her out, I made up a story that we were on our way home from a weekend trip to Alberta, and just decided to stop by since we were in the neighbourhood.

Walking into her house, we knew right away that she wasn't in the puppy mill business, because there wasn't a wall that didn't have a picture of a dog adorning it. Little doggy statues were on the tables, and we both drank our coffees from Lab-pictured coffee mugs. These were definitely not the signs of someone who was just in it for the money. With both of our minds at ease, we expressed our interest in getting one of the puppies that was due in a few weeks' time, and she happily said, "Seeing what great shape your dogs are in, and how easy-going and friendly they are, I'd gladly like for one of my little ones to be going home with you. Would you like a male or a female?"

"Male," we both answered in unison. It wasn't that we didn't like females, but they were more work and things could get messy when they went into heat. The last thing we wanted was having our house turned into a porn film set, with Butch and Sammy trying to hump their brains out all day long. Butch wasn't neutered and although we weren't sure whether or not his newly re-emerged testicles actually functioned, we didn't want to take any chances. Having a litter of puppies on top of three dogs and a cat was unimaginable, because I knew that Franzi wouldn't have been able to give even a single one away, and the vision of *101 Dalmatians* was one that I wasn't eager to experience.

The summer carried on as we waited for our new family member to arrive, and then grow up enough to be brought home. Franzi was very busy at the spa, and not just because it was the height of the tourist season. Much of her clientele turned out to be the local people who had heard that she had "magic hands." This came as no surprise to me, because I knew that she was good, and more importantly, she absolutely loved what she was doing. Not a lot of people out there can say that they love their job, myself included, but Franzi was one of them. She also had an insatiable appetite to learn more and better herself, which led her to enroll in a series of weeklong courses all over North America. "Go for it, girl!" I said.

With Butch a full nine months into his death sentence, he was showing no signs of slowing down, or that his heart was bothering him at all. It was a joy to see him running and playing, and he could still handle a three-hour hike, barking at us near the end because he thought it was too short of an outing. We'd taken him to the vet for his vaccinations and Mark listened to his heart with the stethoscope, declaring that he was still doing quite well. There was a heart murmur that could be heard, but he didn't seem overly concerned about it. "I don't know what you're doing for him with the natural remedies, but combined with the regular heart meds that he's on, it really seems to be working. Then again, you two really stunned me with what you did for his tumour, so I guess I shouldn't be at all surprised. Keep it up." That was really nice to hear from Mark.

The pups were born on July 28th and around five weeks later we made another trip to the breeder so we could stake our claim on which one would be accompanying us home in another four weeks. When you're faced with twelve little adorable puppies, all scampering around their mother, it's not an easy choice. There were six males and six females – all brown – and you could see that the mother was pretty proud of what she'd accomplished. She also kept a guarded eye on us, being the ever-protective mother that she was. The little pups were all scuttling about, with one of the males taking on the king of the pack role, pushing all the other ones around. We quickly deemed him to be the bully of the bunch, so he was off our list. One of the little guys, who'd been body-checked out of the heap by the bully, noticed that there were some different humans observing him, and he tentatively made his way over to where Franzi was kneeling down. She picked the little one up, who easily fit into her hand, and attracted a very evil stare from the mother, who was watching her every move. She didn't do anything, but her displeasure was quite visible. "Dave, this is the one. Just like Sammy – he chose us."

"They all look pretty much the same. How are we going to know which one he is when we come back in a month?" I asked.

"Oh, that's not a problem," the breeder said, as she went into the kitchen and came back with a green felt-tipped marker. She flipped the little guy over on his back and made an X on the inside of his leg where there wasn't any fur. "Have you got a name picked out for him yet, just so I'll know what to call him?"

Naturally we'd been thinking about this for quite some time, with both of us in separate camps. I was fond of the East Indian name Raja, which meant "king," and Franzi liked the Spanish name, Chico, which meant "little" or "small one." The simple fact that our household already had a yellow-furred king meant that my choice for a name was a distant second place. So Chico it would be. It made sense, since he would be the little one, for at least a few years anyway.

"His name is Chico," I told her.

The four-week wait went by quickly, with Labour Day passing and the summer season coming to its unofficial end, and we found ourselves on the road again, going to pick up our new Chico.

He'd grown quite a bit since we'd last seen him, weighing probably about fifteen pounds, and when I searched the inside of his back leg, there was no X to be seen. The breeder said that he was our Chico, proudly stating that she could tell them all apart, and I really hoped that she was right. I didn't want to end up the little bully who had terrorized all his siblings the last time that we were there.

Like Butch and Sammy, he was very disorientated at being separated from his siblings, and he had a look of absolute terror on his face as Franzi tucked him into her jacket to protect him from the chill of the late September day. We let him say hello to his new brothers who were in the back of the truck, with each one of them giving him a good sniff-over, before setting out on the journey to Chico's new home.

We only made one stop during the two-hour drive, for the mandatory safety pee, with the little one going right back to sleep on Franzi's lap when we got him back in the truck.

Maenam, who'd expressed her displeasure at both Butch and Sammy when we brought them home by hissing vehemently, didn't disappoint this time around either. She must have thought, *"Not another one!"* Butch, on the other hand, had taken some time to warm up to Sammy, but was very different this time, wanting to play with the new puppy right from the beginning. Sammy's only real concern seemed to be that the little one was going to steal his bed beside the sofa. When Chico would get too close to it, he'd give a little growl to let him know that it was his bed and his bed only.

Chico grew quickly and soon established himself as one of the boys, mimicking whatever his older brothers did, and he was by far the easiest one to house-train. After only two weeks, he'd run to the door, let out a little yelp to let us know it was time, and then the rest was up to us. If we were too slow, we'd be cleaning. At least he knew how the system worked. Naturally there were still accidents that occurred (like the time he snuck down into the basement and had a very runny poop all over the new vacuum cleaner that we'd just bought the previous day), but these incidents were few and far between. On the whole, he was a pretty well adjusted puppy. There was a lot more action in the house and both Butch and Sammy were acting younger, joining in on the hour-long play rounds instigated by the family's newest member.

The one-year anniversary of Butch's death sentence came and went, which we toasted with a bottle of champagne and a round of cheap steaks for the yellow, black, and brown ones. I often thought that it was a good thing that they only came in three colours. It seemed like we were constantly stepping over or tripping over them. Butch was now living on borrowed time at the ripe old age of nine, but it didn't come as any big surprise to us. He was still acting like he always had, and there have been plenty of medical cases where people have lived well beyond what the doctors had expected them to, so we just looked upon our dear friend as a medical wonder. The doctors might have disagreed with us, but in our hearts, we knew that he still had a lot of living left to do. You could just see it in his eyes.

Chapter 19
Don't Mess With Butch

good friend of ours, Andi, who also hailed from Switzerland, recently had to put one of his two giant Malamute Huskies down due to bone cancer, making for an extremely miserable holiday season. His remaining dog, Kuma, was virtually a giant among dogs, weighing about one hundred and fifty pounds, and at a height where he had to bend his head down to sniff our guys. Kuma was lonely, missing the company of his brother Jasper who he'd grown up with, so when Andi phoned and asked if I'd like to get together for a dog walk to see if it would raise Kuma's spirits, I gladly agreed.

Andi lived fairly close to Chris's farm, so we agreed to walk up there because there was no danger of hunters and the dogs could roam the fields and forests freely – or so I thought. The walk started off well, with Sammy and Butch cruising off on their own, and Chico sticking with Kuma like glue. The little guy must have figured that if he was going to make friends, it was better to have great big friends. *Smart cookie!*

Kuma really seemed to be enjoying himself, never going too far from Andi and me, but with a new spring in his step that hadn't been seen in a while. About an hour-and-a-half into the walk, Sammy decided that he, too, would join up with Kuma, Chico and the two humans, but Butch, who'd only make the occasional appearance, was still off doing his own thing. It was about an hour back to where we'd parked but we decided to cut across a field that would shorten the route to about thirty minutes because Chico seemed to be losing some steam. He was only six months old, and the thought of having to carry him, like I did with Butch as a puppy, wasn't very appealing.

My thoughts of over-exercising the little brown one, as we trekked through the fresh snow, were quickly shattered by some extremely guttural barking that was going on about three hundred yards away in the middle of the open field. It took a few seconds to focus on where the barking was coming from because of the sun, but when I saw Butch standing in the middle of six coyotes, I just freaked out. He was circling, trying to protect himself as they had him surrounded, each taking bites at his rear end to try and bring him down, but he wasn't going down without a fight. Andi grabbed Kuma and Sammy, with Chico cowering behind the three of them, and I took off, sprinting across the field in foot-deep snow as fast as my legs could carry me, yelling at the top of my lungs the whole way.

I'd never seen Butch in a real fight before, and what I saw was a dog who knew the situation – fight or die, simple as that. It was hard to imagine this dog, who only that same morning had been curled up and sound asleep on our sofa, having such a vicious side to him. He was taking a lot of shots, but he was also giving them, despite the fact that he was so badly outnumbered.

As I got to within a hundred yards, the coyotes backed off a bit, and Butch was still on all fours. The sound of this utter lunatic, screaming at the top of his lungs and running towards them must have done the trick. Dogs, they knew; humans, they weren't too sure about. The main thing though, is that the coyotes scattered across the field and into the forest.

In that moment, when I got close to Butch, I could have sworn that I saw a little smirk on his face. He was limping very badly, with his rear end and back legs covered in blood from all the hit-and-run attacks of the coyotes trying to bring him down, but he seemed pretty proud of himself. It reminded me of the first Rocky movie, when Stallone lost and could barely stand up, but in his own mind and everyone else's, he'd won the fight. If his heart could stand that adrenaline rush, we didn't have anything to worry about for quite some time yet. A quick trip to the vet was all it took to fix him up.

As has become customary, the three boys with their uncanny sense of hearing love to greet everyone who comes to our door. They could be in the deepest sleep, or way down in the corner of the basement, but as soon as a car pulled up, they'd bound for the front door, barking their heads off. Beatlemania during the mid-sixties would be a good way to describe their reaction.

We always checked to see who it was before letting them out to greet our guests, as not everyone is as dog-friendly as we are, but when the front door was opened for them, they'd leave the house at about sixty miles an hour, seeing who could be the first one to get to the car and say hello to the newcomers. No one ever seemed to mind, and if they did, well then, too bad. This was our house and this was how it operated. Most of the people even expected this greeting and would bring the boys treats for when they got out of the car. This could've also been a tactic to help them avoid the inevitable dog slobber which accompanied the greeting ceremonies.

In the spring of 2005, on an unusually warm day, Franzi and I were in the middle of our lunch when the three boys started going ballistic. We weren't expecting any visitors so I got up to see who it was before letting the wild pack out. "Franzi," I yelled over the noise, "get over here! It's Stancia." We hadn't seen her since that summer day in 2003 when we took Butch over the Rockies on his medical mission, but we e-mailed and phoned each other quite a bit, with regular updates and the inevitable questions we had about his heart. It had turned into a good long-distance friendship, and here she was, sitting in her car in our driveway.

Franzi popped her head out the window with a quick hello, and yelled to Stancia if it was alright to let the dogs out. Stancia was in the passenger seat, as Paul had driven, and when she opened the car door, we saw that she had a walking cane in her lap. That wasn't a good sign with our wild bunch, but she just said, "Sure, let them come."

Butch, who was still the biggest and strongest of the three, was the first one out the door, followed closely by Sammy, and then Chico. As the three of them stampeded towards the open car, something must have clicked in Butch's head, because he let out a very different bark than any I've ever heard from him before. All three of them stopped in their tracks like they'd just seen a ghost. Butch, who was closest to the car, turned around to look at Sammy and Chico, gave out a short, quiet bark, and then proceeded slowly, all by himself, towards the car. Sammy and Chico just stood there like their feet were nailed to the ground.

We were quite speechless as Butch made his way slowly to Stancia, who was still in the passenger seat. He looked up at her for about five seconds and then gently put his head down into her lap. He stayed like that – totally still for what seemed like an eternity, but was probably only half a minute – as Stancia petted him on the head and scratched him behind the ears. It was a moment frozen in time. Butch had just said "thank you."

It wasn't a long visit, but it was a very enjoyable one, catching up on each other's lives and sharing good food and drink out on the deck in the warm sunshine. Stancia had decided to stop working out of her house and was opening up a clinic in the town where she lived, and Franzi told her that she was thinking of doing the exact opposite; quitting the spa, and working from our house.

Franzi had been at the spa for over a year now, and was getting quite bored with the run-of-the-mill relaxation massages that ninety percent of the customers seemed to want. The last course that she'd taken down in Florida a few months previously was called Lymph Drainage Therapy, which is a well-known and accepted treatment practice in Europe, but is still in its infancy stages in North America. It's a good technique for the relief of swelling, chronic pain, inflammations, and countless other ailments, as well as detoxifying the body.

She found this area of study fascinating and had already enrolled in the next level. Her reasoning was that with lymph drainage, she could achieve much better results with her clients, using only a small fraction of the pressure that she had to employ during even a light massage. This would protect her hands and body from the pain a lot of massage therapists have to endure after a few years in the trade, thus extending her career. Stancia seemed to think it was a brilliant area to branch out in, and even said that it could be of great benefit to our dogs as they aged. She just had to figure out the canine lymphatic system, and then she'd be able to relieve the boys of their aches and pains too.

That was all Franzi needed to hear to make up her mind. Lymph drainage would be her new area of expertise, and her new place of employment would be down in our basement. And that was all *I* needed to hear, as we had a totally unfinished basement. The direct translation meant that as soon as life slowed down at the golf course in the fall, I'd be starting on a major home renovation.

I wasn't a total idiot with a saw and hammer, but the *Dummies' Guide to Home Reno's*, or some such book which I can't recall, definitely came in handy. By the time Christmas rolled around, Franzi had a wonderful massage studio complete with an attached bathroom, and I had a spacious television room with one of those monster screens that allowed you to actually see the puck during a hockey game. I even made a little fit-ness-workout area that looked impressive, but I knew it wouldn't see a lot of action. Watch the hockey game or climb on the treadmill – *tough choice huh?*

Butch had made it to yet another Christmas, and just having him with us was the greatest gift of all as he'd made it well past a year on borrowed time. We were quite happy about that as we toasted to his health on Christmas Eve, but just a day later we were counting our blessings yet again.

The normal evening routine was that before we went to bed, we would open the front door, toss a few treats outside, watch the stampede go by, and then ten or fifteen minutes later they'd bark at the door after doing their business to be let in again. Maybe it was just the mental release of having all the holiday stress behind us, but on this Boxing Day, Franzi was in bed very early and I was left in sole charge of making sure the boys went out and did their thing. "No problem, I'll let them out," I said to her as she was brushing her teeth.

And let them out I did. It was around ten o'clock and Sammy and Chico both came home relatively quickly. Naturally, Butch had to go and say his "good nights" to every tree in the forest so the waiting game for him to come in started in earnest. *"He'll be home soon."* I said to myself as I plopped down on the sofa to watch some mindless action film that had nothing to do with the holiday season, and before I knew it, Franzi was standing beside me, shaking my shoulder.

"Dave, where's Butch? It's one in the bloody morning and he's still not home!"

Having just placed myself at the top of the terrible husband and bad dog owner list by falling asleep on the sofa, I sprung up and got dressed as quickly as humanly possible. Franzi wasn't far behind me, and we both set out on the search for Sir Butch. We called and yelled at the tops of our lungs for about fifteen minutes, but he was nowhere to be seen – not that seeing anything at one in the morning was an easy thing. With no fresh snowfall for the previous couple of days, there was no way of following his tracks either.

Just down the road from our house was a small nine-hole golf course, where he seldom wandered to, but having exhausted all of his other usual haunts, we decided it was worth a try. Sure enough, when we were on the golf course, Sir Butch came wandering over one of the fairways. The words that Franzi spoke to him at that point cannot be printed here, but I'll just say that Butch took second spot on the "You're in Deep Trouble" list, right behind yours truly.

It was very dark as we walked him home, with Franzi keeping a tight grip on his collar, and it was only when we got him inside that we saw the blood covering his bum and rear legs. He'd been at it again with the coyotes, but this time he didn't have a deranged human helping him with his fight. This time he'd taken care of himself, and the fact that he was still alive told us that he'd fought hard to remain so. As we bent down to examine his wounds we both ended up with licks all over our faces, and any anger that had been felt was quickly replaced with concern. *How could you be angry at a dog that had just fought for his life?*

The next morning Butch couldn't even get up off the floor by himself, and when we would help him stand, a few steps was all he could manage. When we got him in to see Mark later that morning, even *he* was shocked by the number of bites that Butch had sustained. It was hard to tell exactly because of the fur, but he figured it was between thirty and forty wounds altogether. "Coyote bites do a lot of internal damage," he told us, and Butch was given the week off from any form of exercise. Antibiotic cream and lots of rest was what the doctor ordered. "Apparently, his heart doesn't seem to be slowing him down any," Mark commented.

Later that week, with Butch still on the mend, it was decided that come springtime when the ground was no longer frozen, we'd be fencing in about an acre of our yard. Their freedom to roam would be gone, but their safety (and our peace of mind) would be ensured. Keeping them safe was all that mattered to us, but those three months really dragged along until we could start on the fence, having to take the three of them outside on their leashes at night to take care of their business.

Once we had the whole yard fenced in, it was like the weight of the world had been lifted from our shoulders. The worrying every time we let them out the door was a thing of the past, and although we still, on occasion, encountered the coyotes when we took them for their walks, it was always during the daylight hours, and Butch seemed to have figured it out that they were animals that didn't need to be messed with. Maybe wisdom *does* come with age.

Chapter 20
No End in Sight

The last few years, from a medical point of view, have been extremely boring, and that is a beautiful thing. Butch is now past his fourteenth birthday – five more than the doctors ever expected him to see. We, on the other hand, expect him to see many more.

To say that he is still the same old Butch would be nice, and to Franzi and me, he is, but when others see him, we're also reminded that he has aged. Sammy and Chico are now the ones who run non-stop during our walks, with Butch being content with the occasional twenty-yard gallop. His back legs sometimes do some funny things – things that even he doesn't expect – but he can still get around just fine. Mark says that it's a nerve thing, with the messages from the brain to the legs somehow getting a little lost in translation, but the main thing is that it doesn't seem to be bothering him. Not once has he yelped or shown any indication of pain, so we just let him do his own thing on the walks. He can still handle a slow two-hour hike, and much to our surprise, he'll be the only one of the three not going for a snooze afterwards. Instead, he finds himself searching for a tennis ball and then standing at the door, barking to be let out for a play round. He truly is an amazing camper.

Three years ago, the idea of putting the dogs to work popped into Franzi's head after one of her clients mentioned that she volunteered at the local long-term care facility, and on occasion they would have pet visitors come in and visit the residents. The only problem was that none of the pet visitors that they received came on a regular basis, so we decided that might be something to try with our guys. We had a little discussion with the Activities Coordinator at the facility and introduced her to the boys, and she fell in love with them right away. Since then, we've been taking them every week.

For many of the residents of the long-term care facility, our visits, or so the staff tells us, are the only times that they ever see a smile on their faces. There are dementia and Alzheimer's patients, as well as people who are just old and worn down. This is their last stop in life and they have little to look forward to in their everyday existence. That's what makes our visits every week so special. Most of the people who are there have had a dog at one point in their lives, and seeing the smiles creep across their faces as they pet our boys, while thinking of their own animals from so long ago, makes it all worthwhile. Our guys are even well-behaved during the visits, which is so unlike when they're at home. They can sense what's going on, and it's not always a rosy experience.

As we've seen on about a half dozen occasions, when Butch goes to a person, with his tail between his legs, and just rests his head on their lap or on their bed, it's pretty much a certainty that their time amongst the living is coming quickly to an end. It's a very uncanny sense and one that I wish he didn't possess, because it's quite a downer when you have to look at that person and talk with them, knowing that they're on the way out. If Butch comes to visit you, and his tail is wagging, then you're still doing alright. We haven't mentioned this special sense to the caregivers at the facility, because then they'd be following us around each time we went there, waiting to see which room was going to be freed up.

The fact that he's doing still so well can be directly attributed to my dear wife. Franzi quit the spa in early 2006, opening up her own practice at home, and continued her ongoing education, specializing in lymph drainage. She's quite the accomplished practitioner now, being booked solid for months in advance, and no matter what kind of a day she has in front of her, be it from eight in the morning to eight at night, or just a simple nine to five stretch – there's not a morning that goes by that she doesn't spend at least fifteen minutes working on Sir Butch. He seems to know that it's good for him, and when he's had enough, he'll give her a lick and walk away.

There was a little scare last year when he suddenly developed a cough, and although we both said to each other that it was nothing to worry about, not wanting to think about the whole cardiomyopathy thing, we decided to play it safe and get a chest X-ray taken. If the fluid was starting to build up in his lungs or in his chest, we'd find a way to fix it, but first we had to know about it.

After Mark had taken the X-ray and had it developed, he came back to the exam room to tell us exactly what we wanted to hear. "No, there's no fluid building up in there, but it never ceases to amaze me, when I see the size of this guy's heart, *twice* the size of what it should be, that he's still going strong. It's just one of those inexplicable things that you simply just have to enjoy." Two days later the cough was gone and we haven't heard it since.

One would think that with an old dog like Butch, the younger ones might try to take over the top dog spot, but neither Sammy nor Chico have ever made any such attempt. If the two younger ones were to see me put just a single bowl of food down on the floor, neither of them would make a move for it, knowing that Butch, the alpha dog, always ate first. I like to think that it's a healthy combination of love and respect. Even our newest family member, Boots, who we'd found as a kitten, practically frozen to death out in the woods last winter after being abandoned or thrown out to die, looks upon Butch as the boss.

Life, as much as you try to plan it out, will almost always deviate from the path you wish it to follow. That's what makes it worth living – the suspense. Just when you think you've got it back on your desired course, there will be a curve ball thrown up that will knock you out of the batter's box yet again. That's just the way it goes. Some things you can control, while other things are totally out of your hands.

There was no way we could control the different illnesses that Butch seemed to be a magnet for, but we could have an influence on how those illnesses were handled.

Determination, stubbornness, and hope are all factors in the continuing existence of My Hope Butch, but more than anything, it was listening to what our hearts told us. I have an enormous amount of respect for doctors, but doctors are also human beings. Their words are not gospel and should not be believed solely for the reason that there are initials behind their names. Knowledge is power, and what doctors do is give us knowledge. What we do with that knowledge is up to us. We can blindly accept their statements and their course of treatment, or we can research their conclusions and look for alternatives.

Had we just accepted Butch's fate, when they told us to come and pick him up from the hospital in Switzerland because there was nothing more they could do for him, he would be dead. Had we just accepted the fact that his leg would have to come off to get rid of the malignant tumour, he might not have died, although with his heart condition the chances were good, but his quality of life would have been drastically reduced. Simple acceptance is very similar to surrendering. When you have someone that you care about greatly, whether it is a child, a spouse, or an animal, one of the greatest healing powers available is hope. Hope is what keeps you going, not letting you give up. It keeps you positive even in the darkest times, and gives you the strength to exhaust any and all avenues.

Butch, whether he knows it or not, has been instrumental in the teaching of hope and unconditional love to both Franzi and me. He's always been there with a smile on his face to greet us when we come home, and he always knows how to cheer us up when our spirits are a little bit down. As Franzi once said, "I'd crawl on my knees to the moon and back for Butch, after everything he's done for us and taught us." And I'd be right behind her.

He's definitely an ongoing story, but right now, as he's standing beside me poking me in the arm with his nose, the centre of his universe revolves around his empty dinner bowl, which he wants filled. Sir Butch cannot be kept waiting, so I'll end our story here.

The End

About the Author

DAVE CASSIDY is a Canadian – married to a Swiss – who called the Alps his home for a dozen years. A business administration graduate by education, he changed direction and attended the "university of travel," backpacking and cycling in over forty-five countries before settling down. He writes because he loves doing it. In addition to writing about his Labrador Retrievers, Dave can be found wandering the backcountry trails of British Columbia, trying to duplicate his only hole-in-one, and stopping frozen hockey pucks with his forehead during the winter months.

Acknowledgments

A very special thank you to Ricki Cundliffe and Avy Nicholson for their advice, help, and support in this endeavor.

Printed in the United States
153747LV00006B/2/P

9 781592 994373